SILENT WARFARE

SILENT WARFARE

UNDERSTANDING THE WORLD OF INTELLIGENCE

Abram N. Shulsky

Foreword by
Roy Godson

BRASSEY'S (US), Inc.
A Division of Maxwell Macmillan, Inc.

Washington · New York · London · Oxford
Beijing · Frankfurt · São Paulo · Sydney · Tokyo · Toronto

Brassey's (US), Inc.

Editorial Offices	*Order Department*
Brassey's (US), Inc.	Brassey's Book Orders
8000 Westpark Drive	℅ Macmillan Publishing Co.
First Floor	Front and Brown Streets
McLean, Virginia 22102	Riverside, New Jersey 08075

Brassey's (US), Inc., books are available at special discounts for bulk purchases for sales promotions, premiums, fund-raising, or educational use through the Special Sales Director, Macmillan Publishing Company, 866 Third Avenue, New York, New York 10022.

Excerpts from *Strategic Intelligence for American World Policy* by Sherman Kent. Copyright 1949 by Princeton University Press. Copyright © renewed 1976 by Princeton University Press. Reprinted with permission of Princeton University Press.

Excerpts from *Secrecy and Democracy: The CIA in Transition* by Admiral Stansfield Turner. Copyright © 1985 by Stansfield Turner. Reprinted by permission of Houghton Mifflin Company.

Library of Congress Cataloging-in-Publication Data

Shulsky, Abram N.
    Silent warfare : understanding the world of intelligence / Abram
N. Shulsky.
        p.   cm.
    Includes index.
    ISBN 0-08-040566-5
    1. Intelligence service.   2. Intelligence service—United States.
I. Title.
JF1525.I6S49   1991
327.12—dc20   90-49399
                                        CIP

British Library Cataloguing in Publication Data

Shulsky, Abram N.
    Silent warfare : understanding the world of intelligence.
    1. Intelligence services
    I. Title
    327.12
    ISBN 0-08-040566-5

Published in the United States of America   Designed by Nancy Sugihara

10 9 8 7 6 5 4 3 2 1

To the memory of
my parents

CONTENTS

Foreword   ix

Preface   xi

Introduction: Writing about Secrets   xiii

1 What Is Intelligence?   1

   The Scope of Intellignce   3
   The Elements of Intelligence   7

2 Spies, Machines, and Libraries: Collecting the Data   11

   Human Intelligence Collection   11
   Technical Intelligence Collection   20
   Comparison of Humint and Techint   30
   Open-source Collection   33

3 What Does It All Mean?
   Intelligence Analysis and Production   37

   What Is Analysis?   37
   The Intelligence Product   53
   Intelligence Failure and Surprise   59

4 Working Behind the Scenes: Covert Action   73

   What Is Covert Action? Some Definitions   73
   Types and Examples of Covert Action   76
   Covert Action and Secrecy   90
   Covert Action and Intelligence   95

5 Spy vs. Spy: Counterintelligence   99

   The Classification of Information   100
   Security   105
   Counterespionage   109
   Multidisciplinary Counterintelligence (MDCI)   115
   Deception and Counterdeception   118
   Counterintellignce Analysis   128

6 Guarding the Guardians:
   The Management of Intelligence   131

   Secrecy and Control   131
   Expertise and Policy   136
   Intelligence and Democracy   144

7 Two Views of Intelligence   159

   Historical Development of the American View   161
   Intelligence and Moral Issues   168

8 Toward a Theory of Intelligence   171

   The Dual Nature of Intelligence   177

Notes   181

Index   217

About the Author   223

FOREWORD

The literature on intelligence, security, and statecraft is large and continues to grow. These "serious" studies are matched in the popular literature by a large volume of espionage fiction. Sifting the wheat from the chaff, however, is not easy. The Intelligence & National Security Library is intended to make available important studies and firsthand accounts by Western and non-Western intelligence practitioners, scholars, and others who have amassed interesting information and analyses. Individual titles are reviewed by an editorial advisory board of scholars and former senior intelligence officials from Western Europe and North America. Though every volume stands on its own merit, the series as a whole is intended to improve our understanding of intelligence and its relationship to security.

This volume provides a unique introduction to the world of intelligence and fills the need for a single, comprehensive, understandable book on this subject. The author, Abram N. Shulsky, has extensive knowledge and experience with intelligence both in academia and in the legislative and executive branches of government. In the early 1980s he was minority (i.e., Democratic) staff director of the U.S. Senate Select Committee on Intelligence, which is responsible for overseeing the entire U.S. intelligence system. He then served as the director of strategic arms control policy at the U.S. Defense Department, and later was a consultant to the president's Foreign Intelligence Advisory Board in the White House.

In this book, Shulsky explains the major missions and products of intelligence agencies, as well as the procedures and activities used to achieve them. He also explores the complex tensions and relationship between a secret intelligence agency and the democratic government and society that it serves. *Silent Warfare* breaks new ground in intelligence studies by proposing a framework that focuses on the dual nature of intelligence—as both a search for knowledge about political, military, and economic matters (with similarities, therefore, to social science) and as an element of the struggle among nations (with similarities to war). Shulsky brings together the knowledge and insights gained in the past decade as intelligence studies mushroomed in the United States, Canada, and the United Kingdom. This book codifies "intelligence" for the professional and the serious student, while also providing a realistic framework for those fascinated by fiction about intelligence agencies and their operatives.

ROY GODSON
General Editor
Intelligence & National Security Library
Washington, D.C.

PREFACE

This book has its origin in a course on intelligence that I taught in 1985 as a visiting professor at the University of Chicago's John M. Olin Center for Inquiry into the Theory and Practice of Democracy. Returning to the academic world forced me to impose some order on my thoughts concerning intelligence, a subject with which I had become familiar in the public policy world of Washington. I am grateful to the Olin Center's director, Allan Bloom, for this opportunity and for much, much else besides.

While working on this book, I enjoyed the hospitality of the National Strategy Information Center, where I held the title of senior fellow, an enviable position with maximum freedom and a minimum of responsibilities. I am grateful to the center's president, Frank R. Barnett; to the director of its Washington office, Roy Godson; and to Jeffrey Berman, *factotum,* for their support.

Through this affiliation, I remained in close contact with the work of the Consortium for the Study of Intelligence and the Intelligence Studies Section of the International Studies Association. This book owes a great deal to the participants in the colloquia and conventions of these two organizations, and I hope that it repays its debt to them by providing an introduction to intelligence studies that they will find useful in their own teaching.

I am particularly grateful to the Lynde and Harry Bradley Foundation for its generous and patient financial support and to its vice president for programs, Hillel G. Fradkin, for his personal interest and sponsorship. I also wish to thank the John M. Olin Foundation for its support of the project's initial stages.

My work on this book was assisted by information and comments provided by the following friends and fellow students of intelligence: Eliot A. Cohen, Diane S. Dornan, Kenneth E. deGraffenreid, Sam Halperin, Carnes R. Lord, and Kenneth G. Robertson. I wish to express my gratitude to them and to Gary J. Schmitt, whose careful critique of the manuscript, to say nothing of his friendship and encouragement, contributed greatly to the final result. I am, of course, solely responsible for its errors and omissions.

ABRAM N. SHULSKY
Washington, D.C.

INTRODUCTION
WRITING ABOUT SECRETS

Another book about intelligence. So much has been published on this topic in recent years that we have almost lost the sense that there is anything paradoxical or even controversial about the public discussion of a subject that has secrecy as an essential characteristic. Of course, in any democracy, government business is the people's business, and there is strong sympathy for a policy of publicizing rather than concealing the government's actions.

Nevertheless, it is also generally understood that safeguarding national security in a dangerous world requires that many government actions be kept secret from foreign adversaries. This, in turn, requires that the domestic public be kept in the dark as well. Indeed, even democratic governments (that of the United States included), to say nothing of undemocratic ones, impose regulations requiring almost complete secrecy about most aspects of intelligence operations and information. Therefore, those outside the government who write about intelligence are sooner or later faced with the questions of *why* are they writing about a secret subject and, perhaps more important, *how* are they able to do so.

In reviewing the extensive literature on intelligence, you can see certain ways in which the question of secrecy has been addressed, although this is more often done implicitly rather than explicitly. According to one view, intelligence has, or should, become less of a "cloak-and-dagger" affair and more like a branch of the social sciences. In fact, intelligence should be a universal social science that seeks to understand, and ultimately to predict, all sorts of political, economic, social, and military matters. As such, it need not be an inherently secretive endeavor. While some secrecy may be necessary to protect the sources of important bits of confidential information, in general, the most important facts—concerning the political, economic, social, technological, and demographic trends that shape a country's behavior in the long run—will not be secret.[1]

According to this view, as intelligence becomes more mature—in the sense of becoming more scientific and more concerned with underlying trends and causes—it relies less on specific secrets and can become more open. As a result, there should be no inherent difficulty in writing about it publicly. In fact, the public discussion of intelligence may help it achieve its proper goal of becoming more like a social science by demystifying intelligence and encouraging the flow of ideas between the intelligence and academic communities.

Other, primarily American, publications on intelligence want to expose alleged misdeeds of a country's intelligence agencies and to bring about some sort of change for the better in the way they operate. Typically, such critiques regard the secrecy with which intelligence agencies operate either as the source of the misdeeds or, at any rate, as a precondition for them.

In this view, the publication of books or articles about intelligence, which destroys that secrecy, is an essential element of any reform program. Whatever damage may be done by publicizing legitimate secrets is regarded as relatively small compared to the damage that could be caused by the intelligence agencies operating in continued secrecy. From this perspective, there is nothing problematic about disclosing information concerning an "unreformed" intelligence agency. In fact, since secrecy is seen as a major cause of, or crucial precondition for, wrongdoing, it is not clear whether even a reformed intelligence agency would be entitled to secrecy.

One of the earliest and best-known books of this sort begins with the assertion that "there exists in [the United States] today a powerful and dangerous secret cult—the cult of intelligence." Publicity is an essential weapon in the fight against "this secret fraternity of the American political aristocracy":

> The aim of this book is to provide the American people with the inside information which they need—and to which they without question have the right—to understand the significance of this issue and the importance of dealing with it.[2]

Silent Warfare belongs to neither category. I believe that intelligence is primarily about the discovery and protection of secrets and that it will remain so in the future. I also believe that the discovery of other nations' secrets and the protection of one's own is, and will remain, so vital to national security that the release of secret information that would impede that work would not be justifiable, despite the catalogue of past misdeeds of the U.S. Central Intelligence Agency (CIA) or allegations that might be made concerning the intelligence agencies of other democratic states. Thus, I face the issue of secrecy and publicity in a more complex manner.

It is possible, by relying on public sources and "leaks," to write a book containing a great deal of apparently classified (i.e., officially secret) information about U.S. intelligence agencies and activities.[3] I have not chosen to do this. This is in part because I have had authorized access to classified intelligence information in connection with my various positions with the U.S. government (not, however, with any intelligence agency). In the course of that employment I promised not to disclose such information.[4] Any attempt to claim that classified information presented in this book was derived solely from public nonofficial sources could be reasonably viewed as a subterfuge. More important, I regard secrecy as essential to intelligence operations and, in any case, do not see the importance of putting into the public domain various esoteric details about the operations of U.S.—or other—intelligence agencies, the vast majority of which appear not to raise significant issues of public policy.

Rather, in this book, while steering clear of classified detail, I attempt to discuss basic concepts in intelligence. My purpose is to enable the reader to think about the general issues of intelligence policy in a way that does justice to the subject's complexities and ambiguities. Thus, my approach is fundamentally theoretical; specific details that are publicly available are provided to illustrate general points rather than to be comprehensive, either with respect to the history of any aspect of intelligence or with respect to its current condition.

While intelligence is becoming a recognized field of academic study at least in the English-speaking world, the theoretical treatment of it remains undeveloped.[5] In this book, I attempt to contribute to that endeavor. At the same time, I recognize that the book's relatively heavy reliance on the Anglo-American experience precludes it from reaching a truly general "theory of intelligence." This reliance is due in large part to the fact that most of the publicly available information about intelligence, not surprisingly, concerns the intelligence agencies of those countries that have the most open political systems. Nevertheless, where possible, I refer to intelligence activities of other societies and try to consider the question of how intelligence agencies vary depending on the nature of the regimes they serve.

This book does not provide readers with any secrets or "inside information," either spectacular or humdrum. I hope it provides a framework for understanding intelligence as well as the many revelations that will, most likely, be forthcoming in the future.

1

WHAT IS INTELLIGENCE?

In popular fiction, and to the public, intelligence has often been synonymous with espionage and skulduggery, with the sexual blackmail of a Mata Hari and the cloak-and-dagger exploits of a James Bond. While activities of this sort have their place within the world of intelligence, the full concept is much richer. Let's begin by looking at the phenomena to which the term "intelligence" is applied; these phenomena include certain kinds of *information, activities,* and *organizations.*[1]

Intelligence refers to *information* relevant to a government's formulating and implementing policy to further its national security interests and to deal with threats to those interests from actual or potential adversaries.[2] In the most obvious and often most important case, this information has to do with military matters, such as an adversary's plans for military action. Potential or actual enemies typically do their best to keep this type of information secret. Of course, other types of secret information may be equally important—for example, information about another country's diplomatic activities and intentions, as well as information about its intelligence activities.

In addition to information of this sort, many types of information about an actual or potential adversary may be useful to know, even though the adversary may not attempt to keep them secret. These could include information about internal political affairs and societal developments as well as economic and demographic statistics. How much material of this sort is actually published depends on the nature of the political regime. In a democratic society, this type of material is almost always publicly available. A totalitarian system, however, often strives to conceal any information about

1

its internal politics, economy, military forces, or society that an adversary might find helpful. Regardless of whether publicly available information is to be considered "intelligence," clearly there must be some process by which it is systematically made available to government officials in a usable form. An intelligence service often performs this function.

Finally, intelligence information typically includes not only the "raw data" collected by means of espionage or otherwise, but also the analyses and assessments that may be based on it. It is this output, often referred to as the intelligence "product," which is typically of direct value to policy-makers. To what extent this intelligence product should strive to present a comprehensive evaluation of a situation, based on all available data, both public and secret, may vary from one intelligence service to another.

As an *activity*, intelligence comprises the collection and analysis of intelligence information—information relevant to the formulation and implementation of government national security policy. It also includes activities undertaken to counter the intelligence activities of adversaries, either by denying them access to information or by deceiving them about the facts or their significance.

Intelligence comprises a wide range of activities. For example, there are various methods of collecting information, such as espionage, photography, intercepting communications, and research using publicly available documents and radio and television broadcasts. There also are different techniques for analyzing the information that has been collected: some of these may be similar to the methods the social sciences use, while others, such as the decryption of coded messages, are peculiar to the intelligence world. Similarly, denying information to others involves various activities, some of which are similar to law enforcement work, such as investigating suspected foreign intelligence agents to learn whether they are in contact with government officials. Others are more esoteric, such as using encryption to protect communications. Finally, various means of deceiving adversaries exist, such as "double-agent" operations and deceptive radio signals.

Looking at this wide variety of intelligence activities, it seems difficult to see any common thread running through them. They all, however, have to do with obtaining or denying information. Therefore, intelligence as an activity may be defined as that component of the struggle between adversaries that deals primarily with information (as opposed to economic competition, diplomatic maneuvering or negotiations, or the threat or use of military force, for example).

Finally, the term "intelligence" also refers to the *organizations* that carry out these activities. One of the most notable characteristics of such organizations is the secrecy with which their activities must be conducted. Many of their methods of operation, such as the use of undercover agents or strict rules concerning access to information, derive from this requirement. Since intelligence agencies are organized to enhance their capacity for secrecy, they also may be given, along with their information-obtaining or -denying functions, the responsibility of undertaking secret activities to advance their government's foreign policy objectives more directly.

Such activity, which in the U.S. intelligence lexicon is referred to as "covert action," may range from the mundane, such as covertly providing critical assistance to a friendly foreign government, to the spectacular, such as orchestrating the overthrow of a hostile one. Whether it should be assigned to the same organizations that collect and analyze intelligence information has occasionally been a controversial question. Even if, for practical reasons, intelligence organizations are given the responsibility for covert action, the more fundamental question of whether covert action should be considered a part of intelligence from a theoretical, as well as a practical, viewpoint would remain.

The Scope of Intelligence

Because not only governments but many other types of organizations operate in an environment characterized by a competitive struggle with adversaries, the concept of intelligence might be applied to them as well. For example, some researchers try to extend the concept to business corporations, treating intelligence as "organized information . . . designed to meet the unique policy-making needs of one enterprise."[3] Similarly, we could speak of the intelligence function of a political party or campaign in trying to figure out what the opposition is up to.

I do not consider these possible extensions of the term "intelligence"; I limit its meaning to the traditional scope, to information and activities relevant to the national security concerns of governments.

This limitation does not adequately define the scope of intelligence, since the term "national security" is itself unclear. Its core meaning has to do with protecting a nation against threats, ultimately military, emanating from foreign nations. When a nation is or is about to be invaded, its national security concerns clearly center on preventing or defeating the invasion and securing itself against a similar situation arising in the future. In less ominous circumstances, it may be much less clear which foreign nations or events can threaten national security and therefore require attention by the nation's intelligence.

The problem is further complicated by the fact that national security interests and threats to them cannot be considered independently of the type of government the nation has (the regime) and its ideological outlook. Although adherents of realpolitik would argue that a nation's interests are determined by the objective factors of the international system, ideological views affect how government perceives them. For example, a regime's ideological character may determine whether it views a given foreign country as a threat. In particular, status quo and revolutionary powers are likely to have different views about what constitutes a threat to national security.[4]

Domestic Intelligence

An even more important area in which the nature of the regime affects the scope of intelligence is what is called "domestic intelligence." Any government must be concerned not only with purely external threats (such as military invasion) but also with threats against its ability to govern, or its very existence, that arise from individuals or groups within the nation's borders. Such threats could come from groups that seek to overthrow the government by illegal means, that seek to use violence to change government policies, or that seek to exclude from the body politic members of a given ethnic, racial, or religious group. How a government defines such internal threats depends heavily on the type of government it is.

A regime in which a dynasty or a single political party has a monopoly of power, for example, is likely to regard any domestic political dissent as a security threat, and its intelligence service will focus a great deal of attention on detecting and thwarting it. In the most extreme case, the government of a totalitarian state may regard all nonmembers of the ruling party as actual or potential enemies. By contrast, the notion of a "loyal opposition," as found in parliamentary and other democratic systems, implies that the government's domestic political opponents do not pose a security threat and hence are not a suitable concern of intelligence.

In addition, there may be many possible types of connections between domestic groups and foreign powers. At one end of the foreign-domestic spectrum would be the activities of an individual or domestic group that acts on behalf, and at the direction, of a hostile foreign power. Then there could be groups or individuals who share common objectives with that power and cooperate in the pursuit of them. Finally, there also could be groups that are seen as subversive of the nation's constitutional order or disloyal to it but without any ties to foreign governments.

Intelligence and Law Enforcement

A related question deals with those transnational threats that do not emanate primarily from a foreign government—for example, narcotics trafficking, international terrorism, or certain types of organized crime. These can be serious threats to a nation's well-being, but they appear to be problems that come within the ambit of law enforcement rather than intelligence. Nevertheless, intelligence is often involved in the fight against them for several reasons. First, they involve activities in foreign countries, where domestic law enforcement agencies have no jurisdiction and where the local law enforcement agencies may be unable or unwilling to be of much assistance. Intelligence may be called upon for information about the foreign aspect of these activities that would otherwise be unavailable.

Second, and more important, the law enforcement approach typically involves waiting until a specific crime has been, or is about to be, committed and then attempting to solve that particular crime and arrest the perpetrators. This may not be an acceptable approach toward international threats. A single incident, such as blowing up a passenger airplane in flight, may cause so much harm that it is necessary to prevent these crimes rather than merely solve them. Furthermore, a specific crime, such as smuggling narcotics across an international border, may be part of a criminal enterprise's operations; if the enterprise is large and well organized, arresting the perpetrators of a single crime may not have much impact on it. Such occasional arrests may even be a tolerable cost of doing business from the perspective of the kingpins. Finally, even if agencies were content to wait until a specific crime occurred, the chances of solving it would depend heavily on their having a great deal of background information available about the organizations involved.

For these reasons, an intelligence approach is often adopted with these types of activity. Instead of waiting for a specific criminal act on which to focus, agencies gather information over a long time concerning various individuals and groups, their motivations, resources, interconnections, intentions, and so forth. Often it is necessary to use informers who penetrate the groups involved and who operate like spies. It also may be possible to intercept communications or use other technical methods of collecting information.

Thus, intelligence agencies are often involved in the fight against such groups. Depending on the regime, agencies' involvement may be limited to the foreign aspects of these activities while domestic aspects remain in the purview of law enforcement agencies. Even in these cases, however, law enforcement agencies often must resort to some intelligence techniques to deal with organized criminal groups. For example, with respect to domestic law enforcement activities, the U.S. Federal Bureau of Investigation (FBI) distinguishes between criminal intelligence investigations and ordinary criminal investigations. The former type of investigation is described as ''broader and less discriminate than usual'': it is not focused on a single completed criminal act but rather on an ongoing criminal organization, whose size, composition, past acts, intended criminal goals, and capacity to do harm must be determined.[5] The dividing line between law enforcement and intelligence, while not a sharp one, generally depends on whether the focus is on punishment of a given criminal act or on an ongoing struggle with an organization engaged in criminal activity.

Economics and Intelligence

Finally, there are questions concerning the function of intelligence agencies with respect to economic issues. Again, much depends on the regime's nature and its economic system. In a system under centralized government control (a ''command'' economy), intelligence would be concerned with the economic aspects of the government's relations with foreign governments, just as it is with all other aspects of its international relations. In addition, intelligence can be used to enhance the state's economic well-being. Acquiring advanced Western technology, for example, is an important function of the Soviet KGB (the Committee for State Security). This activity not only increases the technological level of the Soviet military, but also saves Soviet industry the great expense and difficulty of developing such technology on its own.[6]

In a market economy, however, it is much less clear which economic issues have a national security dimension that justifies or requires the involvement of intelligence agencies. In addition, while many developments in the international economy may have important national security ramifications, it is not obvious that the government should or, in any case, will do very much about such developments; thus, the government may not have a use for information about them. In a democratic society, economic policy is much more likely to be determined by the interplay of domestic economic interests than by any coherent view (whether or not based on intelligence information) of the future world economic environment. For this reason, it is not clear whether the government in such a society would be an important consumer of such intelligence. Private economic interests could probably put it to much greater use, but it is not clear that information gathered at government expense would be distributed to individuals or corporations to further private interests.

Furthermore, most of what an advanced industrial country would find significant would be economic information about the other advanced industrial countries that play a major role in the world economy. Currently, these countries are not political rivals; it is not clear to what extent intelligence capabilities should be used to improve economic competitiveness with otherwise friendly nations.

In general, the relationship between intelligence and economic information depends critically on the extent to which a nation sees its economic situation and relationships in national security terms. For some countries, in particular those with command economies, viewing economics in national security terms may be almost axiomatic. For others, it depends on particular circumstances.

For example, in wartime, intelligence means could be used to gain access to strategic materials (or deny the enemy access to them), a key national security goal. Similarly, in the course of negotiating with a foreign country on economic matters, a nation might use its intelligence capability to learn about its partners' negotiating positions. More generally, the appetite for economic intelligence on industrial, commercial, and financial activity in other countries would probably depend on whether a government has an "industrial policy" bureaucracy that could make use of it.

The Elements of Intelligence

Whatever its scope, intelligence activity can be divided into four parts, often referred to as the elements of intelligence: *collection, analysis, covert action,* and *counterintelligence*. Since these elements are treated in detail in subsequent chapters, they will be touched on only briefly here. The short discussions that follow are meant only to elucidate the nature of the intelligence activity included under each of the four headings and to sketch the relationships between them.

Collection refers to the gathering of raw data, through espionage, technical means (photography, interception of electronic communications, and so on), or in any other manner; thus, it comes closest to what is popularly considered intelligence activity. While collection is obviously fundamental to intelligence work, opinions differ regarding the relative importance of the various methods. For example, students of intelligence have debated the importance of collection from "open sources" (such as publications and radio and television broadcasts) as compared with using methods unique to intelligence services, or the importance of collection through espionage as compared with technical collection.

No matter how good the collected information is, however, it almost never speaks for itself. In other words, some *analysis* of the information is necessary for it to be useful when formulating and implementing foreign policy or military activities. In the vast majority of cases, the collected information is fragmentary, ambiguous, and susceptible to widely divergent interpretations. Thus, the process of analyzing the available information to make judgments about the capabilities, intentions, and actions of another party is a vital part of the intelligence process. Even more difficult is the process of forecasting ("estimating," in American intelligence jargon) the future capabilities, intentions, and actions of a foreign government or political organization.

Conceptually, *covert action* differs from the other elements of intelligence in that, while the others are concerned with seeking and safeguarding knowledge, covert action seeks to influence political events directly. In terms of intensity, covert action can range from persuasion or propaganda to paramilitary action; it has been described as "an activity midway between diplomacy and war."[7]

While the techniques for exerting this influence are many, they have the common characteristic of anonymity, that is to say, the role of the government conducting the activity is not readily apparent or publicly acknowledged. For this reason, an intelligence agency's ability to act secretly often brings it the assignment of carrying out covert action as well. But because it involves implementing policy rather than informing policymakers, there have been occasional suggestions in the United States that covert action not be a function of the same agency (the CIA) that collects and analyzes intelligence. On the other hand, both the United States and Great Britain have discovered through experience that having two organizations involved in running clandestine operations (one for espionage and the other for covert action) can result in energy-sapping rivalries, duplication of effort, or mutual interference.[8]

The proper scope and nature of *counterintelligence* is less well defined and more controversial than the other intelligence elements. In its most general sense, counterintelligence refers to the protection of a society and particularly its own intelligence capability from the actions of hostile intelligence services. In the first place, counterintelligence means denying certain information to adversaries. This protection is accomplished by programs of *security*—actions taken to keep information away from those not authorized to have it; and by *counterespionage*—actions taken to apprehend or otherwise neutralize foreign agents to prevent them from acquiring and communicating secret information. In addition, a society could attack its adversary's intelligence analysis as well as its collection capability; this is done using deception operations that provide false or deliberately misleading information to the adversary to induce him to reach an incorrect analysis.

However, protecting a society or oneself against an adversary's intelligence capability, understood broadly, would require other activities as well. It may be necessary to take steps to ensure that you are not deceived by misleading information deliberately provided by the other party. Thus, counterintelligence must safeguard the integrity of the collection and analytic functions. You would also want to know about a foreign government's covert action aimed at influencing your society and government. Ultimately then, the breadth of counterintelligence activities is determined by the threat an adversary's intelligence activities pose.

2

SPIES, MACHINES, AND LIBRARIES

COLLECTING THE DATA

We begin our examination of the elements of intelligence by looking at the collection of raw data, which can then be correlated, analyzed, and reported. The various methods of collecting these data are usually referred to as "disciplines" and can be broadly characterized as (1) collection from human sources (variously referred to as espionage, human intelligence collection, or, in U.S. intelligence jargon, *humint*), (2) collection by technical means (technical intelligence, or *techint*), or (3) noncovert collection via diplomatic contacts or generally available sources of information such as newspapers or radio broadcasts (open-source collection).[1]

Human Intelligence Collection

Human intelligence collection, or espionage, is what the term "intelligence" is most likely to bring to mind. Its essence is in identifying and recruiting into your service someone who has access to important information and who is willing, for some reason, to pass it to officers of your intelligence service. Typically, such people have access to this information by holding positions of trust in their governments. In some cases (especially in wartime), the person providing the information may not be a government official but a private individual who has the opportunity to observe something of interest, such as ships' arrival in and departure from a harbor.

Ordinarily, individuals in two different roles are involved: an intelligence officer, who is an employee of the foreign intelligence service, and a source, who provides the officer with information for transmission back to the intelligence service's headquarters. The intelligence officer, or "handler," maintains communication with the source, passes on the instructions coming from the intelligence service's headquarters, provides necessary resources (such as copying or communications equipment), and, in general, seeks to ensure the continuing flow of information.[2]

Types of Intelligence Officers

Since they must avoid the attention of the government of the country in which they are posted, intelligence officers cannot simply hang out a shingle advertising their willingness to pay cash for secrets. They require what in intelligence jargon is called "cover," that is, a plausible reason for being in the country, visible means of financial support, a pretext for meeting people with access to sensitive information, and so forth.[3]

In current U.S. parlance, a distinction is made between "official" and "nonofficial" cover. Official cover refers to disguising an intelligence officer as a diplomat or some other kind of governmental official who would be posted abroad. This kind of cover has several advantages. Most obviously, it can provide the intelligence officer with diplomatic immunity. If his espionage activities are detected, international law limits the host government to declaring him persona non grata and expelling him from the country.

In addition, posing as a diplomat improves the intelligence officer's access to potential sources; as a diplomat, he would, without raising suspicions, meet with host-government officials in the course of his ordinary business, as well as with other countries' diplomats stationed in the same capital. Indeed, since other countries also will use official cover for their intelligence officers, he will have innocent opportunities for meeting them as well.

Also, stationing intelligence agents under official cover in an embassy guarantees that, if a national of the host country approaches the embassy with sensitive materials or an offer to provide them, the matter can be handled by intelligence professionals. In this sense, the existence of official cover intelligence officers eases attempts by host-country nationals to make contact with the intelligence service; such positions serve as a useful and perhaps necessary "mailbox," especially in countries that strictly regulate or prohibit their nationals' travel to or communication with the outside world.

Finally, official cover has certain administrative conveniences. The officer can be paid and other personnel matters can be handled through regular government channels, and communication with the intelligence service's headquarters can be maintained through the intelligence "station" (the group of intelligence officers under official cover) located in the embassy.

Alternatively, official cover has several drawbacks. Most important, because of the relatively small number of officials posted to a given host country, that country's counterespionage service may be able to determine, fairly precisely, which "diplomats" are intelligence officers and which are not. This may be done by the obvious, but laborious, methods of maintaining surveillance on each official and noting his movements and contacts, tapping his telephone, bugging his apartment, and so forth. The practice of hiring nationals of the host country to work in embassies in various support capacities probably facilitates such surveillance, especially in those countries, such as the Soviet Union, where it must be assumed that anyone allowed to work in a foreign embassy has agreed to cooperate with the host country's intelligence service.[4]

Actually, less-expensive methods may be able to accomplish the same goal. Materials published by a country might be used to trace the careers of those serving as foreign service officers and to identify patterns that indicate an intelligence connection. For example, it has been claimed that biographic materials published by the U.S. Department of State made it relatively easy to identify intelligence officers under official cover.[5]

Furthermore, while official cover may provide easy access to some potential sources (primarily other diplomats and host-country foreign policy officials), it may block access to others who might be hesitant to deal with foreigners, either in general or with those from a particular country. In any case, potential recruits are immediately put on notice that they are dealing with an official of a foreign government, and that may make them more cautious. In addition, if diplomatic relations are broken off, as might happen in case of an intense crisis or war—when good intelligence may be most necessary—official cover officers must leave the country, thereby disrupting the operation of any network of sources they established.

The advantages and disadvantages of nonofficial cover are, for the most part, the obverse of the considerations already discussed. On the one hand, since they can pose as members of a wide variety of professions or strata of society, nonofficial cover officials (NOCs) can have access to a different, and perhaps wider, spectrum of potential sources. Similarly, they can pose as nationals of the country to which they are posted or of some third country; they thus obscure their connection with the government for which they work, which may help them gain access to information or make contact with potential sources. If diplomatic relations are broken off, they can remain and continue to operate. In general, NOCs also should be much harder for the host government to identify.

On the other hand, nonofficial cover suffers from many disadvantages that limit its use. The expense and administrative difficulty involved in providing nonofficial cover is much greater than in the case of official cover. One method is to persuade a corporation or other private organization to allow an intelligence officer to pose as a member of its staff. (In the case of U.S. organizations, the perceived risks of doing this—in particular, the possibility of public disclosure that will harm the organization's own relations with the host government—have greatly increased in recent years, and it is often difficult for the government to obtain their cooperation.) Alternatively, the officers may themselves establish businesses or engage in activity that provides plausible explanations for their presence in the target country. Not only may this latter course be expensive, it also requires a good deal of time if the cover is to be persuasive, which reduces the time and effort the officer can spend on the primary task of intelligence collection.[6] Communications are likely to be more difficult to maintain, since an NOC cannot make regular use of communications facilities in the nation's embassy without raising some of the very suspicions that nonofficial status is intended to avoid.

A clear distinction between official and nonofficial cover would exist only in the case of a country whose citizens can and routinely do travel abroad for their own reasons and without special government permission. Thus, until the Gorbachev-era easing of Soviet restrictions on foreign travel, any Soviet travel to the West could in some sense be seen as official because permission to travel abroad was a rare and highly prized privilege. In this sense, all Soviet visitors to foreign countries had some sort of official status, and an intelligence officer could equally well take the disguise of a journalist for the Novosti Press Agency as that of a diplomat.

With respect to Soviet and allied intelligence services, in the place of the official cover–NOC distinction, a related one is made between "legal" and "illegal" officers. The reference is not to the officer's status in the host country—whether he is there legally or not—but to his means of communicating with the intelligence headquarters. An illegal officer is one who does not communicate via one of the "legal" establishments in the host country (the embassy, consulate, trade office, or so forth) but directly with the headquarters. In this way, an illegal is similar to an NOC.

Obviously, it will be easier to insert illegal officers into a country that routinely receives a large number of immigrants and visitors and is relatively casual about controlling its borders than into one that does not receive immigrants, generally keeps a watch on visitors, and guards its borders carefully. Thus, it is not surprising to find many more references to Soviet or Eastern European illegal officers operating in the United States and, until 1990, West Germany than vice versa. Judging from instances that have come to light, the Soviet Union is willing to devote immense amounts of time and effort to perfecting the covers, or "legends," of their illegal intelligence officers.

A case that illustrates this point involved Ludek Zemenek, a Czech national who became a KGB officer. Given the identity of a Rudolf Herrmann (the real Rudolf Herrmann was a German who died in the Soviet Union during World War II), he lived in East Germany for about a year. Then, at the end of 1957, he left for West Germany, where he appeared to be an ordinary East German refugee with an East German wife (who had also been recruited by the KGB) and an infant son.

After four years in West Germany, Herrmann was instructed by the KGB to emigrate to Canada, where he eventually established a small business producing advertising and commercial films. He fulfilled various minor tasks for the KGB, such as filing "personality reports" on politicians and journalists he met through his business and maintaining communications with a Canadian professor who was a KGB agent. His most important mission, however, was to preserve his cover so that he would be able, in case of a break in diplomatic relations between the USSR and Canada, to take control of the KGB's network of Canadian sources from the legal "resident" (chief of the KGB station at the Soviet Embassy in Ottawa).

After six years in Canada, he was instructed to move to the United States, where he performed similar tasks for the KGB as he had in Canada. When his son Peter was seventeen, Rudolf explained who he was and what he was doing; the son agreed to work for the KGB as well. Since Peter had been brought to West Germany as an infant and raised from the age of four in Canada and the United States, his background would not give rise to any suspicion; he was to prepare himself for a career in the U.S. government where he could operate as a long-term Soviet source, or "mole." Presumably he would have been able to do so had the FBI not confronted Rudolf Herrmann several years later and, by threatening his arrest and the arrest of his wife and son, obtained his cooperation.[7]

Types of Intelligence Sources

Just as we may classify intelligence officers as official cover or NOC, legal or illegal, we may make some distinctions among types of intelligence sources. One basic distinction is between recruited sources (whom an intelligence officer, after preparing the ground, "pitches," or asks to become a source) and "walk-ins" (who volunteer to assist the intelligence service of a foreign country, sometimes literally by walking into that country's embassy).

While walk-ins have often been sources of extremely valuable intelligence, they are inherently suspect, since there is always the possibility that the volunteer has in fact been dispatched by his own country's intelligence service to pass false or misleading information, to inform his country about the opposing intelligence service's methods of operation, and/or to entrap one of the opposing service's intelligence officers, leading to the officer's arrest or expulsion. On the other hand, an intelligence service that is too suspicious of walk-ins may fail to obtain information that it easily could have. Intelligence lore and history contain stories of walk-ins who were at first ignored or spurned by the country to which they volunteered their services but who turned out to be valuable intelligence sources.

One of the most famous cases of this sort involved Colonel Oleg Penkovskiy, a Soviet military intelligence (GRU) officer who served as a British and American intelligence source during 1961–62. Because of his position as an intelligence officer working in the state committee charged with obtaining Western technology, as well as his close ties to the upper echelons of the Soviet military establishment, Penkovskiy has been regarded as one of the most important Western spies since World War II. It comes as something of a shock, then, to realize that his initial attempts in 1960 to approach the U.S. Embassy in Moscow were rebuffed. It seemed inconceivable to the intelligence officers there that someone of his high rank and position would volunteer to work for the United States; it appeared much more likely that his offer was designed by Soviet counterintelligence as a provocation. It was only in the following year, when Penkovskiy explained his interest in working for the West to Greville Wynne, a British businessman with whom he conducted official business in Moscow, that his espionage career began.[8]

In addition to classifying sources, we might distinguish among the reasons why sources provide information. Sources may be attracted by the ideology or way of life of a foreign country or repulsed by that of their own. They may be greedy; they may be somewhat unbalanced people who wish to bring some excitement into their lives; they may desire to avenge what they see as ill treatment by their government; or they may be being blackmailed. The relative predominance of these motives depends on the characteristics of the society involved, as well as the tactics of the opposing intelligence services.

For example, the history of Soviet human intelligence collection against the United States and Great Britain since the 1930s shows a substantial shift from ideology toward greed and revenge as the motives for Americans or Britons to betray their country. In the 1930s, the Soviets found that the appeal of communism to some Cambridge University students and instructors, including those from prominent families, made the ideological atmosphere very favorable. Among the students recruited at that time who later became major Soviet agents within the British government were Guy Burgess, Donald Maclean, and Harold ("Kim") Philby.[9] On the other hand, Americans and Britons who have been arrested for committing espionage on behalf of the Soviet Union in the late 1970s and 1980s appear to have been motivated mostly by greed.[10] In other cases, most notably that of Edward Lee Howard, the former CIA officer who gave the Soviets important operational details concerning the agency's activities in Moscow, the motive was revenge against the CIA for having fired him.[11]

In general, the popular imagination probably overestimates the prevalence of blackmail as the reason for espionage, although the potential for blackmail may enable an intelligence officer to keep active a source who had become a spy for some other reason but who, later on, wants to quit. Even so, some cases involving blackmail of the sort featured in popular spy novels have come to light. A recent book recounts the blackmailing of a French homosexual by the Czech intelligence service on the basis of photographs of him with some Czech youths who were, of course, indirectly supplied by the service. Following his recruitment, the Frenchman worked successively for Czech, Romanian, and Soviet intelligence until his connection with the Soviets was detected by the French secret service (SDECE), and he was tried, convicted, and sentenced to seven years in prison.[12]

Problems of Human Intelligence Collection

Many of the problems encountered in human intelligence collection are inherent in the nature of the enterprise, while others are more specific to the nature of the intelligence target. Among the former is quality control—the difficulty of ensuring that the information sources provide is genuine.

Sources may, for example, simply fabricate information or imaginatively repackage and embellish publicly available material to make it appear that it came from highly placed inside sources in order to sell it (creating, to use intelligence jargon, a "paper mill"). The history of intelligence contains occasional examples of clever paper mill operators who successfully bilked their clients of large sums of money.

Such paper mills flourished in the late 1940s and early 1950s, taking advantage of the Western intelligence services' difficulty in operating behind the iron curtain. Often, they were run by émigrés from Eastern European countries who were barely surviving as refugees in the West. They soon discovered they could make a living by selling to Western intelligence services information they claimed to be receiving from acquaintances among their former countrymen who had risen to important positions in the new

Communist governments. As many of these émigrés were well educated and politically sophisticated, they were able to embellish and interpret publicly available information to produce convincing intelligence reports.[13]

A potentially more serious quality-control problem arises from the possibility that an agent has been "doubled"—that he is secretly working for his supposed target and that the information he is providing to his supposed employer is intended to deceive. Such doubling can occur when an intelligence source is apprehended and chooses to cooperate with his captors to avoid punishment. Alternatively, the source could have been a double from the beginning, never intending to serve the interests of his supposed employer.

Some of the most interesting and remarkable stories in intelligence history concern this situation. For example, in what was called the "Double-Cross System," the British succeeded in gaining control of, and running, the entire German human intelligence collection effort in Great Britain during World War II. From almost the beginning of the war, the British controlled all intelligence reports that flowed to Germany from its supposed agents in Britain. Among other achievements, these reports helped deceive the Germans about the location and nature of the D-Day landings in Normandy; even three days after D-Day (on June 9, 1944), a message from a British-controlled source was instrumental in retaining a German panzer division in the Calais area (to repel the supposedly imminent landing of a nonexistent main force), thereby helping the real invasion force in Normandy secure its foothold.[14]

Other problems derive from the nature of the target. The more effective and pervasive a target country's internal security apparatus is, the more difficulties it poses for human intelligence collection in that country. By maintaining close control over international travel and communications, as well as over the movements, communications, and economic activity of its people generally, the government of a totalitarian country can make it extremely difficult for nonofficial cover, or illegal, intelligence officers to operate. Official cover agents can be subjected to intensive surveillance, making it hard for them to meet with any citizen of the target country without being observed.

Allen Dulles, the U.S. director of central intelligence under President Dwight Eisenhower, was referring to the effectiveness of such controls when he said, in 1954, that "it's the toughest job intelligence has ever faced—getting good information from behind the Iron Curtain."[15] The result is what is termed, in U.S. intelligence jargon, a "hard target" or a "denied area"—a country in which intelligence activities can in general proceed only under official cover and then with great difficulty.

Other targets pose particular troubles as well. For instance, in attempting to collect intelligence about terrorism, we are hampered by the relatively small, secretive, and tightly knit nature of the terrorist groups. To the extent that membership in these groups depends on long acquaintanceships, family ties, or a history of previous criminal acts, it becomes very difficult to insert an intelligence agent into such a group (in intelligence jargon, to "penetrate" it). Similarly, the loyalties existing within such a group (to say nothing of the discipline it can impose on its members) make it very difficult to persuade an existing member to betray it.

Even when an agent has been inserted into a terrorist group, serious problems continue. To remain a member in good standing of the group, the agent must provide material support for, or participate in, terrorist actions. Yet an intelligence agency must put some limit on actions its agent can take to preserve his bona fides. At the same time, using the information provided by the agent to warn against or otherwise thwart a planned terrorist action runs the risk of exposing the presence of an agent among the terrorists, thus endangering the agent's life. As with organized criminal groups, it is often not until a member has been apprehended that an agency gets an opportunity to look into the inner workings of the group.

Tradecraft

The particular methods an intelligence officer uses to operate and communicate with sources without being detected by the opposing intelligence service are known collectively as "tradecraft." Part of the problem an intelligence officer faces is to defeat the opposing side's surveillance efforts to be able to meet with sources or potential sources without giving away their identity. An officer uses a wide variety of countersurveillance tricks to determine whether he is under surveillance and to attempt to escape it.

For example, an officer may spend several hours traveling to a meeting by a circuitous route, taking several different forms of transportation. If he notices that the man who sat next to him on the westbound subway also happens to be on his eastbound bus, he may reasonably conclude he is being followed. The surveillance team may try to avoid discovery by using a relay system so the same individual is not tailing the officer all the time. The game of surveillance and countersurveillance can be complicated almost indefinitely.

Tradecraft also includes techniques for communicating with a source without having to meet with him at all. For example, an officer may unobtrusively hand off a package or piece of paper to a source as he passes by on the street (a "brush pass"). If done correctly, the maneuver may be unobserved by the opposing side's surveillance. Or the officer may place his briefcase on the floor next to his chair as he enjoys a drink at a café; the source takes the table next to his and places his own briefcase, identical to the officer's, on the floor next to it. When the source leaves, he "mistakenly" takes the officer's briefcase instead of his own.

Similarly, an officer may leave a note at an arranged location, such as in a hollow tree in the park; some hours later, the source retrieves it (a "dead drop"). Again, if the officer places the note without being observed, anyone maintaining surveillance on him to determine his contacts will simply continue following him, not realizing that the meeting has in effect already occurred.

Defectors

So far, I have discussed only intelligence sources who remain in place, that is, who report information while retaining the official position that gives them access to it. This is obviously the best situation from the point of view of intelligence collection, since it implies continuing access to information, as well as the potential to "task" the source to obtain specific documents or pieces of information that are particularly necessary or useful. But it requires that the communications between the source and his handler remain hidden and exposes the source to the risk of being caught. In a denied area, these difficulties are magnified.

As a result, human intelligence collection against such countries often depends heavily on defectors. From the intelligence point of view, these are sources who do not remain in place but rather flee their countries, typically illegally, and are granted asylum. In the post–World War II period, American human intelligence collection against the Soviet Union depended heavily on such individuals.

Despite their importance, defectors present the same problems as walk-ins. It is difficult to be certain that they are genuine defectors rather than loyal citizens sent out by their government to confuse the opposition. Some skepticism is obviously required in dealing with them, at least initially. The conflicting revelations of several major Soviet defectors to the United States—in particular, concerning the presence or absence of a highly placed Soviet mole in the U.S. government—have never been completely sorted out; they bedeviled U.S. intelligence for a quarter of a century.[16]

Technical Intelligence Collection

Technical intelligence collection (or *techint,* in U.S. intelligence jargon) refers to a group of techniques using advanced technology, rather than human agents with direct access, to collect information. Ultimately limited only by the laws of physics and human ingenuity, these techniques for the most part involve long-range photography and the interception of electromagnetic (radio) waves.

Photographic or Imagery Intelligence

Photographic or imagery intelligence (*photint* or *imint*), as the name implies, involves photography to collect intelligence. More specifically, it uses long-range photography to obtain images of places or things to which direct access is not possible. It began as aerial surveillance, which came into being, almost along with aviation itself, immediately before World War I.[17]

At the beginning of the war, in August 1914, the British Royal Flying Corps conducted aerial surveillance of the German troops advancing through Belgium.[18] Once the first period of movement ended, and the German and Allied armies faced each other along a continuous front from Switzerland to the North Sea, aerial surveillance was seen as a substitute for the cavalry reconnaissance patrols that could no longer roam the area alongside and behind the enemy army. As Brigadier General William Mitchell, the American apostle of air power in the interwar period, wrote, "One flight over the lines gave me a much clearer impression of how the armies were laid out than any amount of traveling around on the ground."[19]

From this it was a relatively short step to placing cameras on these reconnaissance planes and developing an aerial photoreconnaissance capability. Unfortunately for the British and French, during most of the stalemate period on the western front following the initial German advances, the main German troop movements were by train and fairly far back from the front. It appears that aerial surveillance was only moderately successful in keeping track of them.[20]

With the further development of aviation and photography, aerial photographic reconnaissance became an important source of intelligence information during World War II. It was used not only to track the deployments and movements of enemy forces, but to follow major technological advances as well. Thus, the British used aerial photography, as well as other intelligence sources, to follow German technical developments, such as the radio-beam systems the Germans developed to direct their bombers to targets in England, new air defense radars, and the V-1 and V-2 missiles.[21]

So far, the examples given of aerial photoreconnaissance have all been from wartime; this is hardly accidental. In wartime the military incentive for conducting this sort of activity is greater and the political obstacles to it are fewer. Not only is it more important to know what is happening in the enemy's country during wartime, but alternative methods of learning about it are fewer. One cannot rely solely on reports from journalists, travelers, diplomats, or attachés; in general, press coverage will be restricted, borders will be closed, and travel within the target country will be restricted, even for the country's own nationals and nationals of neutral countries. At the same time, the international law prohibition against overflying another country without its consent no longer poses a political obstacle.

Even so, U.S. experience in trying to conduct human intelligence collection activities against the Soviet Union during the troubled peace of the years right after World War II was so unsatisfactory that attention again turned to photoreconnaissance. This interest was reinforced after the beginning of the Korean War in 1950, when the West feared that the North Korean invasion of the South foretold a Soviet invasion of Western Europe. It was believed that the Soviets could secretly prepare a massive invasion force that would then be able to attack Western Europe with very little warning. In addition, basic intelligence information about the size of Soviet military forces was often lacking.

Various attempts were made to overcome this deficiency in knowledge about the Soviet Union. One project, code-named Moby Dick, involved launching balloons equipped with downward-pointing cameras in Western Europe. The plan was that these balloons would then drift across the Soviet Union on the prevailing westerly winds until they reached Japan or the Pacific Ocean. At that point, their camera pods would be released in response to a radio signal and recovered. In reality, many of the balloons came down over the Soviet Union, enabling the Soviets to assess the camera's technology. In any case, the random movement of the balloons over the vast land mass of the Soviet Union probably meant that the photographs developed from the film that was recovered yielded minimal intelligence.[22]

On July 21, 1955, at a Geneva "Big Four" (the United States, the Soviet Union, Britain, and France) Summit, President Eisenhower proposed an "Open Skies" plan for mutual aerial surveillance of the United States and the USSR. According to this plan, the two countries would "give to each other a complete blueprint of [their] military establishments, . . . from one end of [the] country to the other" and would "provide within [the] countries facilities for aerial photography to the other country." Each country would have the right to conduct aerial surveillance over the other's territory as it saw fit.[23] The purpose of the plan was to inhibit any attempt at launching a surprise attack, which Eisenhower judged would be impossible if the potential attacker was subject to unlimited aerial surveillance. This mechanism was also seen as a precondition for various disarmament possibilities.

Eight months earlier, on November 24, 1954, Eisenhower had secretly approved the development of a new reconnaissance plane, the U-2, which could fly above the reach of Soviet fighters and surface-to-air missiles (SAMs). Furthermore, it could probably have been foreseen that photographic reconnaissance from satellites would become feasible within the next several years. Thus, Eisenhower's plan was an attempt to obtain by agreement an opportunity to conduct aerial surveillance that technological advance was going to produce (at least for the United States) in any case. Soviet leader Nikita Khrushchev, however, rejected the scheme, characterizing it as an attempt to legalize espionage. On June 21, 1956, Eisenhower secretly approved the first U-2 flight over Soviet territory.[24]

During the next four years, the U-2 flights, both over Soviet territory and along its periphery, yielded a rich intelligence return, providing the United States routine coverage of important Soviet military test facilities and bases for the first time. Although the Soviets lodged confidential diplomatic protests against the overflights, they were at first unable to do anything about them.

It was just a matter of time before the Soviets developed some means to attack the U-2. When the first successful attack occurred, on May 1, 1960, however, the Eisenhower administration was unprepared to deal with the situation, the difficulty of which was increased by the Soviets' capture of the plane's pilot, Francis Gary Powers, and retrieval of its cameras. After U.S. spokesmen had put forward an untenable cover story (that the U-2 was engaged in weather research and had accidentally strayed from its intended route over Turkey), Eisenhower personally took responsibility for the overflights of Soviet territory, which he then ended.

Even before the U-2 incident, however, the U.S. had begun work on a satellite reconnaissance capability. In January 1958, an Air Force major general publicly testified about the ongoing development of an advanced reconnaissance system to be launched by the Atlas booster, as well as about some other reconnaissance capability, with a recoverable capsule (for returning the film to earth), that he optimistically predicted could be launched in the spring of 1959.[25]

Despite being openly predicted, the existence of this satellite photoreconnaissance capability was, during its early years, regarded as classified. Although it could be assumed that the Soviets would understand that some such reconnaissance capability existed, it was not thought expedient to call public attention to the fact. At the time, the Soviets, consistent with their rejection of the Open Skies plan, took the position that space-based reconnaissance constituted espionage just as much as did aerial reconnaissance and was just as illegal. They maintained,

From the standpoint of the security of a state it makes absolutely no difference from what altitude espionage over its territory is conducted. . . . there is absolutely no ground for alleging that espionage at a high altitude, with the aid of artificial Earth satellites, is quite lawful under the existing rules of international law. Any attempt to use satellites for espionage is just as unlawful as attempts to use aircraft for similar purposes.[26]

Given this Soviet position, the U.S. government feared that public discussion of its capabilities and actions in this area would rub salt in the Soviet wounds and prompt them to make a political issue of it. Thus, after some public discussion of space reconnaissance at the end of the Eisenhower administration and seeing no reason to goad Khrushchev by openly asserting the right of the United States to conduct such reconnaissance, the Kennedy administration took "steps . . . to turn the fledgling space reconnaissance program from medium gray to deep black."[27] This policy remained in effect until 1978, when President Jimmy Carter, in a speech designed to assure the American people of the verifiability of the almost-completed SALT II Treaty, publicly confirmed that the United States possessed such a capability; its existence had been, by that time, an open secret for many years.

However good a photographic reconnaissance capability may be, it depends on sunlight and the absence of cloud cover. To get around these limitations, other types of imagery, using radar or infrared waves (emitted by hot objects), may be envisaged. For example, a radar can use the electromagnetic waves it emits not only to detect metal objects, but also, under some circumstances, to obtain a kind of image of the object analogous to an ordinary photographic image; experts use this image to determine some of the object's characteristics. (This differs from the techniques involved in signals intelligence, discussed below, in that it uses the reflection of the electromagnetic waves it emits rather than those emitted by its target.)

Similarly, another part of the electromagnetic spectrum, the infrared frequencies, can be used to detect objects that are hotter than their backgrounds. For example, in the 1930s, the British developed both infrared sensors and radar as means of detecting enemy aircraft. At that time, radar was much more feasible, and the infrared sensors were not developed. In the future, radar and infrared alternatives to conventional photography may be expected to become more important.[28]

Signals Intelligence

Signals intelligence (or *sigint*) is the generic term given to the process of deriving intelligence from the interception of electromagnetic (radio) waves, generally referred to as signals. It may be subdivided according to the type of electromagnetic wave being intercepted:

- The interception of, and derivation of information from, foreign communications signals (radio messages) by other than the intended recipients is known as communications intelligence, or *comint*.
- The interception, processing, and analysis of foreign telemetry (radio signals that relay information from sensors on board a test vehicle to the test engineers concerning the vehicle's flight and performance characteristics) are known as telemetry intelligence, or *telint*.
- The interception, processing, and analysis of noncommunications electromagnetic radiations coming from a piece of military equipment (such as a radar) while it operates are known as electronic intelligence, or *elint*.[29]

In principle, any electromagnetic wave, emitted either as a necessary part or as a by-product of the functioning of a piece of electrical equipment, is subject to interception by a receiver that is properly placed and sufficiently sensitive.[30]

Communications Intelligence (*Comint*)

Of these varieties of signals intelligence, the oldest is comint, which is practically contemporaneous with the use of radio for military and diplomatic communications.[31] Through the end of World War II, comint (combined with cryptanalysis—the breaking of the codes and ciphers in which the valuable messages are transmitted) was more important than any other source of intelligence for the major powers, both in peace and in war, for which we have adequate information to judge.[32]

One of the first uses of comint for which a record is publicly available is the British Navy's use during World War I to give it advance warning of any bid by its German rival to venture out into the North Sea. In addition, at the beginning of the war, the British severed German-owned underwater telegraph cables that linked Germany with the Americas, Africa, and Spain. As a result, Germany's diplomatic "cables" to those areas were sent by radio and were intercepted by the Royal Navy's monitoring stations as well.[33]

Whatever its earlier successes, it is World War II that marks the heyday of British, as well as American, communications intelligence. Under the rubrics "Ultra" and "Magic," vast amounts of accurate and timely information were made available to British and American political and military leaders; measuring the precise extent of its impact on the course of the war remains a huge historical task.

While we would expect that a country's most sensitive radio messages would be encrypted to protect their confidentiality, some areas of communications intelligence are still independent of cryptanalysis. Because of the expense and difficulty involved, some radio traffic is not encrypted; for example, tactical voice communications, such as those between airplanes and ground control stations, are often broadcast "in the clear." In other cases, message traffic is not encrypted because it is believed, rightly or wrongly, that an adversary does not wish to, or cannot, intercept or (because of the large volumes of information involved) process it. Finally, we should not underestimate the importance of simple inertia: for example, the United States has made only belated responses to its discovery that the Soviet Union can, and does, intercept long-distance telephone calls that are transmitted by microwave from one tower to the next.

In addition, a technique known as "traffic analysis" seeks to derive useful information from fluctuations in the volume and other external characteristics of radio communications, even when the content of the messages cannot be understood. For example, if an army headquarters and its subordinate command posts are exchanging an unusually large number of messages, we might conclude that an important operation is about to take place. Similarly, by means of "direction finding," a technique for determining the geographic origin of a radio signal, we can determine the location of the ship, plane, or command post that is transmitting it.

While most comint involves interception of radio messages, messages being passed by wire also can intercepted. This requires physical access to the wires and so is of a less general application than comint involving radio traffic, although in particular cases, it may be important. For example, wiretaps may readily be maintained on telephone lines to an adversary's embassy or consulate in one's own country.

On occasion it may be possible to gain surreptitious access, even outside one's own country, to telephone or telegraph wires an adversary is using. For example, in the divided cities of Vienna and Berlin, in the early and mid-1950s, British and American intelligence managed to tap such wires used by the Soviet military authorities. In the case of the Berlin operation, this involved elaborate secret tunneling from a point in the American sector of the city, under the border between the American and Soviet sectors, to intersect cables running entirely within the Soviet sector.[34]

In addition, through the cooperation of the private companies or government agencies that run the international telegraph service, nations have been able to obtain the texts of other nation's diplomatic telegrams; of course, these messages were typically encrypted, so the benefit from obtaining them depended on a nation's cryptanalytic capabilities. For example, during the 1920s, the U.S. Black Chamber (a secret cryptanalytic office subordinate to the Department of State) worked on encrypted diplomatic cables, the texts of which it presumably obtained from the private U.S. international telegraph companies.[35] At present, of course, radio is more likely to be used for communicating between a government and its embassies abroad.

Telemetry Intelligence (Telint)

The other forms of sigint are newer and reflect the expanding military use of electromagnetic phenomena. Telemetry intelligence (or *telint*) is similar in concept to comint except (1) that the communications on which one is eavesdropping are between a test vehicle (such as a missile) and a ground station and (2) that they consist not of words but the readings of various sensors and other on-board equipment. These measurements of such test characteristics as the acceleration the vehicle is undergoing, the temperature at various points within the vehicle, the rates of flow of fuels, and so forth, taken together, give the engineers on the ground a picture of what is happening on the test vehicle. Just as in the case of comint, the country conducting the test may seek to deny others access to the telemetric information by encrypting it on the missile before broadcasting it back to the ground station.

Electronics Intelligence (Elint)

Elint involves monitoring and analyzing noncommunication electromagnetic emanations from foreign military equipment. By intercepting a radar signal, for example, we can determine various operating characteristics of the radar, such as its beam width (how much space it can scan at one time). Similarly, the maximum operational range of a radar that emits discrete pulses can be determined from the pulse repetition rate (the number of discrete pulses, or "bundles," of radio waves emitted per second).

British scientific intelligence during World War II supplies an illustration of this point. From the fact that the German Freya air defense radar operated at a pulse repetition rate of 500 pulses per second, the British concluded that its maximum range was 300 kilometers. (The calculation is made as follows: the radio wave emitted by a radar travels at the speed of light, or 300,000 kilometers per second. Hence, it can travel 300,000/500 = 600 kilometers between pulses. Therefore, if the wave is to reach the target and return to the radar before the next pulse is emitted, the target cannot be more than 300 kilometers from the radar).[36]

Other Categories of Technical Intelligence

The possibilities for technical intelligence are limited only by the laws of physics and human ingenuity. In addition to photint and sigint, other techniques have been used to collect intelligence. For example, special sensors have been developed to detect and characterize nuclear detonations. These include seismometers, which measure the shock waves associated with underground nuclear tests; devices to detect the radioactivity associated with nuclear materials or the fallout of an above-ground nuclear test; and sensors for the remote detection of the flashes of light produced by an above-ground nuclear test. A different kind of sensor, sonar, uses another natural phenomenon, sound waves, to detect submarines under the ocean's surface; aside from its location, other characteristics of the submarine may be determinable from an analysis of the sounds it emits or reflects.[37]

Platforms for Intelligence Collection

In public discussion and in our discussion so far, the emphasis has been on satellite-based systems to collect intelligence. Satellites have the obvious advantage of being able to overfly any part of the world, without respect for international boundaries. However, they have certain drawbacks as well:

- They are, in general, much more expensive than other reconnaissance platforms.
- They cannot get very close to their targets (satellites in low-earth orbit generally remain at altitudes well above 100 miles, while those in geostationary orbit must be at an altitude of 22,400 miles).
- They are relatively useless a large part of the time even if their orbits are calculated to maximize the intelligence they gather (in other words, a photographic reconnaissance satellite that earns its keep by taking pictures of the Soviet Union nevertheless must, because of the laws of orbital physics, spend a lot of less productive time over the Southern Hemisphere as well).
- Their orbits are predictable, so that the adversary may be able to warn sensitive installations when a reconnaissance satellite will be in range.[38]

Consequently, the development of intelligence satellites has not meant that other kinds of platforms are not used to carry intelligence sensors. For example, airplanes can fly missions along the periphery of an adversary's territory, they can intercept communications that cannot be intercepted from farther out in space, they can take pictures of areas near the territorial boundary, and they can intercept radar signals from the adversary's air defense radars, some of which may have become active precisely to chart the airplane's course.

Ships, such as the ubiquitous Soviet "fishing trawlers," can intercept radio signals from off an adversary's coast. Seaborne or ground-based radars, if they can be located close enough to a site where test missiles are launched or where they reenter the earth's atmosphere, can track an adversary's missile flight tests and determine some of the missile's characteristics. Ground-based sites, depending on location, also can be used to intercept various radio signals.

Legal Issues with Respect to Overhead Reconnaissance

As we have noted, the chief advantage of satellites is in their ability to overfly an adversary's territory without his consent. The U.S. position has been that since a nation's sovereignty does not extend into outer space (beyond the earth's atmosphere), a nation is as free to conduct activities in outer space as it is on the high seas. At the beginning of the space age, the Soviet Union took the position that satellite reconnaissance was as illegal under international law as aerial reconnaissance involving the unapproved overflight of another nation's territory. The Soviets argued that, although outer space did not fall under any nation's sovereignty, it was not a legal vacuum: the presumed illegality of espionage in general applied to space reconnaissance as well.

The Outer Space Treaty in 1967 did not directly address the issue of space reconnaissance. It is often claimed that in the Strategic Arms Limitation Talks (SALT) the Soviets accepted the legality of photoreconnaissance and other forms of satellite surveillance. However, the wording of the relevant SALT provisions (the ABM Treaty, the SALT I Interim Agreement on Offensive Arms, and the SALT II Treaty are the same in this regard) is vague:

> For the purpose of providing assurance of compliance with the provisions of this Treaty [or Interim Agreement], each Party shall use national technical means of verification at its disposal in a manner consistent with generally recognized principles of international law.[39]

The term "national technical means" (NTM) is not defined. While U.S. officials have stated that NTM includes reconnaissance satellites, Soviet officials have been silent about this interpretation. More important, the provision refers to the use of NTM "in a manner consistent with generally recognized principles of international law." Thus, the provision is something of a tautology: if it grants the right to use satellite surveillance at all, it grants it only when such reconnaissance is conducted in a manner *already* regarded as consistent with international law principles and, hence, presumably already permissible.[40] In short, the provision neither legalizes space reconnaissance nor recognizes its legality.

Nevertheless, as a practical matter, the SALT provisions have inhibited any Soviet challenge to overhead reconnaissance; post-Salt writings have ignored the issue. In other regards, however, these Soviet writings have argued against the right to use satellites for direct television broadcasting or for surveying natural resources without the target nation's permission.[41] Thus, the theoretical basis for an objection to space-based reconnaissance still exists. As one Soviet work puts it, "It should be noted, however, that permission to use space objects for functions of verifying compliance with [the SALT agreements] cannot serve as grounds for an extended interpretation of the verification provisions."[42]

Comparison of Humint and Techint

In the past several years, something of a debate has been going on in the United States concerning the relative importance of humint and techint. On one side are those who view technical intelligence as primary and as likely to keep increasing in relative importance as technology advances; on the other are those who think that the United States has overemphasized technical intelligence at the expense of traditional espionage and that it is necessary to right the balance.

Perhaps the most striking recent contribution to the debate has been the spirited defense of techint's primacy in the memoirs of Admiral Stansfield Turner, President Carter's director of central intelligence (DCI):

Now that we have technical systems ranging from satellites traveling in space over the entire globe, to aircraft flying in free airspace, to miniature sensors surreptitiously positioned close to difficult targets, we are approaching a time when we will be able to survey almost any point on the earth's surface with some sensor, and probably with more than one. We can take detailed photographs from very long distances, detect heat sources through infrared devices, pinpoint metal with magnetic detectors, distinguish between barely moving and stationary objects through the use of Doppler radar, use radar to detect objects that are covered or hidden by darkness, eavesdrop on all manner of signals from the human voice to electronic radio waves, detect nuclear radiation with refined Geiger counters, and sense underground explosions at long distances with seismic devices. Most of the activities we want to monitor give off several kinds of signals. Tanks in battle can be detected by the heat from their engines, the magnetism in their armor, or photographs. A nuclear weapons plant emits radiation, has a particular external physical shape, and receives certain types of supplies. One way or another, we should soon be able to keep track of most activities on the surface of the earth, day or night, good weather or bad.[43]

When we consider the sheer technological prowess involved in creating these sorts of technical collection devices, it is indeed breathtaking. Nevertheless, admiration for the technology can easily lead to an overestimation of what techint can accomplish and a concomitant depreciation of human intelligence. In the United States, this view was particularly prevalent during the mid- and late 1970s; since that time, however, humint's importance has received renewed recognition.

The strengths of techint are well described in the passage cited above. For the United States, technical intelligence has been indispensable for collecting the major part of the information it obtains about the Soviet Union. It should be noted, however, that a large part of this information is publicly available in many other countries. Information about the size and general composition of the armed forces and the development of major new weapon systems, for example, is available in most countries from official (especially budgetary and parliamentary) documents. With respect to the Soviet Union, however, intelligence methods are required to collect such information because of the regime's pervasive secrecy on military issues, a secrecy that has continued, in attenuated form, into the era of Gorbachev and *glasnost*.

Thus, much of the technical collection effort is devoted to countering the effects of this secrecy; with respect to many of the categories of information all countries keep secret—such as political and military intentions and plans—human intelligence collection still may be required. Proponents of humint stress that, despite technological progress, old-fashioned espionage remains necessary to provide information about the intentions, political activity, and strategic concepts of an adversary's leadership. Indeed, understanding the adversary's intentions, his strategy, and his perception of the situation in which he finds himself are often the most important intelligence information we could have.

Interception of communications among the highest levels of an adversary's political and military leaders (high-level comint) can also provide intelligence of this sort; it would be similar to having a human agent with excellent access to the adversary's leadership. Obtaining this information through comint, however, is much more difficult than the Turner passage suggests. First of all, an adversary may be expected to encrypt most sensitive communications; as noted in the next chapter, it appears that technological advance (in terms of increasing computer capabilities) aids those trying to develop more secure codes and ciphers rather than those trying to break them.

In this connection, note that human intelligence collection can provide codebooks or other information that facilitates the decrypting of messages. For example, in the early 1930s, the French intelligence service obtained from an agent in Germany important information about the German coding machine, Enigma, including instructions for its use, some details of its construction, and the keys (or daily settings) indicating the position to which the machine was set on a given day.[44] This information was shared with the Polish intelligence service, which achieved the first major cryptanalytic breakthroughs that formed the basis of the eventual British success during World War II.

Second, most comint capabilities can be defeated by keeping messages off the air, that is, transmitting them via wire instead. Intercepting such messages requires gaining access to the wires, which is likely to be difficult in most cases. Furthermore, a new means of transmitting signals, fiber optics, uses coherent light (laser beams) to carry messages and is relatively invulnerable to wiretapping.

In addition, all types of technological intelligence collection, including comint, suffer from a potential "embarrassment of riches." Despite the global reach of the technical collection systems, as described by Turner, there must be some method by which they are told which targets to observe and which to ignore. While it may be correct that "we [soon] will be able to survey almost any point on the earth's surface with some sensor," no one could survey them all at the same time, and even if one could, one would not be able to process all the data the sensors could collect.

Thus, from the existence of technical capabilities such as described by Turner, we cannot conclude that nothing of importance on the earth's surface can escape the notice of an intelligence service with an up-to-date technical intelligence collection capability. Everything depends on the ability to target the sensors appropriately. Human intelligence collection can provide the essential first indication that something of interest is occurring or will occur at a given location. This makes it possible to target the technical systems on that area. Without such clues, the technical systems would be less efficient and might miss important developments either for long periods or altogether.

With respect to some kinds of intelligence information, the problem of correctly targeting the technical sensors may be virtually insoluble. For example, humint is likely to be necessary to collect crucial information about nongovernmental targets (such as terrorist organizations) that lack the fixed facilities or communication networks that are vulnerable to technical collection. In other words, the fewer known locations that a group can be associated with, the harder it is to target technical sensors on it. Intelligence collection against such groups is likely to depend heavily on the ability to infiltrate the group or to recruit its members as informants. If groups of this sort become important intelligence targets, human intelligence collection will become more important as well.

A human intelligence source can also provide the clues to interpret the raw data gathered by a technical collection system. Even with a good picture of a building, for example, an intelligence analyst may not be able to determine its function; a human source familiar with it may be able to explain that the presence of a certain detail, not otherwise remarkable, in fact indicates that the building was designed for a specific purpose connected with a specific military program. Without the human source, it might have been unlikely that the detail would have been noticed or its significance understood. But once this ''signature'' is recognized, pictures of similar buildings can be examined to see if the same detail is present.

As these examples illustrate, humint and techint can serve complementary roles. The intelligence services of a global power such as the United States will continue to require both. Regardless of any technological advances that enhance technical intelligence collection capabilities, human intelligence collection will still be necessary.

Open-source Collection

Publications and Broadcasts

No discussion of intelligence collection would be complete without reference to the gathering of information from open sources, that is, newspapers, books, radio, and television broadcasts and any other public source of information. Even in the case of a society as secretive as the pre-*glasnost* Soviet Union, a lot of valuable information could be gleaned from such sources; with more open societies, even greater amounts of information are openly available.

The importance of open sources in the intelligence process is a matter of dispute and is ultimately tied to some basic questions about the nature of intelligence. One view, expressed by Sherman Kent, is that the bulk of ''high-level foreign positive intelligence . . . must be through unromantic open-and-above-board observation and research.''[45] The more traditional view, on the other hand, has held that while open sources may provide important context and background, the key facts, such as an adversary's specific intentions, must be obtained primarily, if not solely, from nonpublic sources by means of espionage or technical collection.

This question is discussed at length in chapter 7. At this point, the focus will be on the various uses to which open-source information can be put. For example, a standard task of military intelligence officers has been to prepare vast compendia of information concerning countries in which future military operations may have to be conducted. Such compendia should include all information that might be useful to a military staff preparing such an operation. Information concerning the country's geography, its communications and transportation networks, key military and economic facilities, and so forth would all have to be included in sufficient detail to allow the planner to make many decisions, such as determining how quickly troops and supplies could be moved from point A to point B.

Except in the case of the most secretive countries (such as the Soviet Union, where it was admitted in 1988 that previously published maps had been falsified as a security measure[46]), much of this information will be available in open-source literature: road and railroad maps and timetables, newspaper and magazine articles, government economic and statistical reports, and even old travel guides. Collecting and cataloging it are other matters. Huge amounts of information are involved and the resources to collect it for every relevant country are unlikely ever to be available. If, as discussed in the next chapter, the U.S. military force that invaded Grenada in 1983 was not supplied with adequate maps and other information about the island, this was not due to any difficulty in collecting the information but rather to the failure to allocate sufficient resources to what probably seemed like a small, out-of-the-way island.

Similarly, a vast profusion of statistical sources publish economic data throughout the world. Deciding what should be collected, however, requires some sense of what intelligence requirements are likely to be. Economic data may be needed to support the formulation of policies on international trade or economic sanctions, to deal with the effects of shortages and international cartels (such as the Organization of Petroleum Exporting Countries [OPEC]), and so forth. Other kinds of economic data, such as might result from the monitoring of cash flows, could shed light on the international drug trade. Finally, economic data may be needed to support political and military analyses; for example, predictions of Soviet behavior in the late 1980s were dominated by questions of how the Soviet economic situation would affect other areas of policy. Each of these intelligence requirements calls for different sorts of economic data to be collected.

In addition to these obvious types of open-source materials, intelligence analysts require the same sorts of information—speeches by prominent political figures, texts of laws and resolutions, census and other demographic data—that would be required for any academic analysis of the political or social conditions in a foreign country; indeed, the end product may be similar as well.

Depending on the available resources, an intelligence agency may be able to collect specialized data to a degree that would overwhelm an academic researcher. For example, an important technique of kremlinology (the study of Soviet leadership politics) involves tracing the careers of midlevel Soviet officials to determine which midlevel officials are the protégés, or "clients," of which Politburo members or other senior officials. Once these patron-client relationships have been identified, an analyst can, by noting the promotions and demotions of the clients, determine the relative standings of their high-level patrons.

To do this, however, requires the collection and maintenance of an extensive biographic data base. It would involve scanning all major Soviet newspapers and news broadcasts (those originating from the capitals of the various republics as well as those from Moscow, including inter alia the governmental, party, trade union, and military organs); recording every news item that indicates the promotion, demotion, or transfer of an official or that links two officials; and computerizing the resulting data base to make it useful for researchers. A scholar, or even an academic institute, might be hard-pressed to undertake such a task.[47]

Diplomatic and Attaché Reporting

Another means of collecting information, which might be regarded as a composite of humint and open source because it is obtained by human agents but in a straightforward and aboveboard manner, would be the reports diplomats and military attachés file concerning events in the country to which they are posted. Indeed, the line between diplomat and intelligence officer has not always been clear-cut. As one historian of diplomacy primly puts it, "Ambassadors sometimes readily crossed the nebulous line between legitimate gathering of information and espionage and other ill-reputed activities."[48] But even today, when the two functions are separate, diplomatic reports on the political situation in the host country can be an important input to any political analysis. A diplomat who has good access to major political figures in a country should be able to provide insights into the internal political situation that would not be found in the media.

Similarly, military attachés, to the extent they have access to military officers of their host country, can gain insights into the host country's military establishment, such as the personalities of the leading military officers and their competence, characteristic ways of thought, views on military doctrine, and relations with the civilian leadership. In addition, attachés may be invited to observe military exercises or attend reviews or ceremonial occasions where new military equipment is paraded or flown by. They also may be able to travel in the host country and thus observe airfields, harbors, and other military and civilian installations of interest.[49]

Other Overt Human Sources

Diplomats and attachés are not the only foreigners who visit a country and report their observations. For example, the 1987 treaty between United States and the USSR on the elimination of intermediate-range and shorter-range missiles (the INF Treaty) provides that each party send inspectors to specified military facilities of the other party to ascertain whether the country is complying with the treaty's terms. The inspectors have greater access to those facilities than attachés or other visitors would have. Obviously, their reports will contain valuable information concerning their host's military forces.

Similarly, businessmen, scientists, and other travelers learn information about the countries they visit that, while not officially secret, is nevertheless not available in the public media. Whether this information makes its way to their country's government depends, in a country whose citizens do not need special permission to travel abroad, on the willingness of such travelers to report it. The notoriety achieved by the U.S. Central Intelligence Agency has probably meant that, since the 1970s, it has benefitted less from this sort of voluntary cooperation. But the general increase in travel to and from the Soviet Union has meant that the opportunities for such overt human collection have grown tremendously.[50]

3

WHAT DOES IT ALL MEAN?

INTELLIGENCE ANALYSIS AND PRODUCTION

What Is Analysis?

Analysis refers to the process of transforming the bits and pieces of information that are collected in whatever fashion into something that is usable by policymakers and military commanders. The result, or "intelligence product," can take the form of short memorandums, elaborate formal reports, briefings, or any other means of presenting information. This section indicates the breadth of analytic techniques. In describing these activities, standard intelligence terminology is not always used; indeed, analysis does not have any standard categories. Furthermore, the categories that do exist are neither precise nor mutually exclusive. An attempt has been made to arrange the techniques from the most technical, such as the decrypting of coded messages, to the most speculative, such as the predicting of future social and political trends. A subsequent section discusses the variety of intelligence products and the functions they serve.

Technical Analysis

I use the term "technical analysis" here to refer to analytic methods that transform highly specialized data, totally or virtually incomprehensible to everyone but the specialist, into data that other intelligence analysts can use. The examples discussed are cryptanalysis (which transforms seemingly random strings of letters or numbers into the text of a message in a known language), telemetry analysis (which transforms a radio signal into a group of time series describing the performance of a missile or other test vehicle), and photo interpretation (which identifies and measures objects in a photograph).

Cryptanalysis

Cryptanalysis refers to the solving, or "breaking," of enemy codes and ciphers, thereby enabling analysts to transform an intercepted encrypted message into its original, meaningful form. In most cases, the interception involves the reception of radio signals by someone other than their intended recipient. However, the cryptanalytic problem is the same in the case of an encrypted message carried by a captured courier, an encrypted letter opened by postal censorship, or an encrypted telegram obtained by tapping a telegraph cable.

In technical usage, the terms "code" and "cipher" refer to different methods of encryption. In a code, a word or phrase (signifying a thing, concept, or location) is replaced by the group of digits or letters (which may or may not form an actual word) that is found opposite that word or phrase in the codebook. Thus, the message "attack on Saturday" would be encrypted by finding the code group for "attack" (say FGHJ) and that for "Saturday" (say ADFK), thus producing the encrypted message FGHJ ADFK. If a word is not found in the codebook, the sender can either reword the message to use words and phrases in the codebook or spell out the missing word using special code groups of individual letters or syllables.

In a cipher, on the other hand, each letter in the original message—called the "plaintext"—is replaced, following some formula or algorithm, by another letter, thereby forming the "ciphertext." (In a transposition cipher, the letters of the original message are retained, but they are transmitted in a jumbled order, according to some scheme.) For example, a cipher might consist of the rule that each letter be replaced by the letter following it in the alphabet. In this extremely simple cipher, the message in the example used above would be enciphered as BUUBDL PO TBUVSEBZ.

A more complicated cipher (still much too simple to offer any security) would replace the first letter of the message by the letter following it in the alphabet, the second letter, by the letter two places down in the alphabet, and so forth. (For the purposes of such a cipher, the alphabet would be envisaged as written in a circle, with the letter A immediately following the letter Z. Thus, the twenty-sixth letter of the message would be unchanged, while the twenty-seventh, like the first, would be replaced by its immediate successor, and so on.) The message would now read BVWEHQ VV BKEGERPO.

These techniques can be combined in various ways. For example, a coded message may then be enciphered in the same way a plaintext might be. Thus, our example message encoded as before and then enciphered by the first method discussed would yield the following "superenciphered" text:

GHIK BEGL. The advantage of such a procedure is the greater security it offers—to recover the original message, an adversary must break both the code and the cipher. Typically, the code would remain in effect for a long time, while the cipher algorithm would change frequently. The reason is that while the former is quite difficult to change (each change of code means new codebooks must be distributed to each embassy, headquarters, or post that might send or receive messages), it is a simpler matter to change the cipher.

Cryptanalysis refers to the solving or breaking of both codes and ciphers—that is, to reconstructing the adversary's codebook or figuring out the method he is using to encipher messages—using primarily the encrypted messages themselves. (Decryption, on the other hand, usually refers to the intended recipient recovering the plaintext.) Cryptology refers to the more general study of these things, both for cryptanalytic purposes and for devising more secure codes and ciphers. Cryptography is sometimes used to refer specifically to the latter activity (the devising of codes and ciphers) but is sometimes used synonymously with cryptology.

The typical raw material with which cryptanalysis begins is a collection of encrypted messages. Cryptanalysis's task is to discern whatever patterns exist in the apparently meaningless jumble of letters or numbers and to relate those patterns to the known patterns that exist in the language in which the messages were presumably written. For example, in ordinary English text, the letter *E* appears more frequently than any other; therefore, in a group of messages enciphered in the simple substitution cipher discussed above (in which each letter of the plaintext is replaced by one immediately following it in the alphabet), the letter *F* would probably be the most frequent.

Noticing this fact, the cryptanalyst would begin by assuming that *F* stands for *E*. He then might notice that *UIF* appears more frequently than any other three-letter word and assume that it stands for *THE*. At this point, he might well guess that each letter in the ciphertext stands for the letter immediately preceding it in the alphabet and, trying it out, would discover that this was indeed the case.

As may be seen by even this simple example, the amount of raw material a cryptanalyst can obtain is an important factor in determining whether a solution can be achieved. In a short message, *E* may not be particularly frequent: in our example (''attack on Saturday''), it does not appear at all. In a longer message, or series of messages, however, the laws of probability take over, and it would be extremely unlikely for the frequencies of the various letters (or small groups of letters) in the plaintext to differ much from the frequencies with which they appear in ordinary English text.

The history of cryptology is a fascinating one, and it is impossible to go into it in detail here.[1] For our purposes, it will be sufficient to divide that history into three periods, according to the technology that was available for encrypting messages.

In the first period, running from antiquity to the 1930s, messages had to be encrypted by hand. Various techniques were available including codebooks and substitution and transposition ciphers. By the end of this period, codebooks had grown to be cumbersome affairs, with thousands of entries. However, since they tended to be used for long periods, cryptanalysts could eventually reconstruct them. Similarly, cryptanalysts were helped by the fact that the complexity of ciphers was limited because all the steps involved in producing the ciphertext had to be performed by hand. Because the possibility of an encryption or decryption mistake increases as a cipher becomes more complex, it was not always practical to introduce more difficult ciphers.

Of course, the easiest way to break a code is to steal, capture, or otherwise obtain a copy of the codebook, without letting the enemy know about it. Since producing and distributing a new codebook to everyone who would need it is not an easy matter, a code was likely to remain in use for a long period of time, thus enhancing the usefulness of the captured book.

Before and during World War I, all the major European powers had special offices for decrypting foreign diplomatic and military messages. At the beginning of World War I, for example, the British managed to obtain (from captured or sunken ships) copies of the major German naval codebooks. Although the Germans took the precaution of further enciphering the coded messages, the British decrypted them nevertheless.[2]

However, probably the most important British cryptanalytic success involved German diplomatic, rather than naval, codes. On January 17, 1917, British cryptographers decoded a message, known to history as the Zimmermann telegram, in which the German foreign minister directed the Kaiser's ambassador to Mexico to propose a German-Mexican alliance against the United States, in case the United States reacted to German initiation of unrestricted submarine warfare (scheduled for February 1) by declaring war on Germany. Subsequent publication in U.S. newspapers of the telegram, which envisaged Mexico recovering Texas, New Mexico, and Arizona, created a fire storm that did much to make President Woodrow Wilson's decision to go to war inevitable. The release of the telegram was handled so skillfully that the Germans did not suspect that their code had been broken.[3]

The story of American cryptography during World War I and the following decade illustrates how, despite the immense intellectual challenge involved, it was still possible at that time for an individual, working by himself or with a small group, to discover the basic principles of the art and to solve codes and ciphers used to encrypt the most sensitive messages.

Indeed, Herbert Yardley relates how he was able, in several hours on his own, to cryptanalyze a message to President Wilson from Colonel Edward House, Wilson's personal representative then on a diplomatic mission to Germany.[4] Yardley's account of his leadership of the U.S. Army's cryptanalytic unit once the United States entered the war and of the State Department's Black Chamber after the war's end indicates the extent to which cryptography was, at that time, an art rather than a science and how it depended on the insights and intuitions of individuals working essentially by themselves.

However, in the case of cryptology, as in many other areas of military and intelligence activities, World War I marked a crucial stage. According to a historian of cryptography,

> The First World War marks the great turning point in the history of cryptology. Before, it was a small field; afterwards, it was big. Before, it was a science in its youth; afterwards, it had matured. The direct cause of this development was the enormous increase in radio communications.[5]

Increased radio traffic meant a greater advantage to be gained by breaking an enemy's code or cipher. At the same time, the increased amount of traffic meant that, other things being equal, codes or ciphers of the same complexity became more vulnerable to cryptanalysis, since the more raw material (encrypted in the same code or cipher) available, the greater the chance that the cryptanalyst will detect the repeating patterns that make a solution possible.

More radio traffic also meant that manual systems for encrypting and decrypting messages were more and more overloaded. This, plus the desire for more secure (more complex and thus harder to break) encryption systems, led to a second period, in which mechanical or electromechanical devices, such as the American Hagelin, the German Enigma, and the Japanese "Purple" machines, were used to encipher texts.[6]

Such machines incorporated a much more complicated enciphering algorithm or formula than that used by previous cipher systems. More complicated cryptanalytic techniques and procedures were therefore needed to solve these ciphers. Breaking them involved the development and use of primitive computers as well as advances in statistics and other branches of theoretical mathematics.[7] The story of solving electromechanical cipher machines such as Enigma and "Purple" is contained in the literature on World War II cryptography.

We are in the third period, which is characterized by the use of computers both to encipher and decipher messages and to support cryptanalytic efforts. For obvious reasons, this subject is very sensitive, and not much information is publicly available about it. The rise of "public cryptography"—the study and use of cryptography by independent scholars and businessmen—has meant that some information about it has come into the public domain.[8] However, it is not possible, from unclassified sources, to determine how the sophistication of public cryptography's methodology compares to the real thing.

Nevertheless, a few things can be said about the current situation and the relative cryptologic strengths of the United States and USSR. Given the centrality of computers, it would seem likely that the U.S. lead in that area gives it an important advantage; to some extent, this may be balanced by Soviet strengths in the area of theoretical mathematics.[9]

At the same time, it would appear that advances in computer power (in terms of the speed with which the basic arithmetic operations may be performed) favor the defense. In other words, although an increase in computer power enables both the encrypter to use ciphers of greater complexity and the cryptanalyst to solve ciphers of greater complexity, the net effect is to favor the encrypter. A given increment in computer power allows complexities to be introduced into the cipher that the same increment in computer power cannot unravel. If this is so, then the long-term future of cryptanalysis, at least as it attempts to break the ciphers of major powers using the most advanced technology, is in principle not very good. In practice, of course, because of some error in its construction, a given cipher may not take full advantage of the available computer technology and is therefore weaker than it should have been. In addition, mistakes in using the cipher may allow cryptanalysts to solve it.[10] Finally, espionage may bring solutions to cryptologic systems that could not have been solved by cryptanalysis.

Fragility of Cryptanalysis

Cryptanalysis is among the more fragile of intelligence methods, since a country usually changes its cryptographic system if it realizes that an adversary can read its encrypted messages. Thus, it is not surprising that the American and British cryptanalytic successes during World War II were considered to be among the most vital secrets of the war, worthy of the most careful security arrangements that could be devised. In the case of the British success in mastering the German Enigma machine, the secret was kept for about thirty years, despite the large number of people involved in the operation.

The American case was far different. In what might be the worst security breach of the war, the *Chicago Tribune* published, on June 7, 1942, an article on the U.S. victory at the Battle of Midway. Headlined "Navy Had Word of Jap Plan to Strike at Sea," it cited materials derived from decoded Japanese messages. In particular, it included the names of not only the Japanese carriers involved, but also the light cruisers that supported the would-be occupation forces. Furthermore, it asserted that when the Japanese fleet moved toward Midway, "all American outposts were warned" and that U.S. naval intelligence had been able to predict "a feint at some American base [Dutch Harbor, in the Aleutians], to be accompanied by a serious effort to invade and occupy another base [Midway Island]."[11]

A Japanese intelligence expert would probably conclude from the article that the United States had been reading coded Japanese naval messages. Although the matter was referred to a grand jury in Chicago, however, no indictment was brought. It appears that the key U.S. officials ultimately decided against prosecution on the grounds that a trial would only call attention to the article and probably require a public confirmation of the fact that the United States was reading coded Japanese naval messages. (Ironically, on August 31, 1942, this very fact was mentioned by a congressman in a floor speech castigating the *Tribune*'s "unthinking and wicked misuse of the freedom of the press."[12])

On August 14, 1942, the Japanese Navy introduced a new version of its code (dubbed JN-25d by U.S. cryptanalysts). Although the appearance of a new version of the code so soon after the previous version(JN-25c) had been introduced (on June 1) was suspicious, postwar researchers have not discovered any compelling evidence that the change was motivated by the article.[13] Furthermore, the new version of the code "retained the characteristic of the broad JN-25 formula," thus allowing the United States to regain access to the Japanese message traffic more easily than if the Japanese had instituted an entirely new system.[14] In general, the historians who have written on the issue have believed that the existence or, in any case, the significance of the *Tribune* leak escaped the notice of the Japanese altogether and that the August code change was merely a routine one.

Nevertheless, it did take the United States about four months to become as familiar with the JN-25d code as it had been with previous versions. Furthermore, the difficulties involved in developing a new cryptographic system and distributing it to the fleet could easily explain why the Japanese reaction was limited to merely advancing the date of an already planned code change. Recent research has uncovered a reference in Japanese diplomatic traffic to a request to the Japanese Embassy in neutral Lisbon for "newspapers, particularly the antigovernment 'Chicago Tribune,' with as many back issues as possible."[15] Although far from conclusive, this suggests that Japanese authorities were aware of the *Tribune* article on Midway and at least concerned enough about its possible significance to want to see it for themselves.

A more clear-cut example of the fragility of cryptanalysis, involving Britain this time, occurred in 1927. During the preceding years, the British cryptanalytic bureau, the Government Code and Cypher School, had been able to decipher messages between the Comintern headquarters, or the Soviet government in Moscow, and the various Soviet representatives in London (the Soviet Embassy as well as a trade delegation and a trade office of Arcos, the All-Russian Cooperative Society). By this means, the British government tracked the activities of the Soviet diplomats and trade representatives, activities that included espionage and involvement in trade union affairs. In 1927, when the British broke off diplomatic relations with the Soviet Union, these departures from diplomatic decorum were cited as the reasons for the decision. However, the British ministers, when pressed in Parliament to defend their action, were indiscreet in discussing the matter and revealed publicly their ability to read encrypted Soviet messages. The predictable result was that the Soviet Union introduced new ciphers, which the British were unable to break.[16]

A similar case, in which a democratically elected government revealed sensitive cryptanalytic capabilities in order to build support for its policies and thereby lost access to encrypted messages, seems to have occurred in the United States in 1986. Apparently to justify its eventual decision to bomb government facilities in Tripoli, Libya,

> President Reagan [the *Washington Post* reported] and his top advisers made an extraordinary disclosure of sensitive intelligence information . . . to demonstrate that United States has hard evidence that Libya . . . was directly responsible for the bombing of a West Berlin nightclub. . . .
>
> The specifics cited by the president . . . sources said, will make it clear that the United States has the capability to intercept and decode Libya's sensitive diplomatic communications.[17]

The predictable result in fact occurred: "The public disclosure of decoded Libyan diplomatic cables has caused American intelligence analysts to lose a valuable source of information that may take weeks or months to replace, Administration officials said today."[18]

These examples demonstrate a general point about intelligence that applies to other collection and analysis techniques as well: the better the information analysts have available, the more inhibited they are about using it and perhaps alerting the adversary to their intelligence capabilities. This dilemma is strongest in the case of a democratic government that finds itself pressed to reveal detailed intelligence information to persuade the public that its policies are reasonable. But a form of the same dilemma exists for any government, under any circumstances, whenever it possesses specific intelligence information on which it wishes to act.

The problem is most likely to come up in wartime, when the incentive for acting on the intelligence may be very great. For example, during World War II, the British knew, from intercepted and decrypted communications, the precise schedule of the German ships bringing supplies across the Mediterranean to General Erwin Rommel's forces in North Africa. Nevertheless, to prevent the Germans from becoming suspicious about the security of their communications, the British adopted the rule that no ship could be attacked before it was overflown by reconnaissance aircraft, thus providing the Germans with an alternative explanation of how the ship came to be located and attacked.

This point is also illustrated by the story that Churchill knew in advance about the particularly destructive German air raid on the English city of Coventry, but did nothing to alert its air defenses or emergency services for fear of compromising the intelligence source. (The source in this case was the ability to cryptanalyze Luftwaffe messages encrypted on the Enigma machine.) Historical research, however, seems to have established that this story is not true: the available communications intelligence did not allow the British to identify Coventry as the raid's target.[19] Nevertheless, the story provides a particularly dramatic illustration of the moral and strategic dilemmas that a government may face in deciding whether to risk an intelligence source by acting on the information it provides.

Telemetry Analysis

Telemetry refers to the radio transmission of information from a test vehicle, such as a missile being test-fired, to a ground station. The information may concern the vehicle's performance (such as the amount of thrust being generated by its engine or its acceleration), its condition (for example, the temperature of various components or the amount of vibration it is undergoing), or other missile characteristics. The purpose is to provide the data that engineers conducting the test would need to assess the vehicle's operation or, in case of failure, to determine the reasons for it. Using this information, the test engineers can reconstruct the vehicle's flight and assure themselves of its reliability or make modifications.

The same radio signals, however, can be intercepted by a foreign intelligence service, a type of intelligence collection known as telemetry intelligence, or *telint*. Telemetry analysis is the process by which telint data is used to deduce the basic characteristics of the test vehicle. Of course, when the test engineers begin to interpret this data, they already know, from the design of the telemetry system, precisely to which missile characteristic each part of the data stream (or telemetry "channel") refers. The telemetry analysts working for a foreign intelligence service, on the other hand, begin with none of this information; they must figure out, from the raw data themselves, what characteristic of the missile is being measured by each channel.[20] Once the analysts have made these determinations, they can attempt to use the data to create a computer model of the missile, from which such characteristics as initial weight (launch weight) and payload (throw-weight) can be derived.

Since the mid-1970s, U.S. access to Soviet telemetric information has become an important issue in the area of strategic arms control. During the debate over the ratification of SALT II in 1979, it became clear how important access to telemetry was to the United States's ability to verify Soviet compliance with the treaty's provisions. Several aspects of the question figured centrally in the debate.

First, the Iranian revolution in 1979 meant that the United States no longer had access to important "listening posts" (sites favorably located to intercept radio transmissions) in Iran. As a result, the question was raised whether the United States would be able to intercept the needed telemetric signals from Soviet ICBM missile test flights. Second, the treaty explicitly addressed and partially prohibited the Soviet practice of encrypting some telemetric signals, to conceal from the United States the information they contain, but the provision was particularly vague; the question was raised whether it constituted an adequate protection of U.S. access to telemetric information.[21]

In actuality, Soviet encryption of telemetry increased tremendously during the SALT II period.[22] This eventually led to President Ronald Reagan declaring in 1984 and 1985 that

> Soviet encryption practices constitute a violation of [SALT II obligations]. The nature and extent of such encryption of telemetry on new ballistic missiles, despite U.S. request for corrective action, continues to be an example of deliberately impeding verification of compliance in violation of this Soviet political commitment [to abide by SALT II].[23]

It is not clear what the prospects are for any attempts to cryptanalyze encrypted telemetry. In any case, aside from encryption, other methods can be used to deny telemetric information to an adversary's intelligence service. For example, the data may be recorded on a tape inside some kind of hardened capsule (similar to the voice recorder black box on commercial aircraft) that can survive reentry into the atmosphere and the impact of the landing and be recovered. Similarly, telemetric data from a cruise missile or experimental plane may be broadcast at very low power to a "chase" plane flying near it and recorded on board the plane; if the radio signal is sufficiently weak, it might prove impossible to intercept it outside the test range.

Photo Interpretation

Despite the sophistication of the equipment that can take pictures deep within otherwise inaccessible territory, no substitute has been found for the human eye when it comes to interpreting what those photographs show. This is not so simple a task as might be thought: while it is often said that photographs are a particularly persuasive form of intelligence (in the sense that senior officials feel more confident about the intelligence they are getting when they can see for themselves), the average photograph is likely to be unintelligible to the layman. It is only after the photo interpreter (PI) points out and labels the interesting items that ordinary viewers can understand what they are seeing.[24]

A photograph's quality is typically measured by what is called the "ground resolution distance." While the precise meaning of this term is quite technical, it may be thought of as the minimum-sized object (in terms of its length and width) that is distinguishable from neighboring objects or from the background. While many other factors must be taken into account to determine how well a photograph can be interpreted, ground resolution distance is "nevertheless . . . a convenient measure, useful in making gross comparisons and evaluations."[25]

The actual ground resolution distances U.S. photographic surveillance satellites can obtain are classified, because this information would tell adversaries what details (of military equipment, facilities, and so forth) the United States can, or cannot, see. Planners of any deception efforts also would find this information useful, since it would tell them how closely a decoy would have to resemble the real object for the two to be indistinguishable to photographic surveillance.

However good the resolution, all sorts of important information cannot be learned directly from a photograph. PIs must often work from what are called "signatures," that is, specific details that, on the basis of experience or logic, are associated with a certain piece of equipment, the carrying out of a certain activity, the intention to take a certain step in the future, and so forth.

For example, the lengthening of an airfield runway would indicate the probable arrival of a new type of aircraft requiring the longer runway; from experience, a PI might know that a given runway length was correlated with a given type of airplane and could project that aircraft was to be stationed at that airfield. Similarly, in a lighter vein, it might be possible to distinguish a military base for Cuban soldiers from one for Soviet troops by the presence of a baseball diamond, as opposed to a soccer field.

One method of using signatures that the United States has relied on goes by the fanciful name of "crateology"—the correlation between military equipment and the type and size of crate in which it is usually shipped. Once it has been determined that, for example, MiG-21s have been shipped in crates of a certain size, crateology suggests that other boxes of the same size whose contents have not been observed directly may be assumed to be MiG-21s.[26]

The key to using such signatures is the fact that most organizations—military ones in particular—tend to follow routines, to do things by the book. Thus, when the Soviets decided to deploy intermediate-range ballistic missiles (IRBMs) in Cuba, they first prepared the missile base defenses by deploying SA-2 antiaircraft missiles around it in a standard trapezoidal pattern. By observing this pattern, and identifying it as being the same as that used at older IRBM bases in the Soviet Union, analysts could have predicted the future emplacement of IRBMs in Cuba.[27]

The use of signatures can be very productive. But if it becomes known what signatures PIs are using, an adversary can use their dependence on them as a means of deception. In the Cuban missile crisis discussed above, it seems apparent that the Soviet Union did not realize that the trapezoidal pattern of SA-2 emplacements was known to the United States as a signature of an IRBM base; given the effort the Soviets invested in keeping the IRBM deployment secret, their failure to alter the pattern in which SA-2s were emplaced seems simply a mistake.[28] The absence of the typical pattern might have suggested to U.S. intelligence analysts that IRBMs would *not* be deployed in Cuba.

Data Banks (Basic Research)

As already noted in the section on open-source collection, a major function of an intelligence service is often the assembly and maintenance of large data bases covering many topics of interest to a government's foreign and military policy.

In one aspect, this work takes the form of compiling encyclopedias of relevant information on all countries where military activity could conceivably take place.[29] Such compendia are designed to support a military planner, who would be looking at the country as a potential combat zone, and hence contain detailed information about military forces in being, transport and military facilities, and military geography as well as information about the country's politics, demographics, industry, agriculture, and so forth.

While the analytic problems confronted in compiling such an encyclopedia are minimal, it is a major task to try to sort out what information is important and what is not. Decisions on which countries to cover and to what degree of detail can be very difficult to make yet have important consequences if the information is needed to support a military operation. For example, the plan for the invasion of Grenada in October 1983 by the United States and the countries of the Organization of Eastern Caribbean States was developed very rapidly. One consequence was that adequate military maps were not available. According to Admiral Wesley McDonald, commander in chief of U.S. forces in the Atlantic, "The Army, particularly the troops on the ground, were operating initially from roadmaps or other types of maps which made it very difficult for them to determine in [sic] their grid coordinates. That is one of the lessons learned. . . ."[30]

Other types of data banks serve the needs of intelligence analysts themselves. For example, as already noted, collating and analyzing vast amounts of unclassified data can provide insight into a closed society such as the pre-*glasnost* Soviet Union. Biographic data files (containing all newspaper references to party and government officials, their positions, promotions, travel, and so forth), for instance, can be analyzed to shed light on the relationships among officials.

Production of Finished Intelligence

The types of analysis described above are the necessary initial steps of the analytic process; for the most part, the results of this work serve as sources for other intelligence analysts but do not go directly to the policymaker or military commander (the ultimate consumer of intelligence). This section discusses the kinds of finished intelligence produced. The analytic techniques used are neither as technical as cryptanalysis or telemetry analysis nor as unique to intelligence work. In some cases, such as the production of economic or political intelligence, the techniques are not distinguishable from those of the corresponding social science.

Scientific and Technical Intelligence

In the years immediately before and during World War II, the pace at which new scientific and technological principles were incorporated into weaponry increased substantially. A nation's ability to compete militarily became as dependent on its technological level, and its ability to manufacture weapon systems embodying that technology, as on its overall productive capacity, the size of its military forces, or any other measure of military strength. This was particularly true of air warfare, which saw the development and introduction of air defense radar, sophisticated navigational systems for guiding bomber aircraft to their targets, jet aircraft, ballistic and cruise missiles, and finally, the atomic bomb. Understanding new weapon systems that the enemy was developing thus became an important objective of each nation's intelligence agencies. In many cases, it was important to obtain fairly detailed information about the way the system worked in order to develop methods of countering it.

This imposed a new task on intelligence systems: to predict the emergence of new weapons and to understand them well enough to defend against and to counter them.[31] This required that the intelligence agencies have access to specialized scientific and technical knowledge and that this capability be integrated into the intelligence process.

Collection requirements for scientific and technical intelligence have to be more precise than for other forms of intelligence; it is not obvious to someone unfamiliar with the new technology what is to be looked for and where. This in turn means that close coordination is needed between the analysts and the collectors. To some extent, the process must be similar to the scientific method in which hypotheses (formulated by the analyst) are tested, albeit by directed observations rather than by experiments. For example, R. V. Jones, the head of the British Air Ministry's intelligence section during World War II, recounts how his theory concerning the nature of the first system of radio signals the Germans used as a navigational aid for bombers (Knickbein) was confirmed when an aircraft—fitted out with special receivers and flying in an area designated by him—picked up the radio signals he had predicted would be there.[32]

Analysis in the area of scientific and technical intelligence requires the blending of intelligence and scientific or technical expertise. Although the scientific principles themselves are, of course, universal in nature and known to experts throughout the world, the way in which they are put to use in technological developments can differ widely between countries. Thus, this type of analysis requires enough familiarity with scientific and technical developments to understand what an adversary is doing, combined with enough imagination to realize that he might solve technical problems that the analyst has not been able to solve or that he might reach a different, but nonetheless valid, solution to them.

Military Intelligence

Military intelligence deals with information about the military establishment of a foreign country for planning one's own military forces in peacetime or for conducting military operations against it in time of war. The most elementary military intelligence is what is known as the ''order of battle,'' the basic information about a nation's military forces—amount of manpower, numbers and types of weapons, organizational structure, and similar data. (Characterizing this information as elementary does not, of course, imply that it is easy to get or even that it is a simple matter to know which types of auxiliary or reserve troops should be counted and which should not.) Not strictly speaking part of the order of battle, but a necessary complement to it, would be information about the qualitative aspects of a foreign military establishment: how good the training is, what the quality of the leadership is, and so forth.

One step up from this fundamental level would be information about how the forces could be expected to fight: what tactics they have adopted and trained for, how they envisage the nature of a future war (what in Soviet terminology is called ''military doctrine''), and what their strategy would be for fighting it. The raw data for this intelligence can come from open sources (such as military publications), from attachés' or diplomats' overt contacts with the adversary's military, from observing (either directly or via technical collection systems) deployments and exercises, or from human intelligence sources with direct access to military plans. As with scientific and technical intelligence, this sort of analysis calls for blending the intelligence perspective (with its concentration on all available bits and pieces of evidence about the adversary and what they tell about how he thinks) with that of the military specialist (with its understanding of weapon systems' capabilities and the kinds of warfare that can be waged with them).

But above all, it requires the open-mindedness to be able to imagine that the adversary has adopted different solutions to common military problems and that his solutions may well be appropriate for his circumstances and resources or even superior to one's own solutions. In summary,

> strategic planners need intelligence on the *otherness of the enemy*—intelligence that will reveal the enemy's methods of operation, internal disputes, and ways of doing business, as well as the ways in which the enemy differs from [oneself].[33]

Finally, when military operations appear imminent, or are actually taking place, there must be information about the disposition and movement of military forces. This type of information is the primary data for what is known as ''indications and warning,'' which addresses the task of avoiding strategic surprise.

Political Intelligence

Political intelligence consists of information concerning the political processes, ideas, and intentions of foreign countries, factions, and individual leaders. The analysis that produces this intelligence is similar to that underlying all academic and journalistic public writing and speculation on both international politics and the domestic politics of foreign countries. One obvious difference, of course, lies in the existence of secret intelligence sources, human or technical (primarily communications intelligence), that provide information not available to the public commentator.

How important these additional sources are depends on both the nature of the regime of the country being studied and the number and quality of intelligence sources one has with respect to that country. The more democratic and open a society is, the easier it is to study its political life without recourse to intelligence sources. Even in the case of a closed society, however, there may be open-source data that, properly analyzed, reveal much more about its political life than would appear at first glance.

A more important difference between political intelligence analysis and academic or journalistic work has to do with their different purposes. This difference shows itself in various ways aside from the content of the work. For example, intelligence analysts must provide answers in a timely fashion; their work is useless unless it reaches policymakers before they have been forced by circumstances to act. Academic authors, by contrast, generally have the luxury of taking as much time as they feel is necessary to reach a conclusion. Similarly, academics typically work alone and on subjects of their own choice; intelligence analysts, meanwhile, are guided in their choice of topics by the requirements of others, and their work must be coordinated with others before it is completed.

The different purposes the works serve also affect the contents of intelligence and academic analyses. For one, intelligence analyses must emphasize the aspects of a situation that underlie the immediate issues facing the policymakers; the focus in an academic work is presumably determined by those aspects the researcher deems the most fundamental. This question is discussed at greater length in chapter 6 on the overall relationship between intelligence and policy.

Economic and Social Intelligence

Economic and social intelligence deal with the same phenomena as do the various social sciences, at least as far as they are concerned with major contemporary issues. As with political intelligence, the focus of the intelligence analysis should be determined by the information policymakers require. While intelligence analysis in these areas is often less sophisticated—theoretically and mathematically—than corresponding academic studies, this does not seem to be due to differences between either the circumstances under which intelligence and academic work are conducted or their goals.

Not only is the method the same (at least in principle) but the academic scholar is more likely in this area than in any other to have access to the same data as the intelligence analyst, since little of it is acquired by intelligence methods. Nevertheless, in some areas, intelligence methods may be necessary. Much important economic data about the Soviet Union has been and, despite *glasnost,* is still kept secret; this includes, for example, the size of Soviet gold reserves and the Soviets' annual sales of gold on the world market. While intelligence analysts are often forced to estimate these numbers in the same way that any other economist might, an intelligence source might be able to provide important clues or the official Soviet numbers themselves.

In general, however, the contribution of intelligence sources to economic and social analysis is small. Furthermore, the intelligence agencies cannot expect to attract the highest quality analysts in these areas. The freedom of academic life proves more attractive to talented social scientists, even if the salaries are lower. In addition, multinational corporations, banks, and brokerage firms can easily outbid intelligence agencies for the services of highly qualified economists. In general, there is no reason to expect that analyses by intelligence personnel of economic issues not involving societies that keep basic economic data secret would be superior to those of economists in the business world.[34] Of course, much of the economic analysis done in the business world will not be available to policymakers in the government, but at least some of it could be via consulting services and newsletters.

The Intelligence Product

The product of the intelligence process can be any means, from a formal report to a hurried conversation, by which an intelligence analyst transmits analyzed information to the policymaker or military commander who needs it and can use it. In this section I discuss the various forms of intelligence product and the functions they serve. The categorization is general rather than precise; the terminology reflects ordinary usage among U.S. intelligence agencies but is not completely standardized.

Broadly speaking, I divide intelligence output into three groups: current intelligence, basic intelligence, and intelligence estimates. In this, I follow Sherman Kent's lead; he speaks, using his own coinages, of the *current reportorial form* of intelligence, the *basic descriptive form*, and the *speculative-evaluative form* and describes them as relating to information about the present, the past, and the future, respectively.[35] I use primarily U.S. examples to illustrate the different intelligence products because more detailed information is available. The distinctions, however, are generally valid, although the emphasis placed on the different products may vary from one intelligence service to another.

Current Intelligence

Intelligence agencies have a variety of products designed to inform policymakers of major new information that might affect policy. In this regard, agencies serve a function similar to that of the news media.[36] The range of information that should be watched for and reported is as large as the entire scope of the nation's intelligence interest. Obviously, some priorities must be established on the basis of what is, in Kent's words, "positively germane to national problems which are up now and other problems which appear to be coming."[37] While a formal system of priorities may exist, it must be supplemented by the intelligence producers' own judgments about what is important to their consumers. This judgment, in turn, depends not only on the intelligence analysts' common sense but also on their being in close contact with the policymakers.

In the United States, the best-known product of this type is the *National Intelligence Daily,* or *NID,* a sort of classified newspaper containing a series of short (several-paragraph-long) articles on the previous day's events. Prepared by the CIA in coordination with the other major intelligence agencies—the Defense Intelligence Agency (DIA), the National Security Agency (NSA), and the State Department's Bureau of Intelligence and Research (INR)—it is sent to several hundred top national security officials in the government.

A more sensitive daily report is the *President's Daily Brief,* which has a much more restricted circulation. According to Cord Meyer, a former career CIA official, writing in 1980,

It is designed to be read in ten or fifteen minutes by the President at the beginning of each working day. It does not attempt to recapitulate what the news media have reported in the last twenty-four-hour period, but rather to summarize the significance of what secret sources have reported that bears on current world developments.[38]

From time to time, the view is expressed that U.S. intelligence agencies spend too much time and effort fulfilling this "current intelligence" function, to the detriment of their ability to analyze situations in greater depth. For example, a Senate committee report dealing with the CIA's analytic branch, the Directorate of Intelligence (DDI), made the following comments under the heading "The 'Current Events' Syndrome":

> The task of producing current intelligence—analyzing day-to-day events for quick dissemination—today occupies much of the resources of the DDI. Responding to the growing demands for information of current concern by policymakers for more coverage of more topics, [sic] the DDI has of necessity resorted to a "current events" approach to much of its research. There is less interest in and fewer resources have been devoted to in-depth analysis of problems with long-range importance to policymakers. . . .

> According to some observers, this syndrome has had an unfavorable impact on the quality of crisis warning and the recognition of longer term trends. The "current events" approach has fostered the problem of "incremental analysis," the tendency to focus myopically on the latest piece of information without systematic consideration of an accumulated body of integrated evidence. Analysts in their haste to compile the day's traffic, tend to lose sight of underlying factors and relationships.[39]

The very persistence of this criticism over the years probably indicates that the pressure toward a current events approach—the desire of policymakers to be kept informed of the latest hot news—is inherently strong and will often predominate over the intelligence analyst's desire to conduct in-depth studies.[40] The same pressures are probably at work in the intelligence agencies of other countries as well.

Indications and Warning

One of the most important functions an intelligence agency can perform is to provide timely warning of hostile military action; in the nuclear era, it is the most important. And, in fact, the character of the post–World War II

U.S. intelligence system was probably determined more by the failure of the prewar intelligence organizations to provide effective warning of the Japanese attack on Pearl Harbor than by any other factor.

Because of its importance, and because judgments might have to be made quickly, this intelligence function has been (in the United States, at least) systematized to a much greater extent that any other. The system, known as Indications and Warnings (I&W), is based on an analysis of the steps an adversary would either necessarily or probably take to prepare for an armed attack. These hypothetical events—the calling up of reservists, forward movement of military forces, changes in communications patterns, and so forth—are called "indicators"; when the event actually occurs and is observed, it is then referred to as an "indication." Analysts determine how great the threat is by the totality of indications and issue warnings at various threshold levels.[41]

Oleg Gordievski, a KGB officer who worked for British intelligence from 1975 to 1985, has provided a glimpse into Soviet I&W procedures. According to him, in 1981, the Soviet Politburo ordered the KGB and GRU to cooperate on a new worldwide monitoring system to watch for signs of a possible Western nuclear attack. The GRU was responsible for watching the purely military indicators, while the KGB was to watch for signs that the political decision to launch a nuclear attack had been taken. Among the indicators that the KGB residency in Britain (the KGB officers working out of the Soviet Embassy in London) was responsible for monitoring were:

- the pattern of work at 10 Downing Street (the prime minister's residence), the Ministry of Defense, the Foreign Office, the U.S. Embassy, and the headquarters of the British intelligence and security services (for example, were the lights on at night?);

- the frequency with which couriers traveled among those establishments;

- the comings and goings of the prime minister and other key ministers (for example, was the prime minister making an unusual number of trips to Buckingham Palace?); and

- the existence of any unusual civil defense measures, such as stockpiling food or preparing emergency blood banks.

Routine reports were to be made every two weeks, but any particularly striking events were to be reported immediately.[42]

This type of formalized system, in which indictors are determined in advance and can thus guide the collection process to some extent, exists only with respect to the most important questions, such as the possibility of hostile military action. The formal system also ensures that intelligence is fed into the policy-making process and is not ignored. In most other areas, no automatic system is set up to guarantee that the available intelligence is brought to bear when decisions are made.

Following what was widely regarded as the CIA's failure to provide adequate warning of the Iranian revolution of 1978–79, proposals were made to establish a political I&W system to warn of political instability in foreign countries. This would require establishing indicators comparable to those used to warn of military attack. This is a much more difficult proposition with politics than with military matters; it is unlikely that the current state of the social sciences allows this to be done sufficiently to be of real use. Nevertheless, a more formal system would clarify the extent to which intelligence is responsible for warning of potentially serious events, even when the policy-making community is not focusing on that country or region of the world.

Basic Intelligence

Another general type of intelligence product may be termed the "basic intelligence report." Such a report tries to provide as full a picture of a given situation as possible, drawing on publicly available data and relevant information from all intelligence sources ("all-source" intelligence). In the military arena, for example, such products might be an order of battle, the description of a nation's armed forces in terms of numbers and types of combat units, and their manpower, equipment, organization, and subordination of units to higher-level commands. Similarly, a basic intelligence report on a nation's political system could include an account of all the major political forces and personalities, their traditional views and interests, the ways in which they have related to each other, and so forth.

Periodic Reports

Just as I&W represents a systematized form of current intelligence to deal with a specific question of great importance, there may be special series of reports to deal with specific issues. For example, since the SALT I agreements of 1972, U.S. intelligence has produced semiannual reports on Soviet compliance with strategic nuclear arms agreements; these reports present the best intelligence judgments concerning Soviet strategic nuclear forces relevant to the agreements' provisions.

Intelligence Estimates

The most ambitious type of intelligence product is that which not only describes the current situation but also attempts to predict how it will evolve.

Such works are referred to as "estimates" in U.S. intelligence parlance. In particular, a national intelligence estimate (NIE) represents the most authoritative statement on a subject by the U.S. intelligence agencies, all of which contribute to its drafting and review.

These estimates are supposed to take the broadest view of their subject and to project the current situation into the future. In the United States, they are produced by a special staff, with the support of analysts throughout the intelligence agencies. The estimates are supposed to incorporate the views of all the agencies in the intelligence community.[43] A good deal of effort is devoted to finding a consensus position, but, when this is not possible, a dissenting view may be expressed in what is traditionally called a footnote, even though the dissent is sometimes included in the text.

NIEs on some topics of major importance, such as Soviet strategic nuclear offensive and defensive forces, are produced periodically; other topics are covered in response to specific requirements, either self-generated (that is, the idea for the estimate arose within the intelligence community itself) or from elsewhere in the government, most often the National Security Council (NSC). Shorter, more topical estimates, known as Special NIEs (or SNIEs), may be produced in response to more urgent requirements.

In contrast to the U.S. practice, producing estimates in Israel during the period before the 1973 Yom Kippur War was a monopoly of Military Intelligence, a branch of the armed forces. Although other intelligence services existed—the Central Institute for Intelligence and Security (Hamossad), operating covertly in foreign countries; the Shin Beth, responsible for counterintelligence and counterterrorism; and the Foreign Office research department—only Military Intelligence had access to all intelligence information and was responsible for analyzing and distributing it. Furthermore, the cabinet's staff did not have any intelligence expertise, and there was no mechanism by which the political leadership tasked Military Intelligence to provide evaluations of specific subjects.[44] This concentration of power was criticized as contributing to the failure of Israeli intelligence to warn of the Egyptian-Syrian attack on October 6, 1973, which is discussed in the "intelligence failure" section of this chapter.

Variations Among Intelligence Services

While current and basic intelligence functions seem essential to the work of any nation's intelligence services, how integral is the estimative function to the intelligence process? Its importance varies from nation to nation and time to time. For example, in the United States, preparing estimates is seen as the peak of the intelligence process. In the Soviet Union of the 1930s, by contrast, Stalin wanted to keep the estimative function in his own hands; he ordered the NKVD (a predecessor of the KGB) not to send him estimates or assessments of the foreign situation, but to confine itself to reporting the secrets (documents of high-level informant reports) it had obtained.[45] This point has to do with the relationship between the intelligence and policy-making functions of a government, discussed further in chapter 6.

Intelligence Failure and Surprise

Types of Failure

Surprise Attack

The possible failure of intelligence to assess a situation correctly is a danger coeval with intelligence itself. The most dramatic, and potentially most damaging, intelligence failure occurs when there is no warning of an attack, so that a nation's military forces are taken by surprise. Indeed, the U.S. intelligence community owes its current configuration to an effort to remedy the intelligence deficiencies thought to have contributed to the United States being surprised by the Japanese attack on Pearl Harbor on December 7, 1941.

The literature on successful surprise attacks is extensive. The German attack on the Soviet Union on June 22, 1941, and the Egyptian-Syrian attack on Israel on October 6, 1973 (the Yom Kippur War) are, aside from the Pearl Harbor attack, among the most frequently discussed cases, but others have happened in this century.[46] Even during a war, when military forces are presumably much more on the alert than during peacetime, substantial surprise can be, and has been, achieved. Among other examples are the German attack in the Ardennes in December 1944 (Battle of the Bulge) and the Chinese entry into the Korean War in November–December 1950.[47]

Closely related to the failure to anticipate an attack is the situation in which a nation expects an attack but, because of a significant misestimation of where or how it will occur, responds disadvantageously. An impressive example of this kind of intelligence failure is the German reaction to the Allied landings in Normandy on June 6, 1944 (D-Day); the Germans certainly expected an attack, but they were so convinced that the main thrust would be against the Pas de Calais region that they treated Normandy as a diversion and passed up a good opportunity to counterattack in force while the beachheads were most vulnerable.[48]

Other Kinds of Surprise

Although an unanticipated attack may be the most damaging surprise a nation can suffer, it is not the only one. For example, an unexpected political event (such as a shift in alliances or a coup d'état that overthrows a friendly foreign ruler) also may be a serious blow to a nation's foreign policy interests. The American underestimation, in 1978, of the Iranian shah's political troubles and of the seriousness of the opposition to his rule is perhaps the best-known recent example of this type of intelligence failure. It was considered sufficiently damaging at the time to prompt a blunt handwritten note from President Carter to Cyrus Vance, Zbigniew Brzezinski, and Stansfield Turner (secretary of state, assistant to the president for national security affairs, and director of central intelligence, respectively) that stated, with a directness uncharacteristic of government bureaucracy: "I am not satisfied with the quality of our political intelligence."[49]

Similarly, no warning of a sudden, major economic change, such as the failure of U.S. intelligence agencies to foresee the 1973 "oil shock"—the rapid increase in the world price of oil—also may be accounted an intelligence failure, depending on one's opinion of the field of view and responsibilities of intelligence agencies. As has been noted, intelligence's role with respect to economic questions is less settled and more complicated than with respect to political or military matters. In any case, the 1973 oil shock is a complicated example of the problem, since the underlying causes were economic (the previous low price of oil had encouraged rapidly increasing oil consumption and discouraged exploration and development) while the immediate cause was political (the Arab oil states' support for Egypt and Syria in the October 1973 Yom Kippur War).[50]

While the disasters that can flow from being surprised on the battlefield are obvious, the harm caused by the failure to foresee political or economic events is more difficult to assess. In large part, it depends on whether the government would have been prepared to take action had it been warned and whether there were strategies that would have averted the event or mitigated its unfavorable consequences.

For example, it is not clear what, if anything, the U.S. government would have done had it been warned of the 1973 oil shock. Similarly, correctly assessing the shah's political troubles is a vastly different task from determining what, if anything, to do about them; success in the former would not have necessarily guaranteed success in the latter.

Other Kinds of Failure

Most cases of intelligence failure sooner or later involve surprise, since a mistaken view of the external world is likely to cause unexpected misfortune at some point and in some manner. (One exception would be a case in which, through faulty intelligence, an agency is unaware of an adversary's vulnerability, so that it loses the opportunity to take advantage of a favorable situation.) However, in many cases the notion of surprise is perhaps not the most helpful one for understanding the harm intelligence failure causes.

The key intelligence failure is a misunderstanding of the situation, which leads an agent to take actions that are inappropriate and counterproductive to his own interests; whether he is subjectively surprised by what happens is less important than the fact that he is doing or continues to do the wrong thing. Thus, the German intelligence failure with respect to the Normandy D-Day landings resulted not so much in the German Army's being surprised as in its misestimation of the Normandy landings as feints meant to distract attention from the "real" invasion force targeted on the Pas de Calais region.[51] Similarly, the primary cause of the Chinese rout of the U.N. forces in Korea in December 1950 had more to do with a fundamental misunderstanding of Chinese doctrine and tactics than with surprise.[52]

Furthermore, the examples of surprise, involving failures to foresee what action a hostile force would take or with what success it would meet, apply particularly to nations that are on the defensive, strategically or tactically. A nation on the offensive, however, also can suffer through misassessing the opponent's strengths or misunderstanding some other relevant factor. For example, the Allied attack on the bridge at Arnhem, Holland, the "bridge too far," in September 1944 was unsuccessful in large part because of an intelligence failure—the failure, due to overconfidence and a negligent analysis of the available information, to realize that two German armored divisions were present in the immediate area.[53]

Finally, the intelligence failures discussed above involve a misunderstanding that is revealed quickly once one side or the other takes action. Another sort of failure involves the misestimation of a continuing process or condition in which, because nothing occurs to reveal the truth of the situation, it is possible to remain in error for a longer time.

For example, in estimating the size of the Soviet strategic arsenal, the U.S. intelligence community has made both major overestimations and underestimations that colored American strategic views over periods of years. The major overestimations of Soviet strategic weaponry, which produced American perceptions of a "bomber gap" in the mid-1950s and a "missile gap" from the late 1950s until 1961, are perhaps the better known of these errors. But at least equally important was the tendency, throughout the mid-1960s and ending only in the early 1970s, to underestimate the extent to which the Soviet Union was building up its strategic forces.[54]

Causes of Failure

Aside from instances in which relevant information cannot be obtained at all, intelligence failure refers to a disorder of the analytic process, which causes data to be ignored or misinterpreted. Therefore, it is similar to a mistake in any other intellectual endeavor, for example, a mistake by a historian in interpreting an ancient text, leading to an incorrect description of some aspect of antiquity, or a mistake by a meteorologist in assessing the importance of a low-pressure system, leading to an incorrect prediction about the next day's weather.

In addition, however, some peculiarities of the intelligence analysis process introduce further sources of error. While intelligence analysis is an intellectual activity, it is one that, unlike the work of an individual academic, takes place in an institutional setting and according to standard procedures so that the final result is more the product of a system than of any individual. As such, it is vulnerable to certain pathologies that can be addressed in institutional or bureaucratic terms. This section addresses some of the causes of intelligence failure, looking first at institutional ones and then at those that relate more directly to the intellectual content of the intelligence work.

Subordination of Intelligence to Policy

The possibility that intelligence judgments will be made to produce the result superiors wish to hear instead of on the evidence is perhaps the most commonly discussed source of error or bias in intelligence analysis. It is, however, extrinsic to the intelligence analysis process itself (assuming that the analyst realizes he is going against his own best judgment). As rather an issue in what may be called the management of intelligence—the way in which intelligence relates to the higher-level policymakers whom it serves—it is dealt with in the discussion of intelligence and policy in chapter 6.

Unavailability of Information When and Where Needed

Given the large size of the organizations involved in collecting and analyzing intelligence, a possible source of problems is the unavailability of information that is in the system to those who need it when they need it. This unavailability has various causes: for example, security regulations that restrict the circulation of sensitive information, bureaucratic jealousies and power struggles in which control over information becomes one of the weapons, or a simple unawareness in the office possessing the data of another office's information needs.

Similarly, a problem can arise if no central office has both the responsibility to do analysis in a given area and access to all information relevant to it. In this case, different offices may work on different parts of the problem, but a key piece of information may be missed if its significance becomes apparent only in the context of all the available data.

Typically, the Pearl Harbor intelligence failure is explained in terms of a lack of communication between the various intelligence and operational units involved. However, while there may have been some communication problems between the Army and Navy commands in Hawaii, it is not clear that a corresponding difficulty existed between the two services in Washington. A more important difficulty stemmed from the lack of a centralized analytic office with the resources and the responsibility to analyze all relevant intelligence. Instead, intelligence seemed to be handled on the fly by a few people who worked directly for the high-level policy-making officials— an effect of the small size of the U.S. military establishment at that time as much as anything else.

Received Opinion

The success of any intellectual endeavor (scientific discovery, for example, as well as intelligence analysis) can be compromised by the force of received opinion, often referred to as "conventional wisdom"—those opinions about a subject that are generally regarded, without sufficient investigation, as true. While, in one sense, we obviously cannot do without it (we could hardly afford the time or effort to reinvestigate and rethink all our opinions every day), relying on received opinion poses the real danger that we will either misunderstand or perhaps ignore evidence that suggests the truth is otherwise.

However pernicious the effect of received opinion on an individual's thinking, its impact is probably heightened by the bureaucratic environment in which an intelligence service carries out its analysis. While an individual's thought can be influenced by particularly striking evidence that does not fit the preconceived pattern, or even by a chance insight into another interpretation of the evidence, it is unlikely that many people will be affected in the same way at the same time. Thus, individuals challenging the received view are likely to encounter the resistance of the much larger number who remain comfortable with it.

If individuals economize on time and effort by not rethinking all their opinions all the time, the organization may be said to do the same. Given the size and complexity of the organizations involved and the consequent need to obtain the consent (or at least the acquiescence) of many people to the judgments reached, fundamental reevaluation of the evidence with a view toward rethinking all the basic assumptions is a very difficult and time-consuming process.

Thus, if an analyst has to write a report, he is likely first to review what was written the previous year and then merely update it as necessary. This not only saves labor but also offers a degree of security. Because last year's report was approved, if the analyst limits himself to the changes indicated by new evidence, the underlying reasoning does not have to be duplicated, and the sources of potential controversy can be minimized.

Clearly this creates a tremendous opportunity for error in situations involving gradual change. Because intelligence evidence is almost always spotty and incomplete, the accumulation of various bits and pieces of new information may not force a change in the underlying analysis. This may be true even though the preponderance of evidence at some point would suggest to someone starting afresh that a different framework would make more sense. In this manner, an older way of viewing the situation may survive much longer than it should.[55]

Mirror-Imaging

The two problems discussed above apply primarily to intelligence analysis conducted in a bureaucratic setting. Another source of error in intelligence analysis, however, reflects a more common intellectual failure not tied to the setting in which the analysis is conducted. It may be termed "mirror-imaging," by which is meant the judging of unfamiliar situations on the basis of familiar ones.[56] In the case of intelligence, it typically means assessing or predicting a foreign government's actions by analogy with the actions that the analyst feels he (or his government) would take were he (or it) in a similar position.

For example, the failure of Israeli intelligence to foresee the Egyptian-Syrian attack that started the October 1973 Yom Kippur War appears to be due in part to this phenomenon; Israel's intelligence services did not imagine the Arabs beginning a war that they seemed sure to lose.[57] For example, less than two months before the outbreak of war, Moshe Dayan told the Staff College of the Israel Defense Forces that "the balance of forces is so much in our favor that it neutralizes the Arab considerations and motives for the immediate renewal of hostilities."[58]

In retrospect, however, it appears that Egyptian President Anwar Sadat wanted the war to break the stalemate that had developed in Israeli-Arab relations, and he did not, in fact, count on winning it. The initial Arab victories (in particular, the Egyptian crossing of the Suez Canal and penetration of the Israeli defensive line on the other side), although reversed on the ground later in the war, provided the psychological backdrop for the eventual regaining of the Sinai Peninsula. Discounting the possibility of this sort of aggressive risk-taking, foreign to Israeli and U.S. military experience, is an example of mirror-imaging.

Another striking example may be found in the report of the Church Committee, the special Senate committee formed in 1975 to investigate the intelligence community. That report cites the following paragraph from a draft of the 1969 National Intelligence Estimate on Soviet offensive nuclear forces:

> We believe that the Soviets recognize the enormous difficulties of any attempt to achieve strategic superiority of such order as to significantly alter the strategic balance. Consequently, we consider it highly unlikely that they will attempt within the period of this estimate to achieve a first-strike capability, i.e., a capability to launch a surprise attack against the U.S. with assurance that the USSR would not itself receive damage it would regard as unacceptable. For one thing, the Soviets would almost certainly conclude that the cost of such an undertaking along with all their other military commitments would be prohibitive. More important, they almost certainly would consider it impossible to develop and deploy the combination of offensive and defensive forces necessary to counter successfully the various elements of U.S. strategic attack forces. Finally, even if such a project were economically and technically feasible the Soviets almost certainly would calculate that the U.S. would detect and match or overmatch their efforts.[59]

Despite the context in which the Church Committee cites this passage—the Nixon administration in general, and Defense Secretary Melvin Laird in particular, are being taken to task for successfully pressuring DCI Richard Helms to delete this paragraph from the final version of the NIE—its report does not indicate that the judgments in the passage were based on inside information about strategic thinking in the Kremlin. Indeed, the wording (for example, "would almost certainly") suggests instead that the paragraph contains analytic judgments about Soviet thinking rather than direct evidence drawn from documents or high-level informants.

As such it is an example of mirror-imaging not only in the three major assertions (the last three sentences cited) it offers to support its main thesis, but also in the entire way in which the question is framed. The first assertion implies that U.S. intelligence understood what costs the Soviets might consider prohibitive, a judgment that rests essentially on a sort of mirror-imaging—the United States had concluded that this goal was not economically feasible. The second reflects a conclusion common among the theorists of the U.S. strategic community but not necessarily believed by Soviet military thinkers. Finally, the third attributes to the Soviets a mechanistic, apolitical view of the arms race (as an action-reaction cycle) that is common in the United States but not necessarily in the Soviet Union.

Perhaps even more important, the entire manner in which the question is framed in the first two sentences—that is, the equating of "strategic superiority [that] significantly alter[s] the strategic balance" on the one hand, with "first-strike capability" on the other—reflects U.S. mutual assured destruction (MAD) doctrine rather than any attempt to understand what the Soviets might consider significant. It implies that the Soviets would see partial solutions to the problem of countering U.S. offensive strategic forces as insignificant and not worth developing and deploying.

But since this view is merely implied rather than stated, it is not examined on the basis of the evidence. (For example, a careful evaluation of this view would have to deal with the emphasis the Soviets place on strategic air defenses and the Moscow antiballistic missile system, even in the absence of a nationwide ballistic missile defense.) Instead, its attribution to the Soviets seems to be a case of mirror-imaging by analysts who believe that the logic behind the U.S. view is so strong that the Soviets must have accepted it.

Another common form of mirror-imaging, one that affects the ability to assess correctly scientific or technological developments within an adversary's military establishment, is often referred to as the "not invented here syndrome." This syndrome is characterized by an unwillingness to take seriously the possibility that an adversary has developed a weapon or device that one's own military-technological establishment has not thought of, has dismissed as infeasible, or has given up trying to develop. We would expect this syndrome to be more common with respect to an adversary who is regarded as technologically inferior.

R. V. Jones discusses this phenomenon in his account of British scientific and technical intelligence during World War II. In an epilogue to an intelligence report concerning the V-2 ballistic rocket, which the Germans developed toward the end of the war and first fired against London on September 8, 1944, Jones goes through the four possibilities that can exist with respect to a technical development: the British either do or do not succeed with respect to it and the same for the Germans. The not invented here syndrome obtains when

> our experts either fail or do not try, [and] the Germans succeed. This is the most interesting Intelligence case, but it is difficult to overcome the prejudice that as we have not done something, it is impossible or foolish.

Alternatively, our experts in examining the German development are no longer experts but novices, and may therefore make wilder guesses than Intelligence [i.e., intelligence analysts who are not as such experts in the relevant technology], which at least has the advantage of closer contact with the enemy.[60]

Jones's solution to the problem is for the intelligence analyst to be wary of the technical expert's views while trying to make use of his expertise:

[F]rom an Intelligence point of view, it must always be borne in mind that the advice comes from a British, and not from a German expert. If this difference in background is not continually appreciated, serious misadjustments can be made. In the tactical field, Napoleon knew this danger well: he called it, "making pictures of the enemy". In the technical field the same danger exists. . . .[61]

"Solutions" to the Problem of Intelligence Failure

What Is Failure?

More frequently than the popular myth of an omniscient intelligence service would lead us to expect, intelligence reports or estimates contain erroneous statements, and important events occur without intelligence agencies having predicted them. Determining whether such situations constitute intelligence failures requires a standard against which it is reasonable to measure intelligence achievements.[62] Often, it is assumed in discussions of this sort that intelligence performance should be measured against an ideal of clairvoyance. Typically forgotten is that, for the most part, intelligence involves not a metaphorical struggle with nature (as is the case with scientific research that seeks to force nature to reveal its secrets) but a real struggle with a human adversary.

For example, the victim's failure to anticipate a surprise attack is the reverse side of the coin of the attacker's success at achieving surprise. In intelligence work, one opponent is most often trying to frustrate his adversary's attempts to understand the situation accurately. To do so, he will use a whole array of intelligence techniques, including deception, as is discussed in chapter 5 on counterintelligence.

Thus, we cannot compare progress in intelligence techniques to, for example, progress in chemistry. The consequence of progress in chemical research, and the dissemination of the knowledge and insight gained thereby, can be that chemists throughout the world achieve better results in their work. The same is not the case with respect to intelligence; if new insights or procedures enable one group of intelligence officials to achieve better results in its work, this means, in general, that its adversaries' intelligence officials are not performing their own tasks as well as in the past and, in a sense, have fallen down on the job. This is obviously true with respect to questions of deliberate surprise.[63]

Taken to an extreme, speaking of intelligence failure is similar to speaking of "chess failure," defined as the failure to win chess games. Obviously, to improve our chess-playing abilities, it makes sense to critique styles of play, as well as individual moves, as thoroughly as we can. The result should be better individual chess play and, if we share the insights we have gained, by others as well. It cannot be, overall, an increase in the number of games of chess won per number played. Of course, as citizens, we are not concerned with better intelligence in the abstract; we seek to improve our own country's intelligence capabilities and, in so doing, devalue those of our adversaries.

Institutional Solutions

Among the most frequently discussed institutional solutions—solutions that require the restructuring of the institutional framework in which intelligence analysis is carried out—are competitive analysis and the establishment of a devil's advocate.

Competitive analysis refers to the deliberate fostering of separate analytic centers within a government, each of which has the right to formulate and distribute its own intelligence assessments. In principle, each center would have equal and comprehensive access to the raw intelligence data, regardless of which intelligence agency collected it. (In practice, because of the extreme sensitivity of certain types of intelligence information—for example, information that might identify a human source—this result may well be difficult to achieve.)

Typically, some or all of these centers are constituent parts of the major departments and agencies of government or the military services and exist primarily to serve the specialized intelligence needs of their parent organizations. For example, in the United States, the Defense Intelligence Agency is a part of the Department of Defense, reporting to both the Joint Chiefs of Staff and the secretary of defense; each military service has its own intelligence command or service; and the State Department has its Bureau of Intelligence and Research. To some extent, the resulting competition among them reflects the fact that they are subordinated to different government departments, which are themselves in competition.

Alternatively, it might be possible to create separate analytic centers explicitly to compete, most likely on an ad hoc basis to examine a specific issue. An American example for which information is publicly available was the A-B Team exercise of 1975–76, in which a separate team of experts (the B Team) was established to review evidence concerning Soviet strategic developments and determine if it supported conclusions other than those of the writers of the previous years' National Intelligence Estimate (the A Team).[64]

In either case, the virtue of competitive analysis resides primarily in allowing differing points of view to be expressed at high levels, thereby sharpening the debate and focusing attention on whether available evidence unambiguously supports one or the other position. In this way, competitive analysis can act as an antidote to the problems caused by the easy acceptance of conventional wisdom. With competing analytic centers, it is more likely (although not guaranteed) that at least one of them will be skeptical of the received opinions on a subject and will be able to force the other agencies to mount an explicit defense of them. It is an attempt to imitate, within the limiting confines of the government and its regulations concerning security classification of information, the free marketplace of ideas that exists in a democratic society and that presumably furthers the advance of knowledge generally.

From this perspective, the possibility that the competing centers may take positions that are biased in favor of their parent agency's policy preferences or budgetary requests is not such an important drawback. Vigorous debate among the multiple centers will, according to this line of argument, expose the invalidity of positions the evidence doesn't support, while providing a greater chance that new, unconventional ideas will receive a serious hearing.

Of course, it could happen that the conventional wisdom pervades the different parts of the government to an equal degree. In that case, we could not expect the mere existence of competing analytic centers to challenge the conventional wisdom since they would all be infected by the same orthodoxy. This consideration has led to proposals to establish a devil's advocate, that is, an analytic organization whose purpose is to challenge accepted views.

The B Team is an example of an ad hoc devil's advocate established to look at one particular problem and motivated by an already-existing sense that the previous understanding of it had been lacking. The devil's advocate proposal is an attempt to institutionalize this type of practice and, in so doing, protect it from some of the political controversy that surrounded the B Team, which some critics regarded as illegitimate outside (i.e., political) pressure on the intelligence analysis process.

While both of these institutional devices have something to be said for them, neither can be regarded as a panacea, or even as necessarily a step in the right direction. In an article provocatively subtitled "Why Intelligence Failures Are Inevitable," Richard K. Betts has argued that neither institutional solution discussed above, nor any other institutional solution for that matter, can prevent intelligence failure.[65]

Competitive analysis, for example, may air dissents to the conventional wisdom that would otherwise be suppressed; at the same time, however, it presents the policymakers with a spectrum of views, which may leave them confused or may lead them to ignore intelligence altogether and follow their own prior opinions instead. Similarly, the dissents of an institutionalized devil's advocate may lose any real power to force others to rethink their positions, precisely because, in dissenting, "he is just doing his job." Indeed, the perverse result may be that otherwise powerful challenges to the orthodoxy are ignored because they are seen as routine and predictable.

I am not saying, however, that institutional arrangements do not matter or that changing them may not be beneficial. Rather, I am suggesting that the optimal bureaucratic organization of intelligence cannot be determined until we have a sense of what the characteristic problems or deficiencies of a nation's national security apparatus are; the organizational structure should be determined by what would best counteract those bad tendencies. The same solution—for example, competitive analysis—may be helpful or harmful, depending on whether the system suffers from too much conformity with the conventional wisdom (in which case competition might be able to introduce needed new ideas) or from domestic political concerns dominating national security questions (in which case a strong, unified intelligence voice may be necessary to bring international realities to the fore).

Intellectual Solutions

Institutional solutions have the advantage that they can be implemented top-down through managerial decisions and directives; they do not, however, attack the heart of the problem of intelligence failure, the thought process of the individual analyst. Improving thought processes, however, is not a matter that administrative means can deal with directly. Indeed, when we try to be specific about what would be involved, it is not even clear we know what "the improvement of thought processes" means, aside from a general and not very useful admonition to be "smarter."

While it may not be possible to lay down rules that will inevitably guide us to correctly analyze intelligence information, it is nevertheless useful to try to identify intellectual errors or deficiencies that may be characteristic of the analytic process, either generally or as it exists at a certain time and place. In so doing, we can become aware of these tendencies and subsequently try to correct them.

The previous discussion of the intellectual causes of intelligence failure lists mirror-imaging as an important error that must be guarded against. While any intelligence analyst is vulnerable to this error, cultural reasons may make it a particular problem for the U.S. intelligence community. Americans are more open to a belief in the basic similarity of people throughout the world, perhaps because of America's experience in successfully absorbing and assimilating immigrants from diverse cultural and religious backgrounds. Thus, the U.S. intelligence analysts risk being more likely than other analysts to understand and predict the actions of others on the basis of what they would do under similar circumstances.

Thus, an emphasis on expertise in foreign societies and cultures is an important corrective to this error.[66] This expertise can be fostered by a study of the language and history of the country, by an awareness of its religious and cultural traditions, and so forth. A deliberate attempt must be made to see the international situation from its leaders' point of view, rather than our own.

4

WORKING BEHIND THE SCENES

COVERT ACTION

Covert action—especially in its more sensational forms, such as the overthrow of a government or the assassination of its leader—looms large in the public's view of what intelligence is; for professionals and students of intelligence, however, it is something of a question whether covert action should be considered a part of intelligence at all. This issue arises because covert action involves taking action to implement a nation's foreign policy, while collection and analysis are limited to providing the information on which that policy may be based.

What Is Covert Action? Some Definitions

Covert action, in the U.S. intelligence lexicon, refers to the attempt by one government to pursue its foreign policy objectives by conducting some secret activity to influence the behavior of a foreign government or political, military, economic, or societal events and circumstances in a foreign country. As the term implies, the defining characteristic of covert action is that the government conducting the activity do so in a secret or covert manner. However, what secrecy means precisely can vary according to the particular circumstances.

In some cases, the need for secrecy may be absolute, and a government will try to act so that the details and even the existence of the activity do not become generally known. This would be true, for instance, if the covert action involved helping a group of conspirators prepare a coup d'état in a foreign country by smuggling weapons into the country for it. In other cases, the action itself may be public knowledge, but the government conceals its involvement in it. An example would be a government's secret financing of a newspaper or radio station that supported government policies or was hostile to its adversary's. Finally, there may be cases in which a good deal of information becomes public, but for diplomatic or other reasons, the government involved still avoids officially acknowledging its connection with it.

Covert action (euphemistically referred to as "special activities" for bureaucratic purposes) is currently defined by the U.S. government in the most recent presidential Executive Order on U.S. Intelligence Activities, as follows:

> *Special activities* means activities conducted in support of national foreign policy objectives abroad which are planned and executed so that the role of the United States Government is not apparent or acknowledged publicly, and functions in support of such activities, but which are not intended to influence United States political processes, public opinion, policies, or media and do not include diplomatic activities or the collection and production of intelligence or related support functions.[1]

As part of the executive order on intelligence, this definition is valid within the executive branch; for example, it is the definition that would be used in the intra-executive branch process used to evaluate and approve covert action proposals. The term "covert action," however, is also commonly used to refer to a similar but not identical set of intelligence activities about which the president is required by *statute* to provide "timely" notification to the Congress. This set of activities was defined in 1974 by legislation known as the Hughes-Ryan Amendment as "operations [involving expenditure of funds by or on behalf of the Central Intelligence Agency] in foreign countries, other than activities intended solely for obtaining necessary intelligence."[2]

By either definition, covert action is clearly distinguished from the collection and production of intelligence information, which is to say, from what in the United States is typically regarded as the heart of the intelligence function. The distinction is that the goal of covert action is not knowledge but is instead the direct furthering of national foreign policy objectives. In this respect, it more closely resembles the nation's other foreign policy tools, such as diplomacy or military force, than the rest of intelligence. On the other hand, insofar as it is activity undertaken covertly, involving the secret employment or support of agents or allies, it resembles human intelligence collection more than it does the overt policy means a government might use.

While these definitions are clear enough for most practical purposes, they are not absolutely precise. For example, although the executive order explicitly excludes diplomatic activities from the ambit of covert action, it neither defines diplomatic activities nor specifies the dividing line between diplomacy and covert action. Diplomacy also involves attempting to influence the behavior of other governments and their officials and is often carried on secretly; for example, it is often important to keep negotiations between two countries secret from other countries and the public. It may even be that conversations with some officials of a foreign government are not shared with other officials of that same government.

Historically, diplomacy and intelligence have not always been distinct categories. In Renaissance Italy diplomatic envoys, aside from their information-gathering function, which might involve clandestine methods of doubtful legitimacy,

> often became involved in intrigues far from ambiguous. The Venetian secretary and the Milanese *commisarius* at Genoa in 1496, for example, served as intermediaries between their governments and an adventurer who offered to burn up two of [*sic*] three French ships either in the port of Villefranche or at Nice. The two governments agreed to the proposal and to splitting the cost of 400 ducats.[3]

Even today, there are cases that illustrate the artificial nature of the line between diplomacy and covert action. For example, the unpublicized attempts in 1984–86 by State Department and National Security Council personnel to persuade foreign leaders to contribute money to support the Nicaraguan resistance come within the usual scope of diplomatic exchanges.[4] Had they been conducted by intelligence agency personnel, however, they could just as easily have been regarded as covert action.

Another example, less well known, arose from the U.S. response to the kidnapping of the Italian statesman Aldo Moro by the Red Brigades terrorist group in 1978. The Italian government requested the services of a CIA psychologist who had specialized experience in the counterterrorism area. This was considered to be covert action under the Hughes-Ryan amendment definition; delays in preparing the required paperwork led the Italians to turn to the State Department, which, unimpeded by covert action approval procedures, provided a psychologist from its staff. For practical purposes, the line between diplomacy and covert action appears to be drawn in ambiguous cases according to the departmental affiliation of the personnel involved rather than the activity's nature.

It should be noted that the term "covert action" appears to be an American invention, not necessarily used in the lexicons of other intelligence services.[5] For example, the nearest equivalent Soviet term, "active measures" (*aktivnye meropriiatiia*), is broader than covert action—it refers to both "overt and covert techniques of influencing events and behavior in, and the actions of, foreign countries."[6] As such, it does not fall entirely within the sphere of intelligence. Instead, it includes other foreign political activities of both the Soviet government (for example, diplomacy and the use of official media such as Radio Moscow) and the Communist party of the Soviet Union (conducted, for example, through foreign Communist parties or front groups such as the World Peace Council). The term focuses attention on the goal sought—political influence—rather than on the secrecy or openness of the means used.[7]

Regardless of the terminology used, it is important to keep in mind that what is called covert action in the United States is only one tool of foreign policy among many. Because of its unique features and flamboyant past, it has attracted a great deal of attention, and it does pose some particular problems in terms of its secrecy for a democratic government. Nevertheless, the term may be unfortunate in that it emphasizes a characteristic of the means used (their secrecy) while obscuring the fact that the ends sought are, or should be, those of foreign policy as a whole. Because of this focus on the form rather than the substance of the activities involved, the debate in the United States about covert action has emphasized questions of legality and propriety at the expense of more fundamental questions concerning foreign policy goals and strategy.

This chapter will treat covert action as an element of intelligence that is also a foreign policy tool; in chapter 6, the specific issues connected with the use of covert action by a democratic government will be addressed. Because of the ambiguities created by the existence of two nonidentical, official U.S. definitions of covert action, the discussion in the remainder of this chapter deals with activities more inclusive than the covert action category in order to clarify its limits. A more theoretical definition of covert action would not, to be sure, be tied so closely to the vagaries of U.S. law and practice; such a definition, however, remains to be achieved.

Types and Examples of Covert Action

In its most general sense of the secret influencing of foreign behavior, events, or circumstances, the term "covert action" covers a wide spectrum of activities, running from the most pedestrian, such as secretly providing technical assistance (such as security or communications equipment or training) to a friendly foreign government, to the most spectacular, such as assassination or supporting or fomenting a coup d'état. It is therefore difficult to provide a comprehensive list of the types of covert action that intelligence agencies have conducted. In addition, the U.S. intelligence agencies have not developed a standard typology of covert action, nor have those who study them. This section attempts to develop such a categorization.

The purpose of covert action is to influence the actions of foreign governments or events or circumstances in foreign countries. These attempts can be directed at the government of a country, at the society as a whole, or at a particular segment of it. In democratic countries, influence successfully brought to bear on the society may be felt quickly by the government as well; but such influence also can have important effects in the long run in nondemocratic or even totalitarian countries.

Influencing political behavior, circumstances, or events in foreign countries is the very stuff of foreign policy; diplomacy is as directed toward this goal as is covert action. The development and deployment of military forces also may be carried out to influence foreign behavior; this is common in peacetime but may occur during war as well. Thus, it is not surprising that many of the covert action techniques discussed below can be, and are, carried out in a noncovert manner as well. What is or is not considered covert action, for U.S. government purposes, often depends less on the nature of the case than on the peculiarities of the applicable legal and administrative definitions of covert action.

Covert Support of a Friendly Government

In many cases, covert action is carried out through a tacit alliance with individuals or groups with whom one shares common objectives. It is least difficult to do this when the ally in question is a friendly foreign government. In this instance, covert action can be limited to such unsensational activities as secretly assisting it with personal security for its leader or equipment for secure (encrypted) communications.

There is some reason to call such an activity covert action. The support provided to a friendly government helps it stay in power and, in that sense, influence the course of events in that country. In addition the action takes place in secret, in that information is not released to the public concerning the support nor would there be any public acknowledgment of it if word should leak out. But, we could just as easily consider the action a form of secret diplomacy. In fact, the term "covert action" would probably be applied to this sort of activity only if it were undertaken by an intelligence agency; supplying secret aid via diplomatic or military personnel might not be so considered.

Such activities are often small scale and relatively noncontroversial, and hence they are unlikely to make their way into the newspapers. They may, however, be important both technically (by providing capabilities that the friendly government could not provide for itself) and psychologically (as an indication to the receiving government of the reliability and effectiveness of its patron's support). However, this absence of visibility and controversy need not always be the case.

First of all, the same disputes about which governments should be considered friendly and worthy of assistance would be likely to occur as in the case of noncovert foreign aid. The secrecy involved does not change the nature of such disagreements, although it may lead opponents of a program to suspect that it was kept secret primarily to avoid any challenge to it.

Secondly, a dispute might arise from the nature of the assistance, especially if the recipient has an unsavory reputation.[8] For example, in 1974 the U.S. Congress banned the use of foreign aid funds for police training; this came about because of controversy concerning the human rights records of Latin American regimes that were recipients of such assistance.[9]

Intelligence Support

One common type of support rendered to a friendly foreign government may be noted in particular: the providing or sharing of intelligence information. In part because this activity is routine, it would not typically be considered covert action. In cases involving an exchange of information of equal value, and the purpose of providing the other government with information is to receive valuable intelligence in return, it seems more reasonable to view the activity as intelligence collection than as covert action.

In other cases, however, where the exchange is one sided, the major motivation of the party providing the bulk of the intelligence may well be the desire to help the other government. In this case, it seems reasonable to consider it covert support of a friendly government, since it enables another government to achieve objectives it could not on its own, and it is, of course, carried on secretly.

While intelligence would typically be shared only with friendly governments, cases crop up in which a government would pass specific information to another government it did not view as friendly to induce or enable the latter to take a specific step in the interest of both. This possibility, where the motivation is less to help the other government than to make it take a specific action, is discussed below as a method of influencing how a foreign government perceives its situation in the world.

Influencing Perceptions

Unlike the situation discussed above where one is interested in supporting a foreign government whose policies are already favorable to one's interests, the more common and more characteristic covert action tries to change foreign behavior, events, or circumstances to further one's interests. This is done either by influencing the foreign government's actions or by influencing the foreign society, or groups or sectors of it, independently of its government's actions and often against its government's wishes. The ultimate goal is to influence the government's policy or to create the conditions for a change of government. The next two sections discuss how actions, events, or circumstances can be affected by influencing a foreign government's perceptions or those of elements of a foreign society about political, military, or economic matters.

Influencing the Perceptions of a Foreign Government

Agents of Influence

The simplest and most direct method of affecting a foreign government's actions is to use an agent of influence—an agent whose task is to influence directly government policy rather than to collect information. Since an agent who is a high-level official in another government would be in a position to do both, this distinction could be more a theoretical one than a practical one. In such cases, using an agent whose prime function was intelligence collection to influence its government's policy might not be considered covert action. However, an intelligence service might not wish to jeopardize a good source by having that person try to influence his government's policy if, by so doing, he might call unfavorable and potentially dangerous attention to himself.

An agent of influence could be an official of the target government or a prominent member of the target country's political class (an insider, so to speak) who would have good access to government officials, opinion leaders, and the media. If an agent of influence is a high official in the target government, he might, by himself, be able to take actions that benefit another government. The more normal situation in a large, bureaucratic government, however, is that he will be most useful in persuading colleagues to adopt policies congenial to another government's interests. Obviously, he cannot openly advocate policies on the grounds that they are beneficial to some foreign, presumably unfriendly, power; he must seek to influence his colleagues' perceptions of the political situation in such a way that they are naturally led to take positions useful to the government whose agent he is.

A recent example of an agent of influence was Pierre-Charles Pathé, a politically well-connected Frenchman who, in 1979, was convicted of espionage for the Soviet Union and sentenced to five years in prison. As a political insider, he knew a great deal about high-level politics in Paris as well as about the personal lives of major political figures, although he did not have access to classified information. It appears, however, that his real crime was less espionage than being an agent of influence.

In 1976, partially funded by the KGB, he started a political newsletter called *Synthèse (Synthesis)*. During the next three years, this newsletter, which reached a large part of the political elite in France (at one point, 70 percent of the members of the Chamber of Deputies were among its subscribers), denigrated and attacked Western interests and policy; exaggerated differences of interest and policy between France and other members of the North Atlantic Treaty Organization, or NATO (in particular, West Germany and the United States); and defended the USSR and its allies. Pathé was arrested after he was observed receiving some money at a clandestine meeting with a KGB agent in the suburbs of Paris.[10]

The nature of the relationship between an intelligence service and an agent of influence varies according to the circumstances. In the case of someone like Pathé, a sophisticated journalist and political insider whose sympathies for the Soviet Union predated any clandestine connection with the KGB (it is likely that he first came to its attention when he published an article favorable to the Soviet Union in 1959), the relationship was probably a flexible one based on shared interests rather than a strictly disciplined one based on detailed instructions.

Soviet terminology recognizes a spectrum of agents of influence, depending on the degree and type of control exercised by the intelligence service. Pathé would be an example of a trusted contact, that is, someone who is willing to work with a foreign government to advance goals he shares with it but who is not receptive to detailed instruction and would typically not be paid. (The funds Pathé received helped defray the costs of publishing his newsletter but were probably not seen by either party as compensation for services rendered.) He may be contrasted with a "controlled" agent, who receives and executes precise orders and who would normally be compensated monetarily. At the other end of the spectrum would be someone who is manipulated (for example, via his aides or his social contacts) to act in a way that serves the foreign government's interests but who is unaware of this manipulation.[11]

Use of Information and Disinformation

Another method of influencing a government's actions is by providing it with bits of information (or misinformation) designed to induce it to act in a desired manner. A recent example of this is the reported case in which the United States, in 1983, passed to Ayatollah Khomeini specific information about "Soviet agents and collaborators operating in Iran." This resulted in as many as two hundred executions and the "closing down [of] the communist Tudeh party," which "dealt a major blow to KGB operations and Soviet influence" in Iran. The United States reportedly obtained this information when a Soviet "diplomat" in Teheran, Vladimir A. Kuzichkin, defected to Britain in 1982; Kuzichkin was in fact "a senior KGB officer . . . whose job it had been to maintain contacts with the Tudeh party."[12]

Although, in this case, the CIA reportedly participated in the activity, there is no inherent necessity for intelligence channels to be used to pass such information. Absent any intelligence service involvement, such an activity would probably not be considered covert action, although its nature would remain essentially the same. A historically significant example of this type of activity, which would not be considered covert action at all, would be the unsuccessful effort of British Prime Minister Winston Churchill, in April 1941, to warn the Soviet Union of the impending German attack.

Under the circumstances of the time, it is easy to see why Stalin might have suspected Churchill's motives. Stalin, probably possessing an exaggerated sense of English duplicity to begin with, certainly understood that it was in Britain's interest for relations between the Soviet Union and Germany to worsen. Churchill might well have hoped that Soviet defensive measures taken as a result of his message would be misinterpreted by Germany as threatening, thereby provoking further German military measures along the Soviet border, and so forth. As a result, Stalin regarded this true warning as a deception effort and ignored it.[13]

While the two examples cited above involve the passing of true information, there is no reason why misinformation, as long as it is plausible, cannot serve the same purpose. One technique of making such misinformation plausible is called "silent forgery," which is a forged document that is passed privately to a foreign government but is not made available to the media. In the best case, the target government (the government the forgery is designed to influence) accepts the forged document as genuine and does not investigate the matter. The government whose document the forgery purports to be never learns about it and is hence unable to deny its authenticity.

An example of this technique, which failed because the target government did investigate, is provided by Ladislav Bittman, a former Czech intelligence agent. He claims that in 1977 the Soviets prepared a forged memorandum, purportedly from the U.S. Embassy in Teheran and arranged for it to be sent anonymously to the Egyptian Embassy in Belgrade. The memorandum, stamped "Top Secret," discussed a supposed plot by the United States, Iran, and Saudi Arabia to overthrow Egyptian President Anwar Sadat. The covert action failed when the Egyptian government, in response to an official inquiry to Washington, received information that persuaded it that the memorandum was a forgery.[14]

This sort of disinformation effort may be directed specifically against the target's intelligence service, rather than the government as a whole. In this case, the misinformation, instead of being given to the target government, is, so to speak, left lying around for its intelligence services to discover; for example, deliberately misleading conversations may be held over telephone lines the target government's intelligence is known to have tapped. This type of disinformation campaign is usually referred to as a "deception operation" and considered part of counterintelligence rather than covert action. To some extent, this distinction is arbitrary, since the operation's basic purpose and method remain the same. On the other hand, a deception operation is a means of defeating the target's intelligence collection and analysis activities and depends on, and makes use of, a detailed knowledge of the target intelligence service's sources and methods. In these respects, it is reasonably considered a part of counterintelligence.

Influencing Perceptions in a Foreign Society

As opposed to the techniques already discussed, those discussed below are predominantly directed at influencing currents of thought within a foreign society rather than its government. This is a more amorphous task, and it is harder to measure what effect some of these techniques have in any given case. While many of the examples may seem insignificant taken one at a time, the cumulative effect on public opinion over a long period may be large. These techniques, then, are more suitable for use by a government that understands it is engaged in a long-term struggle than by one that deals with each problem or crisis as a separate event.

Agents of Influence

Although this technique would ordinarily involve agents who can more or less directly influence governmental perceptions and policies, one could image an agent whose main task was to affect a foreign country's media. To some extent, Pathé fits in this category, but he is discussed above because of the elite character of his newsletter's readership.

Other examples, involving the Soviet use of agents of influence in Japan, have been recounted by Stanislav Levchenko, a KGB major who defected to the United States in 1979.[15] They include the following: the use of a prominent member of the Japanese Socialist Party (JSP) to prevent another party member, whom the KGB considered to be a Chinese agent, from achieving a leadership position; the use of a senior correspondent of the Tokyo newspaper *Yomiuri* to promote the publication of an article to obtain the release of a Soviet military intelligence (GRU) agent who had been arrested in a double-agent operation; and the use of a young American stringer for the Associated Press to surface a letter purportedly from the wife of a Soviet air force pilot who defected from Siberia to Japan in his MiG-25 that implored him to return to the Soviet Union.[16]

Unattributed Propaganda

One of the more direct ways of attempting to influence a society is by disseminating opinions, information, or misinformation through the available media, that is, by propaganda (as it is pejoratively called). For example, nations with active foreign policies usually have radio stations (such as the Voice of America, Radio Moscow, and so forth) that openly express their views on international questions, much as newspaper editorials express the views of the newspaper's editor or publisher.

At times, however, a government may wish not to be officially associated with the material contained in its propaganda. In these cases, it may put certain opinions or facts into circulation in a manner that does not make their origin apparent. This may be accomplished either by planting them in news media it does not own or control or by means of media that appear to the public to be independent but that are in fact controlled by the government.

There are two major reasons a government might resort to such unattributed (or "black") propaganda.[17] First, the target audience may be more disposed to believe the propaganda if its origin is disguised and the ulterior motive of the propagandist is not evident. For example, anti-Soviet information is more likely to be believed if it appears to come from an independent source than if it comes from the U.S. government. For that reason, as discussed below, the U.S. government established Radio Free Europe and Radio Liberty as apparently private organizations.

Second, for diplomatic reasons, a government may not wish to be associated with certain opinions it nevertheless wishes to propagate to a given audience. For example, during the Iranian hostage crisis of 1979–81, the

Soviet government could take a diplomatically correct position by condemning the hostage-taking at the U.N., while its "black" radio station, the National Voice of Iran, implicitly approved it and sought to inflame anti-American opinion in Iran.[18]

In addition to "black" propaganda media, whose origin is meant to be concealed, one may also speak of "gray" propaganda, whose origin, while not totally or effectively concealed, is nevertheless not publicly acknowledged. For example, the U.S. government established Radio Free Europe and Radio Liberty in 1949 and 1951, respectively, to broadcast to the peoples of Eastern Europe and the Soviet Union. Unlike Voice of America, these stations were not to convey official American views but were designed to provide the target populations with information about their own countries that was not available in their own government-controlled media, as well as with information about the West. They were set up as private U.S. organizations; to support this cover, they even made public appeals for contributions.

In fact, the stations were run by the CIA. According to Ray Cline, "The CIA organized this effort . . . because it was thought the broadcasts would be more effective if their connection with the U.S. Government would be concealed."[19] But while the U.S. government connection was unacknowledged, it was clear that the radios were an American operation. Following the public confirmation by Senator Clifford Case that they had enjoyed covert CIA funding, Congress decided in 1973 to support the radio operations openly via the Board for International Broadcasting, which was established as an independent federal agency.[20]

A similar Soviet "gray" propaganda technique is the use of Novosti Press Agency. Unlike TASS (whose full name literally means the "Telegraph Agency of the Soviet Union"), Novosti is said to be a nongovernmental institution. This is seen as allowing it somewhat greater latitude in disseminating views with which the Soviet government does not want to be associated, although it is unlikely that its "unofficial" status is taken very seriously by anyone outside the Soviet Union.[21]

Another method of conducting propaganda in an unattributed fashion involves planting stories in independent news media or arranging for books to be written and published by authors and publishing houses that have no visible connections with the government or its intelligence agencies. For example, during a covert action campaign directed against Communist influence in Western Europe, the CIA used unattributed propaganda, including secret subventions for publishing books and planting newspaper articles via agents of influence working for wire services or newspapers.

One of the most famous CIA activities of this sort was the publication in various non-U.S. newspapers of a CIA-supplied copy of Khrushchev's 1956 "secret speech" attacking Stalin's "cult of personality." The speech was also published in the *New York Times*, which received a copy from the Department of State but which was presumably aware that the speech had been originally obtained in a clandestine manner.[22] Another example is the CIA's support for the writing and publication of *The Penkovskiy Papers*, an account, based on the actual case materials, of the CIA's premier spy in the Soviet Union in the late 1950s and early 1960s.[23]

A related technique is the use of front groups as a propaganda medium. These groups, while ostensibly broadly based, are in fact under the control of a government and can be relied on to take positions consonant with that government's objectives. They thus serve the same function as unattributed propaganda—they express views that serve a government's interest but in a format more likely to make them acceptable to the intended audience. Among the numerous Soviet front groups in operation, the World Peace Council is the best known; others include international organizations of lawyers, students, and women.

Forgeries

Another technique for putting material into circulation without taking any responsibility for it is the preparation and circulation of forged documents. In recent years, many forgeries purporting to be official U.S. documents have come to light.[24] While in most cases it is difficult to prove their origin, the indicators point to the Soviet Union.

All of these techniques serve the same general purpose: to influence a target audience's perceptions so it will take desired actions. The material used to do this—the arguments advanced by an agent of influence; the content of the propaganda, attributed or unattributed; or the text of the forgery—must be plausible to those whom one is attempting to influence. In general, therefore, one would expect the false material to be mixed in with some truths to enhance its plausibility. The resulting amalgam, which has the effect of misleading the target audience in some important respect, is often referred to as "disinformation" (from the Russian word *dezinformatsia*, which is used to refer to the active measures technique of misleading an audience to induce it to act in one's own interest).[25]

Of course, it is possible that a totally true message (or one that was believed to be so by those propagating it) could have the desired effect on a target audience. The most effective part of the Khrushchev secret speech (in the sense of reducing communism's prestige in Western and Eastern Europe) consisted of the revelations concerning Stalin's crimes and the "cult of personality." Publicizing it was an effective CIA covert action even though the text was authentic.[26] Similarly, the British release of the authentic Zimmermann telegram, discussed in the previous chapter, was a masterstroke of unattributed propaganda.

Support for Friendly Political Forces

Another way of influencing events in foreign countries is the provision of material support to friendly political forces, such as political parties, civic groups, labor unions, and media. While this can be, and sometimes is, done openly, covert aid may be more palatable to the recipient groups and is less likely to lead to politically damaging charges of foreign interference in the target country's internal affairs.

Traditionally, the Soviet Union facilitated this type of activity by a fictitious distinction between the Soviet government and the Communist party of the Soviet Union. While the former could pursue correct diplomatic relations with other states, the latter, through such organizations as the Comintern, the Cominform, and the International Department of Central Committee, maintained relations with, and provided support for, "progressive" forces throughout the world. In response to Soviet activity of this sort in Western Europe after World War II, the United States engaged in a covert action program of aid to democratic political and cultural groups and trade unions.

The immediate impetus was the Truman administration's fear (in late 1947) that the Communists would win the Italian elections scheduled for the following spring. To support U.S. overt propaganda efforts, the CIA conducted such activities as providing financial and other support (for example, training in electoral campaign techniques) to the non-Communist political parties. It also attempted to influence the Socialist party against cooperation with the Communists. As Ray Cline, former deputy director of the CIA, explained,

> These kinds of financial and technical assistance to the Christian Democrats and other non-Communist parties, as well as the efforts to split off Socialists from the united front group dominated by the Communists, had to be covert. Italian party leaders could not afford to let Communists obtain evidence that they were supported by foreigners because it would blunt public anger at the Communist Party for its own financial and policy dependence on the Soviet Union. Hence CIA got the job of passing money and giving the technical help needed to get out the vote and win the election.[27]

Following the electoral success of the non-Communist parties, the CIA "was instructed to propose specific information programs and other political action that would negate Communist efforts to expand Soviet political influence in Western Europe."[28] As described by the Church Committee, the resulting program involved "subsidies to European 'counterfront' labor and political organizations" that were

intended to serve as alternatives to Soviet- or communist-inspired groups. [There were e]xtensive . . . labor, media and election operations . . . in the late 1940s, . . . Support for "counterfront" organizations, especially in the areas of student, labor and cultural activities, was to become much more prevalent in the 1950s and 1960s, . . .[29]

As Ray Cline has emphasized, much of this funding went to organizations of the non-Communist left that were not necessarily sympathetic to specific U.S. foreign policy positions. He cites specifically the Congress of Cultural Freedom and political journals such as *Encounter* in England and *Der Monat* in West Germany.[30] This strategy was presumably dictated by the view that the major ideological battleground in Europe was on the left and that the more conservative organizations would, in any case, have fewer problems in obtaining funding domestically. It points out, however, a typical ambiguity in covert action: it is often possible to work with people with whom one has major disagreements; the embarrassment the revelation of such an arrangement would cause becomes another reason for secrecy.

A more recent, and more controversial, U.S. program of this sort was conducted in Chile following the inauguration of the Marxist Salvador Allende as president in 1970. This program was designed to provide opposition political parties and media with the financial resources to survive the country's economic chaos and hostile regulatory action by the government. The controversy surrounding it focused on two issues (aside from the larger question of what the U.S. policy toward the Allende regime should have been).

First, the program was condemned as unnecessary, since, according to the Church Committee, CIA national intelligence estimates during the Allende period indicated that "despite attempts to harass and financially damage opposition media," the opposition press (and in particular *El Mercurio* [the nation's largest newspaper and the most important anti-Allende medium]) remained free and that "the traditional political system in Chile continued to demonstrate remarkable resiliency."[31] However, the committee noted that those responsible for the estimates were unaware of the covert action program: "Thus, there was no estimate of whether those sectors would survive *absent* U.S. money."[32]

Another controversy concerned the purposes for which U.S. aid was given. A strong attempt was made to keep U.S. assistance away from those groups that were actively seeking to overturn the government (such as the trucker's union, whose long, damaging strikes provided the occasion for the military coup) and to limit it to opposition parties and media. According to Gregory Treverton, a critic of covert action who was a staff member of the Church Committee, "The pattern of deliberations within the U.S. government suggests a careful distinction between supporting opposition forces and funding groups trying to promote a military coup. The attempt to draw that distinction was, so far as I can tell, an honest one. . . ."[33] Nevertheless, as Treverton concludes, this distinction was fundamentally artificial, one that existed "in the minds of Americans, not Chileans."[34] The opposition groups chose their own strategy for achieving their objectives and picked their tactics and allies accordingly; if the various anti-Allende forces wished to cooperate with each other, then U.S. support for some groups helped their allies as well.

Influencing Political Events by Violent Means

In the public mind, covert action is most often associated with violent methods of influencing political events. As the discussion so far has shown, many nonviolent techniques can be covertly employed to influence political behavior, events, and circumstances in foreign countries. In addition to these activities, which make up the vast majority of covert action operations, there are techniques that involve the supporting or use of violence, to which we now turn.

Support for Coups, "Wars of National Liberation," and "Freedom Fighters"

Support for political groups need not be limited to the peaceful opponents of a foreign government but can be extended to groups that seek either to influence that government's policy through violent means or to overthrow it. This could involve the support of an existing group or the creation of a "puppet" group to carry out these activities.

The precise type of support would depend in part on the group being supported and the strategy it followed. It could take the form of military aid for an insurgent fighting force, operational support for a coup d'état, external political and economic pressure and internal subversion directed against the target government, or training and economic support for the development of cadres for a long-term guerrilla struggle. The two large, basically overt, "covert" actions undertaken by the United States during the Carter and Reagan administrations (support for the guerrilla struggle against the Soviet-supported Afghan regime and support for the *contra* resistance in Nicaragua) exemplify this type of covert action.

A particular form of this sort of activity that has received a great deal of attention is patron-state support for international terrorism. The support governments provide to terrorist groups can vary greatly in magnitude and importance. At the low end of the spectrum, a patron state might provide training facilities or a haven where terrorists would be safe from arrest while planning their attacks or to which they could flee afterwards. At the higher end, this support could include money, weapons, genuine or forged passports, or use of the diplomatic pouch to send weapons or explosives into the target country. The amount of control the patron state exercises over the terrorist group's activities can also vary; in some cases, it may be fairly detailed, while in others almost nonexistent, as long as the general nature of the activities is consistent with the patron's interests.

Paramilitary

At the borderline of real covert action are cases in which a government uses irregular (or volunteer) forces in a military conflict, either alone or in alliance with similar groups or indigenous forces. Because a relatively large-scale effort of this sort can hardly remain secret for long, we might argue that this type of activity should be excluded from the category of covert action. On the other hand, since intelligence services are likely to be tasked to carry it out, it is usually grouped with more covert types of action. In any case, since the activity would not be publicly acknowledged by the government carrying it out, it remains covert action in that sense, regardless of how transparent the pretense of noninvolvement becomes.

Specific Acts of Destruction or Violence, Including Assassination

Finally, covert action can take the form of specific acts of violence, directed against individuals (such as the assassination of foreign government officials, key political figures, or terrorists) or property (such as the French blowing up the Greenpeace ship *Rainbow Warrior*).

The CIA's bungled attempts to assassinate Fidel Castro, as well as its involvement with the political forces responsible for assassinating Patrice Lumumba of the Belgian Congo (now Zaire) and Rafael Trujillo of the Dominican Republic, were among the main issues that surfaced during the investigations of the agency during the mid-1970s and were minutely studied by the Church Committee.[35] One result of these revelations was the inclusion in President Gerald Ford's executive order on intelligence of an explicit ban on "engag[ing] in, or conspir[ing] to engage in, political assassination."[36] This provision was retained in the executive orders on intelligence promulgated by Presidents Carter and Reagan.[37] This issue resurfaced in the late 1980s in connection with U.S. policy toward Panamanian strongman Manuel Noriega, when it was alleged that the provision prohibited the CIA from assisting anti-Noriega members of the Panamanian Defense Force in planning a coup (for fear that it might involve or, at any rate, result in Noriega's assassination). From this point of view, the provision thereby contributed indirectly to the U.S. invasion of Panama in December 1989, which achieved the same result but at a much higher price.

One of the better-known recent covert actions involving violence against property was the blowing up, by French intelligence agents, of the *Rainbow Warrior* in 1985. This ship, which was attacked while at harbor in New Zealand, was owned by the environmental organization Greenpeace, which intended to use the ship to protest and interfere with French atomic weapon tests in the South Pacific. A Portuguese crew member on board was killed in the explosion, and two of the French agents involved were caught before they could leave New Zealand.

Covert Action and Secrecy

Although secrecy appears to be at the very heart of covert action, its actual importance and function, as noted at the beginning of this chapter, is not at all a simple matter; it depends very much on the type of covert action and the circumstances in which covert action is undertaken. The degree of secrecy required, and the motivation for it, can differ greatly from case to case.

In some cases, secrecy may be essential to the operation's success. Admiral Stansfield Turner, director of central intelligence under President Carter, in the course of congressional testimony, provided an example of such a covert action. The operation involved sending a CIA agent to Teheran to facilitate the escape of six Americans who had taken refuge in the Canadian Embassy after the American Embassy was seized in November 1979.[38] Any revelation of the operation (even if the identities of the CIA agent and the six in hiding were not revealed) would have endangered the safety of the seven people involved by heightening Iranian vigilance, by leading Iran to invade the Canadian Embassy, or by complicating the process of extracting from Iran the Americans using false passports.

Similarly, keeping certain details of an operation secret may be needed to prevent interference with it, even though the broad outlines of the program are generally known. For example, we might consider U.S. assistance to the Mujahedeen in Afghanistan. A specific channel used to transfer supplies might be vulnerable to sabotage or diplomatic pressure by the Soviet or Afghan governments if they knew about it. Thus, with respect to this detail of the covert action, absolute secrecy would be necessary, regardless of the publicity the operation as a whole received.

Cases such as this, where secrecy about either the entire operation or a specific part of it is crucial to carrying it out at all, are probably rare. In many other cases, however, secrecy is very important for the operation's effectiveness. In this category, we could consider the kinds of unattributed propaganda or support for political activity that have already been discussed.

These activities are carried out covertly on the grounds that public awareness of the foreign source of propaganda or of funding for political activities would diminish the effect they could have. The concept of "black" propaganda, for example, is that information that would be questioned or rejected were it known to come from an adversary or from some other foreign source with an obvious ulterior motive will be more acceptable if its origin can be hidden or falsely identified. (In some cases, secrecy would be required because the funding of political organizations would violate the law of the target country.)

In addition, "black" propaganda can be used to sow dissension in the adversary's ranks by falsely attributing to him provocative words or actions. In this case, secrecy concerning the true source of the propaganda is necessary to support its credibility. Sefton Delmer, who ran British "black" propaganda operations in World War II, claimed that "the simplest and most effective 'black' operation is to spit in a man's soup and cry 'Heil Hitler!' "[39] Similarly, many Soviet forgeries of recent years have involved fabricating U.S. government memorandums that evince a hostile attitude toward a third country.

In other cases, secrecy may be necessary to secure the cooperation of a third party that is willing to help only if the activity is concealed, thus enabling that party to avoid damaging its other foreign relationships. For that reason, even in a case in which the contours of a covert activity could be safely made known, keeping it secret might be important to gain the cooperation of a third country.

A final category deals with cases where public awareness is avoided less because it would endanger those carrying out the operation or harm its effectiveness than because diplomatic reasons make it desirable not to acknowledge governmental involvement.[40] For example, the lack of official acknowledgment of an operation may inhibit an adversary's response, even if the adversary is aware through intelligence information of the involvement. This is particularly true if the adversary is a democracy in which the government must obtain public approval or understanding for any response it might make; the adversary may be inhibited from trying to obtain public support by the fear that publicizing the incriminating evidence will jeopardize the means by which it was collected. Thus it makes sense for a state that supports international terrorism, such as Qadhafi's Libya, to disavow any connection with a specific terrorist event, even when its complicity otherwise becomes known.

For example, the U.S. government's ability to respond to the Libyan-supported terrorist bombing on April 5, 1986, of a discotheque in West Berlin, in which an American serviceman and another person were killed, ultimately depended on U.S. willingness to divulge sensitive intelligence information proving Libyan involvement. While the U.S. government was willing to do this, it paid a heavy price; the Libyans were made aware of the extent of U.S. intelligence capabilities directed against them and hence were able to reduce the effectiveness of those capabilities.

More generally, although governments are understood to engage in covert action (as in espionage), covert action is frequently illegal under the laws of the country in which the covert action is taking place. It also may be said to be contrary to the norms of international law, for which nonintervention in the internal affairs of sovereign states is a basic premise.

For these reasons, it is less provocative and less disruptive to diplomatic relations not to acknowledge an operation even if the country adversely affected by it is well aware of one's involvement. The target country, either in the interests of good relations, or because it cannot effectively prevent it, may ignore the covert action; it is much harder for it to do so if the government conducting it publicly acknowledges what it is doing.

Plausible Denial

Closely related to this is the doctrine, long considered axiomatic, that even if a nation's involvement in covert action becomes known, the chief of state should be able to deny that he authorized or even knew of the action. He should be able to assert, with some plausibility, that it was carried out by subordinates who acted without his knowledge or authority.

In the post–World War II period, this doctrine came to public attention most forcefully when President Eisenhower disregarded it and publicly admitted that he had authorized overflights of the Soviet Union by the U-2 reconnaissance plane. Eisenhower's action came in May 1960, after a U-2 plane, whose high-flying altitude had previously made it invulnerable to air defenses, was brought down by a Soviet surface-to-air missile while on a reconnaissance flight across that country. (Although not covert action, this incident, involving an apparent violation of international law, raised the same issue of plausible deniability.)

In his memoirs, Soviet First Secretary Nikita Khrushchev claims that it was Eisenhower's admission of responsibility, rather than the flight itself, that caused him to scuttle the Paris "Big Four" summit meeting scheduled for later that spring.[41] Eisenhower, however, felt that he could not deny knowledge without suggesting that he did not effectively control U.S. military forces, especially given the large infrastructure necessary to support the flights. While it is possible to disavow the actions of a small group of secret agents, who can be portrayed as renegades acting without or contrary to orders, it is another matter to disavow an operation that obviously required the cooperation of many people at various air bases around the world.

An example of plausible denial in recent years arose from the case of the French intelligence agents who blew up the *Rainbow Warrior*. The French government maintained that official involvement in the affair went no higher than Defense Minister Charles Hernu, who was responsible for the DGSE (Direction Générale de la Sécurité Extérieure, the French foreign intelligence service subordinate to the Ministry of Defense) and who resigned three months after the attack. President François Mitterrand escaped essentially unscathed.[42]

In the United States, the doctrine of plausible denial was in effect abolished by Congress in connection with its investigations into intelligence matters in the mid-1970s. At the end of 1974, following revelations about a covert action program in Chile, the U.S. Congress passed the Hughes-Ryan Amendment, which prohibited CIA covert actions

> unless and until the President finds that each such operation is important to the national security of the United States and reports, in a timely fashion, . . . to the appropriate committees of the Congress, including [the Senate Foreign Relations Committee and the House Foreign Affairs Committee].[43]

Congressional consideration of the amendment focused on the part that required the executive branch to inform Congress about covert actions. However, the amendment's requirement that the president find that proposed covert actions are important to the national security destroyed the president's ability to plausibly deny involvement in any covert action operation that became publicly known.[44]

In the course of the Iran-Contra investigation, Admiral John Poindexter's claim that he did not inform President Reagan about the diversion of the proceeds from the Iranian arms sales to the Nicaraguan resistance represented an attempt to revive the plausible denial doctrine. In particular, Poindexter testified that he did not tell the president about the diversion in order to "provide some future deniability for [him] if it ever leaked out."[45]

The Abandonment of Secrecy

Because of the increased congressional role in controlling covert action, among other reasons, the United States has, in effect, abandoned secrecy in recent years with respect to some operations that would ordinarily be (and, often, still are) called covert action. For example, the question of aid to the Afghan and Nicaraguan insurgents was openly discussed and debated in Congress and in the press. The United States even asserted, in connection with the 1988 Geneva agreement on Soviet withdrawal from Afghanistan, a right to continue aiding the rebels as long as the Soviets provided aid to the Kabul government. Despite the fact that these activities are called covert action, they are overt in many respects (although some details may remain secret).

In other cases, the United States has abandoned secrecy altogether for activities that previously would have been considered to require it. In 1973, for example, after CIA funding of Radio Free Europe/Radio Liberty (RFE/RL) had been publicly confirmed, Congress replaced the covert funding mechanism with overt government funding via a newly created independent federal agency, the Board for International Broadcasting. While this change was not undertaken voluntarily, it may not have had much effect on RFE/RL's credibility in the target countries. Regardless of how the initial disguising of sponsorship enhanced RFE/RL's effectiveness, it would seem that, by 1973, the radio stations already had a long track record by which their audiences could judge them.

Similarly, following President Reagan's speech in London on June 8, 1982, in which he called for strengthening the infrastructure of democracy on a global basis, the National Endowment for Democracy (NED), a federally funded private organization, was established in 1983. It provides overt support (directly and via affiliated institutes of the AFL-CIO, the U.S. Chamber of Commerce, and the Democratic and Republican parties) for institutions—trade unions, business associations, other civic organizations, media, and political parties—that can make possible or contribute to democratic life in foreign countries where democracy is weak, threatened, or nonexistent.

This effort was to some extent modeled on the international activities of the political foundations associated with the West German political parties;

these foundations were funded by the West German government and work through similarly minded political organizations in other countries to promote democracy. They are generally credited, for example, with providing vital support for the non-Communist parties in Portugal during the turbulent and dangerous period following the overthrow of the Caetano dictatorship in 1974. In certain respects, this type of overt support for democratic institutions partially replaces the covert support the United States provided to democratic forces in Western Europe right after World War II.

Covert Action and Intelligence

Having reviewed the wide range of activities that come under the heading of covert action, we now look at its relation to the rest of intelligence. Two questions suggest themselves. First, should covert action be conducted by the intelligence-gathering and analysis agencies, or should it be lodged in a separate bureaucratic structure? Second, should covert action, from a purely theoretical perspective, be considered part of intelligence?

Should Covert Action Be Separate?

Arguments Against a Separate Covert Action Agency

As noted in the first chapter, both the United States and Britain have discovered through experience that having two organizations involved in running clandestine operations—one for intelligence collection (espionage) and one for covert action—can create serious practical problems. During World War II, the British Special Operations Executive (SOE), charged by Prime Minister Winston Churchill with "setting Europe ablaze," was separate from the Secret Intelligence Service (SIS, or MI6) and reported to the minister for economic warfare. This gave rise to the inevitable interdepartmental rivalries as the two agencies competed for scarce resources.[46]

Similarly, in the United States, a special CIA component called the Office of Policy Coordination (OPC) was set up in 1948 to conduct covert action. Although administratively part of the CIA, it operated on the basis of policy guidance provided by the Departments of State and Defense, and its head was appointed by the secretary of state.[47] This office was separate from the CIA's Office of Special Operations (OSO), which collected intelligence via espionage. Eventually, this arrangement was found to be unworkable, and the two offices were consolidated in 1952 into the newly created Directorate for Plans.[48] According to the Church Committee, this step was due to (1) the anomalous position of the director of central intelligence in having an office (the OPC) for which he was administratively responsible (and which was funded through the CIA) that nevertheless took policy guidance directly from the Departments of State and Defense and (2) the competition between the OPC and the OSO for the services of the same agents and the difficulty, given the rivalry, of ensuring operational cooperation between them where necessary.[49]

Although conceptually different in function, covert action and human intelligence collection rely on similar means, especially the secret cooperation of agents able to operate effectively in the target country. In many cases, the agents who would be useful for one function can perform the other function as well; two separate offices could easily find themselves competing for the services of the same individuals. In addition, many of the support functions, such as assuring communications between officers and agents or making clandestine payments, are similar or identical and require similar skills, contacts, and resources. Close coordination would be necessary to ensure that the operations of one office in a given country did not inadvertently interfere with those of the other; such coordination might be difficult to achieve, especially if it required that one office's interests be subordinated to those of the other. Thus, a strong case can be made for combining these functions in a single organization whose operations in a target country or region of the world would be controlled by a single chief.

Arguments for a Separate Covert Action Agency

Despite the operational convenience of consolidating these functions, it has been argued that the different nature of the tasks involved makes consolidation inadvisable. In particular, the argument is made that giving the same organization responsibility for implementing policy (via covert action) with respect to a given country, on the one hand, and collecting and analyzing intelligence about that country (including assessing the results of the covert action), on the other, jeopardizes the objectivity of the analysis. In essence, this is the same argument that is made for the existence of a *central* intelligence agency—that is to say, one that is not a part of a policy-making and policy-implementing ministry or department of the government.

Is Covert Action a Part of Intelligence?

Aside from this organizational question, the more theoretical issue remains of whether covert action should be considered a part of intelligence. In including covert action among the elements of intelligence, I have noted that it is typically a function of intelligence agencies; this alone does not address the question of whether it makes sense to consider it a part of intelligence for theoretical purposes.[50]

To answer this question, let's get a better sense of just what covert action is. As already noted, the term itself is taken from the U.S. intelligence lexicon and does not necessarily have a clear counterpart in the usages of the intelligence services of other countries. Furthermore, the various U.S. definitions of covert action were developed in the context of attempts to regulate it by law or executive order; they are not necessarily useful for the present theoretical purpose.

In reviewing the types of covert action, some (such as secret support for a friendly regime) seem almost indistinguishable from diplomacy, and others (such as paramilitary activity) shade off into guerrilla or "low-intensity" warfare. What seems to be uniquely covert action is a middle ground between diplomacy and war that involves the secret manipulation of the perceptions of others to induce them to take actions that one sees as in one's interest. As such, is covert action reasonably considered a part of intelligence?

On the one hand, it has been argued that covert action—a means of implementing policy—is so different from the rest of intelligence, which deals with obtaining the information on which policy should be based, that it is a mistake to consider it a part of intelligence. From this point of view, it is more reasonably categorized as one of many foreign policy tools—such as diplomacy, economic aid, "most favored nation" tariff status, overt propaganda, exchange programs, Peace Corps–type programs, public diplomacy, military aid, and the threat or use of military force—that a nation uses to advance its interests.

On the other hand, it may be countered that defining intelligence as the obtaining of information is too narrow: if obtaining information is so important, then the denial of valuable information to one's adversary also must be an important part of intelligence. As becomes clear in the next chapter, an effective and particularly profitable way of preventing one's adversary from learning the truth is to deceive him into believing a falsehood. From this perspective, covert action and counterintelligence look similar: both involve affecting the adversary's behavior by manipulating his perceptions.

The question of whether covert action is a part of intelligence is intimately tied up with the question of what intelligence is. I will return to this question in the concluding chapters of the book.

5

SPY VS. SPY

COUNTERINTELLIGENCE

Of all the elements of intelligence, counterintelligence is probably the hardest to define. In its most general terms, counterintelligence refers to information collected and analyzed, and activities undertaken, to protect a nation (including its own intelligence-related activities) against the actions of hostile intelligence services. Under this definition, the scope of counterintelligence is as broad as the scope of intelligence itself, since all manner of hostile intelligence activities must be defended against.[1] In a narrower sense, however, counterintelligence often refers specifically to preventing an adversary from gaining knowledge that would give him an advantage. I examine this notion of counterintelligence first.

In conceptualizing what is involved in such a defense against an adversary's intelligence collection, let's first distinguish between passive and active measures. The most important passive measures, which seek to deny the adversary the information he is seeking simply by blocking his access to it—by, as it were, building a wall around it—are usually referred to as "security."[2] I discuss the nature of the wall—prohibiting access to sensitive information by individuals whose trustworthiness has not been ascertained, the protection of documents and communications in safes and by encryption, and so forth—in the section on security, below. First, an organization must decide what information is important enough to protect—what information must be kept within the walls.

The Classification of Information

Levels of Classification

A classification system categorizes information according to its sensitivity, which is to say, the amount of damage its revelation to a hostile foreign power could cause and, hence, the importance of protecting it. In the United States, the first such system for protecting national security documents was promulgated by the War Department in 1912; it and the Navy Department set up their own classification systems during World Wars I and II.[3] President Harry Truman established the first governmentwide system of classifying information in 1951.[4] The system is currently governed by an executive order President Reagan promulgated, setting out the definitions, rules, and procedures for operating the system.[5]

The U.S. classification system attempts to classify information according to the degree of harm to the national security its unauthorized release to an adversary would cause. The more sensitive the information, the more carefully it is to be protected and the fewer the people who are "cleared" for it (authorized to have access to it). Under the current system, the basic levels of classification are confidential, secret, and top secret, which are defined in terms of the damage to national security their unauthorized disclosure reasonably could be expected to cause:

- top secret: "exceptionally grave damage"
- secret: "serious damage"
- confidential: "damage"[6]

In addition, numerous other classifications are used to restrict further access to information. For the most part, these classifications refer to information about technical intelligence collection techniques and capabilities and are imposed by the director of central intelligence by virtue of his responsibility, under the National Security Act of 1947, to "protect intelligence sources and methods from unauthorized disclosure."[7] The years have seen, however, a proliferation of these special classifications (or "compartments") as various entities within and outside the intelligence community have tried to protect information they see as particularly sensitive. Periodically, attempts are made to systemize this process, and DCIs have contended that they should have sole authority to authorize these special compartments. It seems, however, to be an unending struggle, and the repeated admonitions not to create new classifications testify to the strength of the incentives to do so.

Need to Know

As noted above, the more sensitive the information (in terms of level of classification), the fewer are the number of people authorized to have access to it. In principle, however, mere clearance is not enough to obtain access to the information. People seeking access also must establish a need to know the information in order to perform their official responsibilities. This part of the information-control system is much less formal than that dealing with clearances; in general, anyone controlling classified information is responsible for ascertaining a requester's need to know before providing the information.

It is questionable whether this requirement constitutes an effective barrier to the unnecessary dissemination of classified information. In 1985, a Department of Defense (DoD) Commission to Review DoD Security Policies and Practices, headed by retired Army General Richard Stilwell, observed that "the principle that a cleared individual is authorized access only to that information he 'needs-to-know' is generally not enforced."[8]

What Should Be Classified?

The basic answer to the question of what should be classified, at least as far as the U.S. government is concerned, is contained in the definitions of confidential, secret, and top secret given above. These may seem straightforward in principle, although the key terms "damage," "serious damage," and "exceptionally grave damage" are vague, both in themselves and as applied to a concept as general as national security.

In fact, the real situation is much more complicated. The very way in which the problem has been posed—what information should be walled off from public access and discussion—presupposes a fundamentally liberal view of government and society in which the free flow of information is the rule and its denial, by means of classification, the exception. This view is probably the exception rather than the rule as far as history goes. The more common tradition has been that of governmental secrecy, broken when the government itself sees some advantage in disclosing information.[9]

Consider, for example, the fact that democratic countries routinely publish large amounts of data about their defense budgets. Although the notion of classifying a democratic country's entire defense budget is out of the question, both the United States and the Soviet governments have believed, judging by their actions, that publishing their defense budgets is harmful to themselves and useful to their adversaries. With respect to the Soviet government, until 1989 it regarded the amount spent on defense as a state secret.[10] U.S. intelligence, meanwhile, devotes considerable resources to determining the size of the Soviet defense budget and its major elements. If this information were not considered helpful to the U.S. government, these intelligence resources would presumably be employed on other tasks. Similarly, if the United States did not disclose its defense budget, the Soviet intelligence system would at the very least have to redirect some resources from their present tasks to that of determining its size; Soviet intelligence would also be less certain about American military developments and less confident in its assessment of them.

What this example is meant to show is not that a democracy should classify its defense budget but that the reason it does not do so has more to do with internal political considerations than with abstract criteria for classification.[11] The key dilemma can be stated as follows: almost any organization—political party, business corporation, football team, or whatever—that is competing with other organizations will want, other things being equal, to keep secret most information about its strategy for carrying on that competition, the resources it has available, and so on. Thus any information that is released damages its competitive position.

The same is true of the government's national security activities. The question is always one of balancing the potential harm to national security against the requirements of the domestic political order. No natural harmony exists between these two standards, and no unambiguous line can be drawn.

Despite the tendency to secrecy, any government, but especially a democratic one, often finds it useful or even necessary to release information to explain its actions and build public support for them. As noted in the previous chapter, the Reagan administration, to justify and secure public support for the 1986 bombing raid on Libya, released information derived from decrypted Libyan cable traffic implicating Libya in the terrorist bombing of a West Berlin discothèque. In alerting the Libyan government that its cable traffic was being read, the administration risked losing an important intelligence capability.

Overclassification

It has been a recurring complaint that the U.S. government classifies too much information and at too high a level. This criticism has been made not only by congressional committees and nongovernmental critics of the intelligence agencies or a given administration, but by insiders as well. For example, a 1985 DoD commission on security practices noted that too much information appears to be classified and much at higher levels than is warranted. Current policy specifies that the signer of a classified document is responsible for the classification assigned but frequently, out of ignorance or expedience, little scrutiny is given such determinations. Similarly, while challenges to improper classifications are permitted, few take the time to raise questionable classifications with the originator.[12]

To some extent, as already noted, secrecy is a natural characteristic of any government. Given the great and, to some extent, unique openness of the American political system, the practice seems particularly anomalous and has raised greater objection in the United States than elsewhere. In recent years, the same issue has surfaced in other countries, particularly Great Britain, where the laws governing the release of governmental information are much stricter than in the United States.

Aside from the primary harm—the unnecessary denial of information to the public, reducing its ability to understand and debate national security policy issues—overclassification also could have the secondary drawback of reducing the credibility of the classification system, leading to a tendency to disregard its rules. If many innocuous documents are classified, the inhibitions against the unauthorized disclosure of classified information are bound to be weakened.

Whether such pervasive overclassification exists in the U.S. government is a much more difficult question to answer. While any system that deals with millions of documents each year is bound to produce some dubious results, the major sources of disagreement arise from different views of what standards should be applied to the classification decision.

A common claim of those who believe that overclassification is rampant is that documents are often classified to save government officials from embarrassment or censure. These people claim, in other words, that classification serves to shield officials from public accountability for their actions. While this is an unacceptable motive for classification, the situation is often more complicated; the embarrassment is often not simply to an official who may have done something improper vis-à-vis the public, but to the government itself vis-à-vis foreign powers.

As was discussed in the treatment of covert action, secrecy is sometimes desired more for diplomatic reasons than because it is operationally necessary. The same is true with regard to foreign policy altogether. As in the case of covert action, however, governments have generally tended to be more open about many facets of foreign policy and less concerned about diplomatic niceties. Governments are more likely now than previously to admit that they conduct espionage and other intelligence activities. Thus, there is less room for invoking the excuse of governmental embarrassment. Nevertheless, valid diplomatic reasons may exist. For example, in 1977, the *Washington Post* asserted that King Hussein of Jordan had received subsidies from the CIA, a claim that could only be harmful to him politically.[13] Keeping such a relationship secret to avoid embarrassing and weakening the political position of a friendly head of state is a legitimate motive for secrecy that is not, strictly speaking, operationally necessary.

Underclassification?

Although it is often claimed that governments overclassify, it is worth considering whether the opposite is more likely in certain areas. This might occur with information developed outside the government that is significant enough to national security to justify its being classified and controlled. The most obvious example of this is information relating to nuclear weapons technology. We would expect that information that could facilitate nuclear proliferation would be carefully controlled.

In the United States, this issue was addressed in the Atomic Energy Act of 1954, which defined restricted data as "all data concerning (1) design, manufacture, or utilization of atomic weapons; (2) the production of special nuclear material; or (3) the use of special nuclear material in the production of energy, . . ."[14] Under the act, this type of information is subject to controls regardless of whether it was developed inside or outside the government. (The same act also prohibits the dissemination of unclassified information relating to the design of, and security measures for, various facilities for the production or utilization of nuclear materials.[15])

Nevertheless, considerable amounts of information about nuclear materials and weapons exist in the public domain in the United States. Thus comes the occasional report that a bright physics graduate student, working at a public library with unclassified sources, has drawn up plans for a nuclear bomb that unspecified experts have acknowledged as viable.

Other information that cannot be classified, but that might, under certain circumstances, deserve some protection include:

- financial information that would enable one to earn illegitimate (insider) profits on financial or commodity markets,
- technological information a nation may wish to prevent adversaries from obtaining, and
- personal information that might enable a hostile intelligence service to recruit government officials either by offering money to those with financial problems or by blackmailing them.

Protecting this sort of information has involved communications security, discussed below. However, it can, on occasion, involve other issues. For example, efforts have been made in the United States to apply the regulations concerning the export of technology to the dissemination of scientific papers dealing with these technologies; however, no feasible scheme for accomplishing this has been developed. In 1982 the deputy director of central intelligence, Admiral Bobby Ray Inman, noted the problem in a speech to the American Association for the Advancement of Science. Speaking of theoretical and applied cryptologic research, he expressed concern "that indiscriminate publication of the results of that research will come to the attention of foreign governments and entities and, thereby, could cause irreversible and unnecessary harm to U.S. national security interests." Among the areas where publication of technical information could harm national security, Inman included "computer hardware and software, other electronic gear and techniques, lasers, crop projections, and manufacturing procedures."[16]

Other than the rarely invoked Patent Secrecy Act of 1952, which allows the government, on national security grounds, to order that an invention be kept secret and to that end to withhold any patent for it, no effective mechanism exists for dealing with these issues. Attempts to invoke general export controls to prevent, for example, the dissemination of technical papers at conferences attended by foreigners have, by and large, been abandoned in the face of public controversy.[17]

Security

Security measures are steps taken to obstruct a hostile intelligence service's ability to collect intelligence. Such measures are designed to prevent a hostile intelligence service from either gaining access or exploiting any access it may have to personnel, documents, communications, or operations to gain important information; they constitute the wall surrounding classified information. The more traditional aspects of security—which deal with protection against the adversary's human intelligence collection efforts—are discussed in this section; those that deal with his technical collection capabilities are discussed later under the heading "multidisciplinary counterintelligence."

Personnel Security

Personnel security involves procedures for screening potential employees before hiring them for a job that gives them access to information a hostile intelligence service might wish to collect and for ensuring that current employees continue to meet the standards for access to such information. A screening procedure's primary function is to judge the potential employee's willingness and ability to keep classified information secret. The key elements of this judgment involve the potential employee's character and loyalty.[18] Judgments about character must consider both the individuals' mental stability and whether, for any reason, they would be vulnerable to blackmail by a hostile intelligence service.

In the United States, the screening investigation determines whether an individual is granted a security clearance, that is, authorized access to classified information. The investigation relies on information supplied on a security questionnaire by the individual, supplemented and verified by a national agency check (interrogation of the data banks of various law enforcement and other government agencies), and depending on the sensitivity of the information to which access is to be granted, interviews with friends and acquaintances, present and former neighbors, work- and schoolmates, and so forth. In the case of particularly sensitive information, a periodic reinvestigation is required to maintain access.

Background investigations of this sort are probably not very effective in assuring the loyalty and character of personnel to be granted access to classified information. Various legal prohibitions, discussed in the next chapter, prevent the FBI or other government agencies from collecting and maintaining membership lists of what used to be called subversive organizations such as the Communist party of the United States, even if the organization openly advocates the violent overthrow of the U.S. government.[19] A member of such an organization, who was prudent about discussing his membership with acquaintances and who did not disclose the membership on the security clearance forms, could reasonably hope to remain undetected.

In addition, societal changes in the United States have made it considerably harder to get candid responses from acquaintances, colleagues, neighbors, and others. First of all, there is a typically American resentment at government snooping, which means that respondents are disinclined to pass on negative information. In addition, the increased geographic mobility of U.S. society implies that past acquaintances and neighbors are harder to locate and may have only a superficial knowledge of the candidate. The changed political climate means that respondents are less likely to take questions of loyalty and subversion seriously. The same is true with respect to questions about character and life-style. For example, the vast increase in narcotics usage among the middle class (and, in particular, its young) during the 1970s makes it harder to distinguish the cases in which past drug usage indicates a real personality problem and potential vulnerability to blackmail from those in which it does not.

Finally, there is the question of whether informants can be assured that their candid remarks will remain confidential. Under the Privacy Act of 1974, individuals have extensive rights to access government files about themselves; while an exemption exists that allows an investigative agency to withhold the name of an informant who requests anonymity, this may not be entirely reassuring to potential informants who would be quite embarrassed, or worse, if their identities were revealed.

First, such a potential informant may worry about the possibility that his name or some identifying fact (such as a phone number) will be released inadvertently. Second, he may be concerned that, even though his identity is not explicitly revealed, the subject of the investigation will be able to deduce it from the substance of the information the government file contains. (In other words, the release of a seemingly insignificant detail, which, however, only the informant knew, could give away his identity. Since the officer reviewing the file before its release would not likely be aware that this detail provided a solid clue to the identity of the informant, he might well release it, unaware of the damage he was causing.) Finally, as a Department of Justice official told the Senate Judiciary Committee in 1978, "In theory, the [Privacy and Freedom of Information] acts provide an adequate basis for protecting our sources, but whether they in fact do so is largely irrelevant as long as our sources think they do not."[20]

One method of augmenting the background investigation as a protection against unsuitable personnel is the use of the polygraph machine, commonly known as the lie detector. This technique has been used primarily by U.S. intelligence agencies. Neither other Western intelligence services nor non-Western ones place as much faith in it. Within the United States, the CIA places the greatest emphasis on the polygraph. The agency requires that any candidate for employment take a polygraph test, and that all personnel be subject to periodic retesting as a condition of continued employment. However, extension of polygraph use to the rest of the U.S. government has been strongly resisted, most notably by former Secretary of State George Shultz. On the other hand, following the arrest for espionage of Geoffrey Prime, an employee of the British Government Communications Headquarters (GCHQ, the British communications intelligence agency), U.S. officials urged that the polygraph be adopted by GCHQ as well. (Prime is believed to have compromised various comint capabilities that involved close U.K.-U.S. cooperation.) The implicit threat was that the United States might be less willing to cooperate on communications intelligence matters if this were not done.

While use of the polygraph appears to have a strong deterrent effect, and in many cases induces the revelation of information that was otherwise concealed, its overall accuracy remains controversial.[21] Aside from the question of the frequency with which innocent subjects fail the test and are unfairly rejected for employment or forced to resign as a result, foreign intelligence services apparently have developed methods for beating it.[22]

The Changing Nature of the Threat

Since the mid-1970s, a succession of espionage cases has involved employees of U.S. government agencies or contractors.[23] In these cases, the motivation has been primarily financial, although occasionally compounded by emotional instability. Thus, these cases differ from the famous American and English espionage cases of the 1940s and 1950s, in which the motivation was primarily ideological. This pattern suggests additional steps that could be taken to improve personnel security, such as developing detailed psychological profiles and instituting a system for alerting security officials when individuals with access to classified information either run into financial difficulties or appear to be living beyond their means of support.

Physical Security

Physical security refers to the steps taken to prevent foreign intelligence agents from gaining physical access to classified information. It deals with such matters as the strength of safes in which classified information is kept and alarm systems to detect any unauthorized intrusion into the areas in which officials deal with classified information. For the most part, the requirements of physical security are not arcane and differ only in degree, if at all, from those a commercial establishment might take to prevent thefts of merchandise or equipment.

One major difference, however, is that physical security seeks to safeguard not only the material objects, such as documents, that contain information but also the information itself. This requires much stricter controls on access to the relevant areas, since an intruder can quickly and unobtrusively implant a bugging device that would give a hostile intelligence service access to what was being said within the classified work area. Therefore, it is important to control what is taken into the area as well as what is removed.

Similarly, it is important to have some means of ''sweeping'' an area to detect any bugging devices so they can be removed. This in turn leads to the development of less-detectable systems for monitoring conversations. The high level of technical sophistication to which this spiral can lead has come to public attention, most recently, with the problems concerning the new building the United States is constructing to serve as the chancery (office building) for its Moscow embassy.

The building is constructed with precast concrete columns and beams the Soviets manufactured without any U.S. surveillance. The Soviets took advantage of this to design a bugging system that could use the entire structure as an antenna for picking up signals and relaying them. The system appears to be quite sophisticated, and the United States has had difficulty understanding how it was intended to work. As former Defense Secretary James Schlesinger testified in 1987,

> In past years, the Soviets were sufficiently behind us that we were able to detect penetrations, and neutralize them. . . . We now face a rising curve of Soviet technology, with no gap between what the Soviets can do and what we can do; indeed, in some areas they have been ahead of us. . . .

> With respect to both embassy construction and operations, we have a lot to learn from the Soviets. The Soviets have thought long and hard about how to design embassies for security, and they have thought long and hard about the construction process, . . .[24]

Counterespionage

The security measures discussed above are passive, since they do not go after the hostile intelligence threat directly but seek to deny it access to information. More active measures that try to understand how a hostile intelligence service works to frustrate or disrupt its activities and ultimately to turn those activities to one's own advantage are usually referred to as "counterespionage."

Surveillance Operations

An obvious way to learn about the activities of a hostile intelligence service is to mount surveillance operations (keep under constant observation) against its officers wherever they operate. Such surveillance tries to determine where the officers go and with whom they communicate or are in contact; these contacts can then be used as leads for further investigation.

While simple in concept, this is in practice a complex task. The officer's tradecraft, which was discussed earlier in connection with human intelligence collection, is devoted primarily to frustrating this sort of operation. Not only will the officer be trained in evading surveillance, but techniques such as brush passes and dead drops may be used to conceal the identity of the person with whom he is in communication. In addition, if the surveillance is observed, it may prompt the officer to cancel any planned meeting to avoid endangering his contact. Thus, it is important to hide the surveillance. To do this is difficult and requires a great deal of manpower, since an officer trained in countersurveillance techniques will notice if the same person is trailing him for any length of time.

Because this sort of surveillance is cumbersome and expensive, it is important to target it on actual intelligence officers. One place to look, of course, is at the kinds of official cover positions available to the hostile intelligence service: diplomats, consular officials, trade representatives, journalists (for government-owned media), and employees of international organizations such as the U.N., when the employees are selected by their own governments. The problem is to determine which individuals holding these sorts of positions are really intelligence officers and which are what they appear to be.

This problem can be attacked in several ways. In general, the more knowledge an agent has about the operation of, for example, a given foreign embassy, the more likely he can tell which officials seem engaged in actual diplomatic or consular activity. If an official does not seem to be engaged in such activity, he may be involved in intelligence work instead.

Similarly, it may be possible, by observing patterns of rotation and replacement of personnel, to determine who is replacing whom; if X has been identified as an intelligence officer, X's replacement is likely to be one as well. Also, the same techniques used to collect intelligence in general may be targeted on the hostile intelligence service and its presence in the agent's own country. The more an agent learns about that service and the way it operates, the more effectively surveillance can be targeted. Finally, using double agents, as discussed later in this chapter, may enable him to determine the identities of hostile intelligence officers.

Intelligence Collection

The most direct way to achieve counterespionage's goals is to collect intelligence directly from the hostile service, either by human or technical means. (To distinguish this type of intelligence collection from the methods peculiar to counterintelligence, it may be referred to as ''positive'' foreign intelligence.) Thus, the recruitment of a KGB official who was involved in all espionage operations against the United States could solve the major U.S. counterintelligence problem immediately. In this respect, counterintelligence would not differ much from intelligence collection in general; its target, however, would be the adversary's intelligence service rather than the governmental leadership, armed forces, or other institutions.

Defectors

As with other types of humint collection targeted on a closed society like the Soviet Union, recruiting and running an agent within the KGB or GRU (military intelligence) is extremely difficult. Thus, the United States and other Western countries have relied heavily on defectors from Soviet intelligence services for counterespionage information. The most prominent recent example was Vitaliy Yurchenko, the deputy chief of the KGB department responsible for espionage against the United States and Canada. After defecting in the summer of 1985, he provided information about Soviet espionage successes against the United States. For example, although he did not know their real names, the personal and operational details he provided led to the arrest of Ronald Pelton, a former employee of the National Security Agency, and the surveillance of Edward Lee Howard, a former CIA employee.[25]

Double-Agent Operations

The other major method of conducting counterespionage is through double agents. They are agents who, while pretending to spy for a hostile service, are actually under the control of the country on which they are supposed to be spying. Such agents may have originally been real spies who, upon being detected, were "turned," or converted, into agents of the country on which they were spying. Or they may be agents who pretended to volunteer to spy for the hostile intelligence service but who in fact remained loyal to their country ("dangles"). In between would be those who, having been approached by a hostile intelligence service, report the recruitment attempt to their own country's authorities and are encouraged by them to play along.

These three double-agent operations all serve the same counterintelligence purposes. At the simplest level, they allow the counterintelligence organization to penetrate the adversary's cover mechanisms and identify officers of the hostile intelligence service engaged in running agents. As a result surveillance can be concentrated on the actual intelligence officers, while less attention need be paid to the other officials who, although they have the same cover status, really are diplomats, trade officials, and so on.

In addition to identifying the hostile intelligence officers, these operations also enable counterintelligence agents to learn their adversaries' operational methods. Agents can observe how they pass instructions to their agents and receive information from them, when and where they prefer to meet them, what precautions they take against being detected, and so forth. In short, by knowing how and when the adversary communicates with his agents, counterintelligence learns about its adversary's tradecraft and can better counter it. In addition, knowledge about the adversary's tradecraft, and the general pattern of his intelligence officers' activities, contributes to counterintelligence's ability to identify them. Finally, if a double agent is provided with some special piece of equipment, such as a radio transmitter specifically designed for use by agents, his contact gets the chance to examine it. This might lead to, for example, the interception of radio traffic between the intelligence officers of the hostile service and their real agents.

From the instructions handlers give the double agents, his contact might be able to learn about the hostile service's collection priorities. This could provide valuable clues to the adversary's thinking about major issues.[26] Alternatively, lack of interest in an area that would seem very important might indicate that the adversary already had good sources of information about it; this could provide an important clue for counterintelligence investigation.

In addition to obtaining information about the hostile intelligence service, its modus operandi, and its collection priorities, double agents can exert some control over the service's actions. The mere existence of a double agent achieves this purpose to some extent: if the hostile service believes it has an agent with access to specific information, it may not bother to recruit another one. By deflecting the service's activities, the double agent can protect an important area of information. In any case, the handling of the double agent absorbs the hostile intelligence officer's time and effort, thereby reducing the resources for recruiting and running real agents.

Furthermore, the window one double agent provides into the operations of the hostile service may allow counterintelligence to dangle successfully another double agent, perhaps one who has or appears to have access to information the hostile service is particularly anxious to obtain. The first double agent might also be able to support the bona fides of the second; for example, the first agent could confirm the supposed fact that the second had just received a promotion that gave him expanded access to sensitive data or that he was having financial difficulties and desperately needed an additional source of income. Finally, counterintelligence can use double agents to deceive an adversary, leading him to misunderstand the situation and draw the wrong conclusions, because it controls the information the double agents pass to their supposed employers.

Double agents obviously must provide *some* information to their handlers to remain credible. Frequently, this problem is solved with "chicken feed"—ostensibly classified, sensitive information that is, in fact, not very important. Alternatively, the double agent can provide true, important information that the adversary is thought to have already obtained through some other channel. In these cases, counterintelligence must balance the advantage of keeping the double agent credible against the damage done by releasing the information, however trivial or duplicative, by which this credibility is maintained. The goal is to provide as little useful information as possible without raising the suspicions of the hostile intelligence service.

A more ambitious use of double agents involves having them provide a judicious blend of information and misinformation designed to mislead the adversary. This to some extent controls not only the adversary's intelligence collection but also his analytic capabilities. The payoff from doing this can be enormous, although the difficulties involved are huge as well.

Deception is discussed more fully below. In this section, I look at two examples of large-scale, very successful, double-agent operations, one conducted during a war and one in time of peace.

Wartime Double Agents: The Double-Cross System

One of the best-known examples of a large-scale double-agent operation is the Double-Cross System, by which the British, during almost all of World War II, *"actively ran and controlled the German espionage system in* [their] *country."*[27] Starting with a single German agent who was detained on his return to Britain from Germany at the beginning of the war, the British were able to build up, under their control, a large network of supposed German agents and keep the Germans believing in them until the end of the war.[28]

Among other things, the original agent sent back information the Germans used to produce false identification papers for additional agents to be sent in by parachute or boat, thus facilitating their capture by the British. In other cases, new agents were told to contact ones already in place (and already controlled by the British) for money or other aid. For the rest of the war, helped by some lucky breaks, the British kept control of the entire German espionage network by intercepting new spies on their arrival.

John Masterman, the MI5 (British security service) officer who ran the system, listed seven objectives for it:

- to control the enemy espionage system,
- to catch fresh spies being infiltrated into the country,
- to gain knowledge of the personalities and methods of the German secret service,

- to obtain information about the codes and ciphers of the German service,
- to get evidence of enemy plans and intentions from the questions asked by them,
- to influence enemy plans by the answers sent to the enemy, and
- to deceive the enemy about Britain's plans and intentions.

The advantages for the British were enormous. For example, in 1940, the original agent was given a code for communicating with Germany. Since this code turned out to be "the basis of a number of codes used by the Abwehr [German military intelligence]," possession of it led to Britain's "early and complete mastery of the [Abwehr code] system."[29] Later in the war, when the British became more confident of the Double-Cross System, they achieved the last two objectives, which involved deceiving the Germans. The climax came in 1944, when double agents were used to bolster the deception campaign that induced the Germans to expect the main D-Day landing at Calais rather than in Normandy.

Because of its cryptologic success (Ultra), British intelligence was in a position to observe the German reaction to the information and misinformation reported by the double agents. Among other things, it could tell which reports were forwarded to the top leadership in Berlin and whether they were believed. This feedback was crucial for achieving the deception objectives, because it allowed the British to emphasize points the Germans had missed or modify the message to relieve any German doubts.

Controlling the enemy's espionage network had its price: the network had to produce enough intelligence to keep the Germans satisfied with it. Furthermore, the information it produced could not be easily contradicted by information available to the Germans through other intelligence channels, including any uncaptured spies. (It turned out there were not any, but, of course, the British could only become aware of that over time; at first, they had to assume there might be other agents of whom they were unaware.) However, this seemed a reasonable price to pay; since the Germans were likely to have an espionage network in Britain in any case, it made sense for the British to run it.

In retrospect, the manager of the Double-Cross System believed that the British running it were probably too cautious in the sense that the British probably surrendered more true information than they had to and did not make full use of the deception potential. Not only did the Germans possess fewer other intelligence channels against which the double-cross information could be checked (as noted above, they had no loyal agents), but they also proved to be remarkably trusting of the agents they thought they had.

This high degree of trust is illustrated by the failure of the following ploy:

> On one occasion an agent was deliberately run in order to show the Germans that he was under control, the object being to give them a false idea of our methods of running such an agent and thus to convince them that the other agents were genuine. The theory was sound and the gaffes committed were crass and blatant, but the object was not achieved . . . the Germans continued to think of the agent as being genuine and reliable![30]

Cuban Double-Agent Operations Against the United States

On August 12, 1987, the *Washington Post* reported that a defector from the Cuban foreign intelligence service, the DGI, had told CIA debriefers that "an undetermined number of Cuban government officials, once believed by the United States to be secretly working for the CIA, were feeding the agency misleading or useless information prepared by the Cuban DGI. . . ."[31] Following this revelation, Cuban media published detailed accounts of the operations of many of these double agents, including photographs of them engaged in supposedly clandestine activities. That their activities were known to the Cubans in such great detail tends to confirm they were double agents for part, if not all, of the time they were purportedly spying on Cuba. According to Cuban sources, some of the agents, apparently aware that the United States now knew their true allegiance, sent farewell messages to their U.S. handlers.

Without a careful analysis of the information provided by these double agents, it cannot be determined whether Cuba was attempting systematically to mislead the United States to take steps contrary to its interests. Even without such an ambitious plan, the operation would have paid its way from the Cuban point of view by absorbing large amounts of CIA time and effort that otherwise might have obtained useful information; by revealing CIA operational methods, thereby helping to counter its real agents, if any; and by feeding U.S. intelligence analysis random pieces of information and misinformation that confused it and prevented it from forming any coherent picture of events in Cuba.

Multidisciplinary Counterintelligence (MDCI)

What Is MDCI?

Just as the hostile intelligence threat posed by a technically up-to-date adversary is not limited to human intelligence collection, so active counterintelligence cannot be limited to counterespionage. Rather, it must take into account the full range of the adversary's technical intelligence collection capabilities, including overhead photographic reconnaissance and communications and signals intelligence.

Thus, the first task of MDCI is to assess the effectiveness of the adversary's technical intelligence collection capabilities. This knowledge, in turn, indicates where one's own information, communications, or activities are vulnerable and how best to protect them. The actual measures that can be taken may be labeled ''security'' or ''technical countermeasures'' and vary from technology to technology. The multidisciplinary perspective, however, is important because it encourages one to look at the problem from the adversary's point of view.

Communications Security

Just as the interception of messages, both those in written and, more recently, electronic form, is a major method of collecting intelligence, so protecting the contents of messages has long been a major counterintelligence task. In the twentieth century, this has focused on protecting electronic telecommunications transmitted either by wire or radio.

Messages transmitted by wire can be safeguarded by preventing the line from being tapped (reading the message either by drawing a small amount of current from the line or by sensing the fluctuations of the magnetic field around the line caused by the current flowing through it). Radio signals, on the other hand, cannot be protected; any receiver within range can pick them up. Some signals, such as microwave transmissions (which are used to carry long-distance telephone calls, among other things), are highly directional (not dispersed in all directions but concentrated in a beam pointed at the intended receiver), but even they can be intercepted if a receiver is properly placed in line-of-sight contact with the emitter.

The contents of radio messages have been protected primarily through encryption. Written messages can be encrypted in the ordinary fashion before transmission. For voice messages, ''secure phones,'' or ''scramblers,'' are used; they distort the voice signals in a complex manner. Anyone intercepting such a signal receives a meaningless jumble of sounds analogous to the jumble of letters of a ciphertext. Restoring the original voice message is comparably difficult.

Very secure scrambling devices are expensive. Few are available within the U.S. government and the defense industry, and they are used only to discuss classified information. Outside the government, they are practically nonexistent. Thus, most long-distance telephone communication, which uses microwave transmission either across a network of microwave towers (terrestrial microwave) or between ground stations and satellites, is vulnerable to interception.

In the mid-1980s, in the United States, this situation came to the public's attention because of the controversy surrounding the location of the new Soviet Embassy in Washington. Built in the Mount Alto neighborhood several hundred feet above downtown Washington, the Soviet buildings look out over the downtown and northern Virginia areas, including the White House, State Department, Pentagon, and most other government buildings. From this and other official Soviet buildings in the United States (consulates and trade representatives in New York, Washington, and San Francisco; the U.N. mission in New York; and residential and recreational facilities in New York City, on Long Island, New York, and on Maryland's Eastern Shore), Soviet intelligence can intercept large volumes of long-distance telephone calls.

In addition to government officials using ordinary nonsecure phones, targets probably include high-technology corporations, commodity traders dealing in products the Soviets buy or sell in large amounts (grain, oil, and gold), and financial institutions. The Soviets also may target individuals with access to classified information to try to learn compromising personal details that can be used to blackmail them.

Various countermeasures have been suggested to reduce this vulnerability. For example, one could redesign the microwave network to eliminate those links passing near the Soviet intercept facilities and replace them with underground cables. Alternatively, one could encrypt all signals transmitted by microwave by scrambling the signal when it first goes on the air and decrypting it when it has finished the microwave portion of its journey. Both solutions have some technical weaknesses and would be expensive to implement. In the future, the situation may be eased by the widespread use of fiber-optic transmission, which is being adopted by communications companies for economic reasons. Fiber-optic cables are virtually untappable and, because of their great capacity (ability to transmit many signals simultaneously), tend to be cheaper than conventional copper cables or terrestrial microwave.

Emanations Security

Any piece of electrical equipment radiates electromagnetic waves; by intercepting these waves, it is possible, in theory, to deduce the characteristics of the electrical signal that caused them. Thus, from these waves, called "emanations," someone could reconstruct the text of a document being typed on an electric typewriter or being transmitted from a computer to a printer. This can be guarded against, for example, by shielding the electrical equipment to reduce the intensity of the emanations, making them harder to intercept.

Other Technical Countermeasures

Countermeasures can be devised to guard against other technical intelligence collection means as well. With respect to satellite photographic reconnaissance, for instance, it is possible, assuming we can identify which of the adversary's satellites are for photographic reconnaissance, to predict their orbits and to warn military or other sensitive installations to stop activities and move sensitive equipment under cover when the satellites are able to photograph them. Of course, the more we know about the satellites' capabilities, the easier it is to prescribe the necessary countermeasures. For example, after we have determined the points on the earth's surface directly beneath the satellite's orbit, we still must know at what distance to the side objects are still within the cameras' range. Similarly, electronic or telemetry intelligence collectors may be beatable by encryption, by jamming, by shifting to frequency ranges the collector cannot pick up, or by ceasing emissions when collectors are within range.

Deception and Counterdeception

So far, the discussion of counterintelligence has examined ways in which an adversary's intelligence collection capabilities may be countered. If done successfully, the adversary will presumably lack the information needed to analyze the situation in which he finds himself, and his actions, being blind, will be less likely to serve his purposes. As the treatment of double-agent operations has indicated, however, we can try to counter the adversary's intelligence operations more ambitiously by targeting his analysis capability, that is, by taking steps to mislead him.

What Is Deception?

Deception is the attempt to mislead an adversary's intelligence analysis concerning the political, military, or economic situation he faces and to induce him, on the basis of those errors, to act in a way that advances one's own interests rather than his. It is considered a form of counterintelligence because it attempts to thwart a major purpose of the adversary's intelligence operations; in addition, it often involves counterintelligence methods, such as double-agent operations.

Deception and intelligence failure are related concepts. Indeed, one side's successful deception implies the other side's intelligence failure. The reverse, of course, need not be true; a side may make important mistakes in its intelligence analysis even without any deception by the other side. Nevertheless, it is often possible, in cases of intelligence failure, to identify some effort at deception by the other side. To what extent that effort is responsible for the failure is a more complicated question.

Deception can be attempted in wartime or in time of peace, although one would expect deception to be much more common in wartime. Deception ranges from tactical to strategic. Any battle that begins with a feint in one sector, while the main weight of the attack falls on another, exemplifies tactical deception. Examples of strategic deception are less common but often very important, such as the Allies' World War II deception operation that misled the Germans about the location of the Normandy D-Day landings.

Peacetime deception operations are not common, tend to be less well known, and are sometimes hard to identify as such. Among the more spectacular was one known as the "Trust," a Soviet organization that pretended to be hostile to the new Communist regime but which was in fact established and run from 1921 to 1927 by the forerunner of the current Soviet KGB, the Cheka.[32] Using this fake opposition group, the Soviets made contact with anti-Communist émigré organizations and Western intelligence services, thereby channeling and neutralizing any hostile activities they might undertake; induced potential opponents within the Soviet Union to make contact with it, thereby allowing the Cheka to learn their identities; and disseminated abroad false information about the internal state of the Soviet Union.[33]

During the 1950s and early 1960s, the Soviet Union engaged in deception operations to convince the United States that the USSR possessed larger offensive strategic nuclear forces than it in fact did. At a ceremonial flyover in July 1955, for example, the Soviets "displayed" twenty-eight Bison (Mya-4) bombers—probably more than they had in their entire inventory—by having the first group of planes circle around out of view of the spectators (including the U.S. air attaché) and return for a second pass.[34] Similarly, in the late 1950s, Soviet leaders, drawing on the prestige derived from the initial successes of their space program, made a series of exaggerated claims concerning the Soviet ICBM program.[35] In this way, the Soviets contributed to the bomber gap and missile gap fears in the United States (that held that the Soviets were about to surpass the United States in these measures of strategic nuclear capability). The Soviet deception appeared aimed at inducing the West to make political concessions—such as concerning the status of Berlin—that it would otherwise be insufficiently motivated to make.[36]

The content of the deception—the false view one side wishes the other to adopt—obviously depends on the situation and on how one wishes his adversary to react to it. In wartime, for example, one might wish to launch a surprise attack on the enemy, in which case the deception would be devoted to convincing him that no attack is on the way. Sometimes, as in the case of the Normandy D-Day landings, the enemy fully expects to be attacked, and it is unlikely one could convince him otherwise. In such a case, the deception is to convince him that the attack is coming at a time, in a place, and/or in a manner other than what the actual plans call for.

In time of peace, on the other hand, it is less obvious what goal the deception should pursue. One might wish to convince an adversary that one is stronger than one really is to induce him to make political concessions that he would not otherwise feel compelled to make. Alternatively, one might wish to conceal one's actual military strength to lull one's adversary into complacency and not provoke him into increasing his own military forces. If one's forces are limited by an arms control treaty, one could have the goal of concealing a treaty violation, thereby leading the other party to continue to limit his own forces.

The Prerequisites of Successful Deception

Blocking True Signals and Manufacturing False Ones

If we visualize the intelligence process as the reception and interpretation of signals emitted by the activities of the side under observation, then implementing a deception operation involves blocking, to the extent possible, the true signals (those that reflect the actual activities) and substituting misleading signals. To use a simple example: the actual tank at point X is camouflaged, while a dummy plywood tank is placed out in the open at point Y. If an enemy reconnaissance plane flies over the area, it may miss the tank at X (the visual signal having been blocked by the camouflage) and report one at Y (assuming that the false signal emanating from the plywood dummy is similar enough to a true one). In the case of double-agent operations, the real documents, for example, remain in government safes, while false ones, produced as part of the deception operation, are passed on by the double agents to their handlers.

The first half of the task is the problem of security. If too many true signals get through, the adversary is unlikely to be deceived, although he may be so confused by the mixture of true and false signals that he cannot form a coherent picture of the actual situation. Thus, the first prerequisite of successful deception is the ability to block most, if not all, of the channels by which the adversary collects intelligence information about one's activities. In general, this is easier to do in wartime than in peace, which is one (among several) reason successful deception is more likely to occur in the former than in the latter.

Blocking intelligence-gathering channels requires, among other things, comprehensive knowledge of the intelligence channels by which the adversary receives signals. A good counterespionage capability is necessary, since one well-placed human source could reveal the actual situation or, for that matter, the deception plan itself. Beyond that, one must know about the adversary's technical intelligence collection capabilities in order to thwart them. Thus, ships and planes can adopt radio silence (more properly "emission control," or "emcon," since radar and other electronic emissions could give away the vehicle's position as quickly as would radio transmissions) to avoid detection by enemy comint or elint. If ground forces can rely on landlines (communication via telephone or telegraph wires) rather than radio, as did the German forces before the December 1944 Ardennes offensive, the same effect may be achieved. Similarly, if the orbits of the adversary's photographic reconnaissance satellites are known, then activities can be halted and equipment moved indoors or camouflaged when the satellites are overhead and able to photograph them.

The second half of the task, manufacturing false signals, is also planned with the adversary's human and technical intelligence collection capabilities in mind. Double agents can pass whatever fake document or report one wishes, as long as they can produce a plausible explanation for their access to it. Deceiving technical collection systems is more complicated but possible. To achieve surprise at Pearl Harbor, the Japanese did not merely impose radio silence on their attack fleet on its trip across the Pacific. In addition, the fleet's radio operators were kept busy passing bogus messages to each other using transmitters based in Japan. Thus, if the radio signals had been intercepted (it does not appear that they were) and the transmitters' locations determined, the United States would have concluded that the Japanese aircraft carriers were engaged in exercises in home waters.[37] Similarly, photographic reconnaissance can be fooled by dummy weapons or vehicles; to know how accurate the dummies must be to be indistinguishable from the real thing, one needs to know how good the adversary's photographic reconnaissance capabilities are.[38]

Feedback

In conducting a deception operation, one faces major uncertainties:

- Were all the real signals blocked?

- Did the manufactured signals reach the adversary?
- Did he draw the desired conclusions from them?

To answer these questions, successful deception typically employs some method of finding out how the adversary is assessing the situation. If he is not alert enough to have noticed the false signals, or if he has not interpreted them as the deceiver wished him to, then more can be manufactured to get his attention and lead him to the desired interpretation. If he begins to sense anomalies in the (false) picture of the situation the deceiver has planted in his mind, new signals can be created to explain them away. If enough true signals have reached the adversary to enable him to understand the situation correctly, one may wish to abandon the deception and change plans.

Feedback can be obtained in many forms. In some cases (of wartime deception or of deception in support of a surprise attack), the adversary's actions (or lack of them) may be sufficient indication of whether he has been deceived. Thus, the absence of any signs of heightened military activity (which would have been easily observable) by the Hawaiian-based U.S. fleet in the first week of December 1941 told the Japanese what they needed to know. In other cases, adequate feedback may require good intelligence about the other side's views of the situation; in the case of the British World War II Double-Cross System, this feedback was provided by the Ultra intercepts, which gave the British good access to the internal deliberations of the German high command.

The more long-term and strategic the deception, the more important good intelligence feedback becomes. The deceived party's responses to such deception take longer to become manifest; thus, one needs some other way of knowing whether the bait has been taken. In general, peacetime deception operations require better intelligence feedback than those conducted in wartime. In wartime, the adversary is more likely to have to act quickly based on his understanding of the situation, thus perhaps revealing whether he has been deceived. During peace, the adversary is under less pressure to take actions that indicate his understanding of the general situation.

Deception and Self-Deception

The false view of the situation one wishes an adversary to adopt must be determined by the action one wishes the adversary to take. Nevertheless, the view must be plausible to the adversary; in fact, success is more likely if the deception scenario is based on what the adversary thinks is the case anyway. For example, the D-Day deception worked so brilliantly in part because Hitler was already convinced that the Allied landing would take place at

Calais, where the English Channel is narrowest. Thus, the manufactured signals only had to reinforce this view and prevent it from being undermined by any true signals that managed to get through; this is an easier task than having to induce the adversary to adopt the deception scenario in the first place. Thus, it is not accidental that most of the impressive deception successes involve a large element of self-deception.

Counterdeception

Experience shows that defeating every attempt an adversary might make at deception is very difficult. Even as they were running Double-Cross, the British were being similarly tricked by the Germans with respect to their intelligence and guerrilla-type operations in the Netherlands. Starting in the late summer of 1941, with the arrest of a Dutch intelligence agent working for MI6 (the British foreign intelligence agency), the Germans managed to catch all subsequent British agents sent to the Netherlands by the Special Operations Executive (SOE, whose mission included sabotage and support for anti-German resistance groups).

Having broken the cipher system used by these agents, the Germans continued to send messages to Britain that purported to come from the agents, who had in fact been arrested. Some arrested agents cooperated in preparing and transmitting the messages; in other cases, German radio operators impersonated them. Among other things, these messages made the arrangements for additional airdrops of agents and supplies, which were in turn captured immediately. The operation, which the Germans called *Nordpol* (North Pole) and *Englandspiel* (the match against England), continued until two of the captured agents escaped from the camp in which they were being held. At this point, concluding that the game would be given away in any case, the German military counterintelligence officer in charge of the operation chose to end it with a plaintext message to London on, appropriately enough, April 1 (1944).[39]

One incident from this operation shows how strong the psychological resistance is to the idea that one is being deceived. When British agents in Holland enciphered their messages for transmission back to London, they were supposed to include a security check—a specified deviation (which would appear as a simple, random error) from the cipher system that would indicate to those receiving the message that they really were who they were supposed to be and that they were operating freely and not under German compulsion. An agent might be instructed to make a "mistake" in the fiftieth letter of each outgoing message. If the Germans obtained the ciphering system but did not understand the principle of the security check, any message they sent would be treated as bogus, since it would not contain the required error.

In this particular incident, the Germans used their own radio operator to transmit messages in the cipher system they obtained from a captured British agent. Since a radio operator can often be identified by the manner in which he hammers out the dots and dashes of Morse code (his "handwriting"), the first message explained that a new operator had been recruited in Holland because the original agent had sprained his wrist. This message contained no security check at all and should have been recognized as bogus by SOE headquarters in London; this was, after all, the very situation for which the security checks had been devised. Instead, the staff officer in London, disturbed by the failure to follow proper procedure and seemingly oblivious of the reason the procedure had been instituted, replied with an order to "instruct [the new radio operator] in the use of his security check."[40]

In any case, understanding deception is the first step toward figuring out how to avoid being deceived; by understanding the factors that facilitate deception, one can at least be alert to the possibility of deception and recognize some warning signs. One is particularly vulnerable to deception when one is dependent on a small number of channels of information and when the adversary is aware, at least in general terms, of the nature of these channels and their mode of operation.

For example, a heavy dependence on photographic reconnaissance satellites, whose identities and orbits most likely will become known to those whom they are photographing, may make one vulnerable to being deceived. The adversary, knowing when his facilities can be photographed, may make sure certain things are not seen: the items may be moved into garages or sheds or covered with camouflage or tarpaulins whenever a photographic reconnaissance satellite passes overhead. Similarly, the adversary knows when to display dummy equipment to increase the chance of its being noticed and mistaken for the real thing.

The situation is obviously worse (from the point of the potential deception victim) if the adversary can find out ahead of time not only which sites can be photographed but which *will* be photographed. Similarly, it is also worse if the adversary knows the satellite's precise capabilities. If he knows the satellite's ground resolution distance (roughly speaking, the smallest object the satellite can detect), for instance, he knows how similar to the real thing the fake pieces of equipment have to be to appear identical to the satellite. For this reason, it was an important intelligence coup for the Soviets to obtain the manual for the U.S. KH-11 photographic reconnaissance satellite. They bought it for a mere $3,000 from William Kampiles, after he resigned his position as a junior CIA officer in November 1977.[41] It is also for this reason that satellite photos (which might indicate the degree of detail the satellite detects) are classified.

Once one understands the risk of being deceived that comes from heavy reliance on a single known channel, one decides what to do about it. The best corrective is to maximize what might be called "unexpected collection"—taking photographs at times and places the adversary does not anticipate. Given the predictability of orbits, this is hard to do in the case of satellite reconnaissance; along the borders or coasts of the adversary's territory, where aerial photography is possible, this is easier to achieve.

Nevertheless, certain steps are possible even with respect to satellites. Although the adversary may be able to determine (by studying its orbit, for example) which satellites conduct photographic reconnaissance, it takes him some time to do this and to warn his military facilities accordingly. During the satellite's first few hours of flight, it is likely that the pictures it takes are unexpected. Hence, it makes sense to consider carefully which facilities should be photographed on a satellite's first few orbits. Similarly, thought could be given to ways to prolong the period of unexpected collection, perhaps by varying the launch and orbit characteristics of the satellites, so that it takes the adversary more time to determine their function.[42] Finally, if it were feasible to have several photographic satellites in orbit at the same time (including, if possible, dummies the adversary could not easily distinguish from operating satellites), the adversary might find it impossible to protect sensitive military equipment and operations against all of them without impeding his activities to an unacceptable degree.

Conversely, many proponents of signals intelligence (and, in particular, communications intelligence) argue that they prefer it to other types of intelligence collection because several factors ensure the reliability of the information it collects. Comint may be collected in vast quantities, which implies that the true signals are more likely to get through. By the same token, it would take a larger effort to deceive comint by means of a fake radio network (which would still require the use of real resources and personnel to create the signals) than that involved in displaying dummies or turning an agent and running him as a double.[43]

Even more important is the fact that the adversary will ordinarily be unable to tell which of his many communications channels others may be reading; he may well transmit fake messages that are never intercepted, while some of the real ones are. However, even this is not foolproof: via espionage or some technical means an adversary may learn on which frequencies or communications lines others are eavesdropping. If so, these communication channels might be used in a deception effort.

A complicated situation of this sort, which illustrates the difficulty of assessing potential deception operations, took place in 1953–56. The United States and Britain dug a tunnel from the American into the Soviet zone of Berlin to tap a set of telephone and telegraph cables that linked the Soviet Air Force headquarters at Karlshorst with the city. The tunnel was built jointly by MI6 and the CIA. Unfortunately, George Blake, a senior MI6 officer in Berlin, was a Soviet spy. (He was finally tracked down, arrested, and convicted in 1961.)

Blake presumably told the Soviets about the tunnel as soon as he learned about it. Even if he were not directly involved in the tunnel project, the operation was so large and complicated that it is hard to believe that any alert British or American intelligence officer in Berlin would not have quickly picked up some idea of what was being done. Thus, one can assume the Soviets learned promptly of the tunnel's existence and purpose.

However, the Soviet telegraphic communications being transmitted on the tapped lines were encrypted. According to John Ranelagh, whose history of the CIA seems to have benefited from a considerable amount of information from its former officers, the *real* secret of the affair was the existence of a technique that enabled the CIA to recover the clear text of the encrypted messages.[44] This technique was not shared with the British; hence Blake should not have been able to betray it. Thus, even knowing of the tap, the Soviets might have continued to use the telegraph line for sensitive messages in the belief that their encryption rendered them secure.

On the other hand, the British shared in the intelligence collected from the Berlin tunnel operation. According to Ranelagh, "The British were to carry out the analysis of half the material" produced by the intercept.[45] If so, then it should have become evident that the United States had some method of decrypting the intercepted messages; if Blake were aware of this, the Soviets would have learned that the tunnel posed a real threat to them.

The tunnel operation ended April 21, 1956, about a year after the first message was intercepted, when it was ostensibly discovered by Soviets in the course of repairing one of the tapped cables that had been damaged by heavy rainfall. At the time, the CIA, not knowing of the existence of a Soviet spy in the MI6 Berlin office, regarded the Soviet discovery as accidental. In retrospect, of course, one would have to consider the possibility that the Soviets contrived to make the discovery appear so to protect Blake.

The interesting question is to what extent the "take" from the operation should be regarded as potentially deceptive. On the one hand, it seems likely that the Soviets, via Blake, would have learned about the operation quickly; that they let it go on so long suggests that they were using it to deceive the United States and Britain. On the other hand, one would have to look at the actual information the operation produced; if it were very valuable then it becomes less likely that the Soviets realized that the line was insecure (Ranelagh claims that the first indications that the Soviets had an agent in MI6 in Berlin were acquired by the tunnel operation[46]). The intelligence take would have to be studied as a function of time to determine if the Soviets became aware of the operation before their ostensibly accidental discovery of it and, if so, when.[47]

In any case, even without knowing that the adversary is listening to a particular communications link, a deception operation could create an entire net of radio transmitters whose sole purpose is to send messages the adversary might intercept; if the net is big enough, the adversary is bound to stumble across it. This would be an expensive and elaborate measure, and it is perhaps feasible only in wartime. In wartime, however, it is clearly possible: before the D-Day landings, the United States and Britain created such a radio net to help deceive the Germans into believing that there existed a large First U.S. Army Group, based in southeastern England, that was poised to conduct the invasion against the Calais area. In fact, the Army Group contained very few real soldiers; most of its divisions and other components existed only on paper and in the radio chatter among the station operators of the false network.

This was a key part of the D-Day deception operation; it not only supported the prelanding deception, but it also helped prevent the Germans from moving reserves into Normandy in the crucial days following the landings there. It allowed the Germans to interpret the Normandy action as a diversion, a means of distracting their attention from the invasion that was to come. According to a study of deception in World War II,

> The networks which were set up to carry the fake radio traffic were extensive and complicated. At the peak there were 22 fake formations [i.e., the supposed headquarters of the army group and its constituent armies and divisions]. . . .

> There is little doubt that the simulated radio traffic, most of which was carried on within a very short distance of the enemy and was therefore easy to monitor, was—after the contribution of the double agents—the most important factor in the overall deception.[48]

The same factors help one determine the risk of being deceived by humint collection capabilities. In particular, if one's human intelligence collection capabilities depend heavily on defectors, it increases one's vulnerability to being deceived. First, unlike the case in which one has an agent in place, the adversary knows the defector's identity. He can determine, more or less, what information he had access to. Although he cannot prevent the defector from telling what he knows, he can take account of that information in any deception plan he develops. In this respect, information that comes from a defector is similar to "expected collection."

Second, the adversary can relatively easily plant a defector with false (deceptive) information designed to mislead one. If one relies heavily on defectors, the adversary may provide several of them, whose reports, although false, will nevertheless support each other. Suspicions that the Soviet Union may have done just that to the United States, starting in the early 1960s, led to some of the most severe internal conflicts in the history of the CIA between those who took this possibility seriously and those who found it overblown. The latter group finally triumphed when the CIA's counterintelligence chief, James Angleton, the major proponent of the former view, was fired by DCI William Colby in December 1974.[49]

Counterintelligence Analysis

As the discussion of double agents and deception indicates, protecting the integrity of one's own intelligence operations can become very complicated, involving much more than catching the occasional spy. In fact, cases may be linked to each other in various ways; the overall task of guarding one's own intelligence apparatus against penetration and deception requires a special office dedicated to counterintelligence analysis to serve as an institutional memory and to analyze these connections.

The best way to determine whether one's own intelligence apparatus has been penetrated is to acquire a high-level source in the hostile service (either an agent in place or a defector). Even in this best case, however, it would be a rare stroke of luck if the source could identify by name the spies in one's ranks. This would be the case only if the source were directly involved in handling them or were a very high-ranking officer of the hostile service. In the much more likely scenario, one's source will be able to provide only clues to the spies' identities. Analytic work will be necessary to make those clues yield results.

For example, one may discover that the adversary has had access to several classified documents on a subject. Assuming they all came from the same agent, one could review the distribution lists for the compromised documents and note which officials had access to all of them. Alternatively, the source may know that the spy held a meeting with his handler in a certain foreign city on a specific date. Reviewing travel records would indicate which officials with access to relevant information were in that city then.

In addition, other clues may be available that suggest penetrations of some sort. Thus, if one's operation fails (an agent is discovered or a technical collection system is thwarted) in a way that suggests the adversary was aware of the operation before it took place, it is necessary to investigate how he may have learned of it. There will no doubt be many avenues (individuals with access to the information as well as security vulnerabilities or lapses) by which the information could have reached the adversary. If there is a series of such failures, however, it may be possible to narrow the options; for example, maybe only one particular individual had authorized access to all of them. In any event, such a series should alert an intelligence service to the possibility that its adversary has effective human or technical intelligence collection capabilities that must be discovered and neutralized.

6

GUARDING THE GUARDIANS

THE MANAGEMENT OF INTELLIGENCE

The preceding four chapters have discussed types of intelligence activities and some issues that arise with respect to them. I now turn from the intelligence activities themselves to the relationship between intelligence and the government of which it is a part and to questions concerning the management of intelligence by its nonintelligence superiors, or "political masters."

The management of intelligence presents two major sets of issues. The first set arises from the secrecy in which intelligence activities are necessarily conducted; it centers on the special difficulties that secrecy creates for the political superiors whose job it is to oversee and control intelligence activities. The second set arises from the uneasy relationship between expertise and policy-making. It deals with the problems of determining the appropriate weight the views of the experts (who claim special knowledge or expertise) should be given in governing the actions of the policymakers (who have the actual authority to set policies and make decisions) and of ensuring that the experts' views receive the attention they deserve.

Secrecy and Control

In a modern government, with its many thousands of employees arranged in complicated bureaucratic structures, the problem of controlling their myriad activities, and ensuring that they are in accordance with the law and the policies of their superiors, is bound to be difficult. With respect to intelligence agencies, this basic problem is compounded by secrecy, even though the secrecy springs from the legitimate need to keep knowledge of

131

certain intelligence sources, methods, and activities secret from the public and restricted to the smallest possible number of officials within the government. This secrecy hinders the management and control mechanisms that are common elsewhere in the government.

In principle, of course, control of government activities is organized in a hierarchical fashion, so that every official is ultimately responsible, through a chain of command, to the head of the government. Thus, the minimum condition for control is that each superior have the right to know all the information to which his subordinates have access. In general, this condition is probably met, although the notion of plausible denial raises some important questions in this regard.

Having theoretical access to information about an activity is not, however, the same as knowing enough to control it effectively. In other areas of governmental activity, the direct top-down control exercised by superiors is supplemented by other mechanisms, both formal and informal: examinations by auditors or inspectors general, challenges and complaints by competing parts of the bureaucracy, investigations by law enforcement agencies, legislative oversight, press coverage, and complaints or other feedback from the public.

Applying these mechanisms to intelligence activities would require spreading knowledge about them beyond the narrowest possible circle of officials whose need to know derives from their actual involvement in them. How far the knowledge is spread depends on the mechanisms, since one may involve informing only a few additional executive branch officials; another, members of the legislature and their staffs; and a third, the public at large. In each case, a balance must be struck between the danger of widening the circle of those with access to the information and the benefit derived from the increased capability of the intelligence agencies' political superiors to control their work.

Plausible Denial

Because these control mechanisms all involve more dissemination of information, one could say, in general, that a tension exists between secrecy and effective control. With intelligence activities, however, achieving effective control may be complicated by the doctrine of plausible denial, which suggests that even fundamental top-down control by superiors may be placed in doubt. According to this doctrine, intelligence activities that might cause embarrassment (because they violate international law or for some other reason) should be planned and executed in a way that allows the head of government plausibly to deny that he had anything to do with them or even knew they were occurring. As already discussed, this doctrine is associated with covert action, although it is also applicable to other intelligence activities, such as espionage or aerial photographic reconnaissance violating the target's airspace.

This doctrine of plausible denial can complicate the control of intelligence activities to which it is applied. To be effective, it requires not only that knowledge of the activity be restricted to the smallest possible number of officials but also that there be no formal procedure by which it is approved and no paperwork in which the approval is recorded. The activity itself should be conducted with a minimal amount of record keeping, and any files created in the course of carrying it out would probably be destroyed once the activity is completed. Obviously, this creates the conditions for misunderstandings and uncertainty as to whether a specific action was authorized. In particular, without a written record (or paper trail), it could easily prove impossible to determine whether an activity had been approved by the head of government or other senior nonintelligence officials.

All this does not mean that intelligence agencies in general, or any one in particular, is, in the phrase attributed to Senator Church, a "rogue elephant." It suggests, however, that, other things being equal, an intelligence agency may more easily "jump the rails" than other governmental organizations. Against this inference, on the other hand, one should note that intelligence agencies investigate the character of a potential employee more carefully than other government offices and that the opportunity for illicit personal enrichment in an intelligence agency is less than in many other government offices that deal with economic statistics or regulation or that conduct business on behalf of the government by, for example, awarding contracts or leasing government lands for private exploitation.

Although Senator Church, chairman of the Senate committee formed in 1975 to investigate the intelligence agencies, used the term "rogue elephant" early in the investigation to describe the CIA, that characterization was generally abandoned by the time the investigation was completed. In the view of Loch Johnson, a Church Committee staffer sympathetic to Senator Church, the chairman's use of the term "derived from a sense that the evidence needed to be dramatized to have an effect upon the public," and the final report of the committee "carefully steered clear of the 'rogue elephant' theory."[1]

Of the major CIA actions the committee criticized, the attempts to assassinate Fidel Castro raised the most important questions about the agency jumping the rails. According to the committee's report on the CIA's involvement in assassination plots,

There was insufficient evidence from which the Committee could conclude that Presidents Eisenhower, Kennedy, or Johnson, their close advisors, or the Special Group [the interagency group that reviewed covert action proposals] authorized the assassination of Castro.[2]

Instead, the record the committee found was bewilderingly vague about authorization. The key CIA officials said they felt they were fully authorized to do what they did, but that this authorization had not been conveyed in so many words, either orally or in writing. In short, the committee confronted precisely the sort of record, or rather lack of record, that one would expect to find in a situation ruled by the doctrine of plausible denial. President John F. Kennedy and his brother, Attorney General Robert F. Kennedy (who played a major role in formulating policy toward Cuba), could have plausibly denied any involvement or contemporaneous knowledge of the assassination attempts.[3]

Thus, despite the a priori argument that control of intelligence agencies by their political superiors may be problematic, the Church Committee record does not actually show that this was the case regarding attempts to assassinate Castro. Rather, it demonstrates the plausible denial doctrine working successfully to shield the president from blame. This, of necessity, leaves open the possibility that the CIA was out of control, but it seems unlikely, given the lack of outrage from administration figures.[4]

For Whom Does Intelligence Work?

In any case, it is a peculiar control by a head of government that is consistent with the plausible denial doctrine. It is unlike the ordinary control the head of government exerts over departments or ministries through an official chain of command and written orders, cabinet decisions, policy statements, memorandums, and so forth. Its basis is a direct, or personal, loyalty of the intelligence service to the head of government, rather than bureaucratic subordination.

In past ages, intelligence services commonly worked for a monarch, chief minister, or commander in chief in a personal capacity outside the ordinary governmental structures. For example, Sir Francis Walsingham, the powerful secretary of state to Queen Elizabeth I of England, supported a very effective intelligence service largely out of his own funds and nearly went bankrupt in the process.[5] Similarly, the Duke of Marlborough, the British commander in chief during the War of the Spanish Succession, used a traditional $2\frac{1}{2}$ percent commission on the British-paid salaries of his army's foreign troops, as well as other perquisites (or tradition-sanctioned kickbacks, to use less elegant language) on various procurement contracts, to finance an apparently successful secret service. He regarded these funds as properly expended by him for "procuring intelligence and other secret service," but he was later prosecuted by his political opponents for embezzlement for his pains.[6] In both instances, the distinction between public and private funds or activities was cloudy. Clearly, this sort of arrangement cannot easily accommodate itself to a modern bureaucratic state, in which the separation between officials' public duties and their private interests is supposed to be absolute.

But the issue goes beyond ensuring accountability for public funds. There is the more fundamental question of who can authorize anyone to engage in such activities at all. This is particularly important in a constitutional government like the United States in which the powers of government are divided among the branches of government and political officials are responsible to the electorate. Under the U.S. Constitution, the president claims the power to engage in intelligence operations on the basis of his foreign policy and military responsibilities. It is not clear how the president's subordinates can claim the right to exercise these powers without his authority. At the same time, as discussed in chapter 4 on covert action, Congress has insisted on a complete paper trail leading back from intelligence activities to those who authorized them. Thus an important effect of congressional involvement in this area has been to subject intelligence activities to formal bureaucratic control within the executive branch.

But congressional involvement went beyond the question of how intelligence activities should be authorized and controlled within the executive branch. The House and Senate intelligence committees successfully asserted a right to be kept "fully and currently informed of all intelligence activities" and to receive "any information . . . concerning intelligence activities which is in the possession" of any intelligence agency.[7] Taken together with a reinvigorated power of the purse (the power of Congress to appropriate or withhold funds for intelligence, as for all other governmental, activities), Congress could use and, to some extent, has used these levers to establish a joint authority with the president over intelligence.

The result, in the words of former Deputy Director of Central Intelligence Robert M. Gates,

is that the CIA today finds itself in a remarkable position, involuntarily poised nearly equidistant between the executive and legislative branches. The administration knows that the CIA is in no position to withhold much information from Congress and is extremely sensitive to congressional demands; the Congress has enormous influence and information yet remains suspicious and mistrustful.[8]

This discussion of congressional involvement in intelligence matters helps to explain a further problem of control: however adequate informal direction can be for a head of government to control an intelligence service, it will not let a legislative body feel it is exercising its authority over the service effectively. For that, more formal means of control are necessary, such as those already noted (formal right of access to information, notification of certain types of activities, and the requirement that funds for intelligence activities be appropriated by law). Thus, in the United States, the result of congressional involvement has been to subject the CIA, as well as other intelligence organizations, to full executive branch control and to the same system of legislative oversight as any other part of the government.

Expertise and Policy

The previous section dealt with issues concerning how to manage intelligence services that must conduct many activities secretly. Another set of problems involves the difficult relationship between expertise and policy or between those who possess specialized knowledge about an issue and those who are authorized to determine and implement government policy concerning it. This relationship is a problem in all parts of the government, regardless of the policy areas with which they deal, and is thus a recurrent theme in public administration theory.

Many issues and conflicts typically arise between expertise and policy. At the center is the question of what role expertise ought to play in the policy-making process. How should one reasonably draw the line between the functions and responsibilities of the experts, on the one hand, and the policymakers, on the other? Clearly, we want policy to be guided by the best information available; we would be very critical of a policymaker who ignored the available facts and based his actions on his unsupported views of what the world was like. At the same time, we want policy to be made by those to whom the political system (via election or appointment) gives the leadership authority; in any case, they must take ultimate responsibility for their policies, regardless of the information on which the policies were based.

Theoretically, contemporary social science resolves this problem by means of the "fact-value" distinction: social science can provide the facts, (including contingent predictions such as "if the government follows policy X_1, it will obtain result Y_1"), but policymakers have a monopoly on choosing the values to be pursued (whether to prefer result Y_1 to result Y_2, or vice versa).

This theoretical solution provides, however, very little useful guidance in practice. First of all, the social sciences are far from being able to make contingent predictions with any confidence in most areas; certainly with respect to the national security issues with which intelligence deals, this type of predictive ability is not available. Second, most if not all of the debates in the national security arena center much more on differing assessments of the factual consequences of policies than on disagreements concerning which values should be sought. Everyone can easily agree on peace, liberty, and prosperity as goals, but the means to achieve them are debated endlessly. Conversely, if it could be stated with any certainty that a given policy would attain these goals, the policy-making role would be diminished to the point of extinction.

Since intelligence can provide only the roughest approximations of what will happen, the theoretical fact-value distinction does little to illuminate the appropriate roles of intelligence and policy. In practice, policymakers' choices depend more on their views about the consequences of policies than on their choices of goals. (Indeed, the choice of ultimate goals is considered so self-evident that the issue is rarely addressed at all.) Thus, what policy-makers do is not so clearly separated from what experts do as it first seemed; hence, it is not surprising that the intelligence-policy relationship holds a certain amount of tension. Each side often views the other side's actions as infringing on its territory.

"Killing the Messenger"

From the intelligence officer's perspective, the difficulties between intelligence and policy look like the latter's fault. The difficulties stem, in their view, from the policymakers' tendency to disregard intelligence reports that do not support the policies they wish to adopt or have already adopted and to which they are committed. Intelligence officers think policymakers are interested in the intelligence product only insofar as it can be used to support their policies, which they have adopted for completely different reasons. When the intelligence product does not support their policies, they either ignore it or try to "cook" it by using political pressure to change its contents.

This perspective has led to the view, which tends to predominate in both academic and political discussions of intelligence, that the most important characteristic of any intelligence-producing organization is its independence from policymakers. Only an independent intelligence agency, in this view, can resist the political pressures that policymakers would otherwise bring to bear on it to conform its analyses to their policy preferences.

In the American context, this has provided the most important argument for the existence of a *central*—nondepartmental—intelligence agency with its own collection and analysis capability. Such an organization, the argument runs, will be free of the biases that would distort the output of an intelligence service that was part of the Department of State or Defense and forced to take account of its parent organization's policy preferences or budgetary interests.

This independence permits the intelligence agency to be guided entirely by the data, without having to worry about how its product will affect the policy process. Independence helps negate what may be called the "killing the messenger" syndrome, the tendency to blame the messenger—the intelligence analyst—for bringing unwelcome news—analyses of the situation that do not support the favored policy.

The common understanding of this syndrome is that it reflects some irrationality on the part of the policymaker; it may perhaps best be illustrated by a passage from Shakespeare's *Antony and Cleopatra*. After threatening the messenger who has informed her that Antony has married Octavia, Cleopatra explains her behavior as follows:

> Though it be honest, it is never good
> To bring bad news: give to a gracious tiding
> A host of tongues; but let ill tidings tell
> Themselves when they be felt.[9]

Not to be forewarned of unpleasant developments until they come up and bite is an idea that obviously cannot guide an intelligence agency. Any policymaker who adopted such a position would indeed be acting irrationally.

However, a policymaker need not be influenced by this irrational motive to wish to prevent an intelligence agency from reporting unwelcome news. In a modern bureaucratic state, no official, even the head of state or government, receives intelligence information or assessments bearing on a given policy that other high officials do not receive as well. Some of these other officials may have been enemies of the policy and can be expected to use any negative intelligence information or assessment to question and try to overturn it.

This difficulty is only exacerbated when intelligence is routinely shared not only with the official's colleagues and bureaucratic rivals, but also with his political opponents (for example, the opposition party in Congress). From this perspective, then, it is not at all irrational for a policymaker to wish to ensure that intelligence provides the "right" answer.

Of course, what is in the interest of any one policymaker need not be in the nation's interest. From the national point of view, we should seek whatever will bring about the best implementation of the best policies. Unfortunately, these two goals may have conflicting requirements. Formation of the best policy requires that all of the relevant intelligence product be available to everyone engaged in forming the policy. Intelligence information and analyses will most likely support arguments for and against any proposed policy; all these arguments should be weighed in reaching a final decision. Suppressing pieces of information or lines of argument, or keeping them from certain participants in the policy-making process will, in principle, bias the process and reduce the likelihood of its yielding the best result.

Implementation, however, poses a different problem; once a policy is chosen, the arguments against it must be ignored. Attempts to reargue the basic policy question whenever a tactical decision must be made or to reorient the policy in response to each new piece of intelligence can only lead to a weak, confused, vacillating, and ultimately ineffective policy.

The wide dissemination of the intelligence product, parts of which are bound to contradict the assumptions on which the policy was based or to reflect poorly on its progress, can look like a needless evil to the official in charge of implementing the policy. In the earthy language of former President Lyndon Johnson, the problem is as follows: "Policy making is like milking a fat cow. You see the milk coming out, you press more and the milk bubbles and flows, and just as the bucket is full, the cow with its tail whips the bucket and all is spilled. That's what the CIA does to policy making."[10]

"Imperial Intelligence"

While the intelligence analyst may often feel that the policymaker's attachment to a policy leads him to ignore or to try to distort or suppress relevant information, policymakers may feel that although intelligence often offers only tenuous judgments, policymakers are expected to treat those judgments as gospel and to make decisions accordingly. In many of these cases, it is not clear why the intelligence judgment should be treated as more authoritative or objective than anyone else's, including the policymaker's.

For example, often an intelligence judgment dealing with major political issues is based not on a sensitive nugget of hard data (for example, the report of an agent inside the adversary's cabinet or general staff), but rather on data available to the policymaker (or to a journalist, for that matter) as well. In this case, the policymaker may feel justified in deciding to trust his own judgment rather than that of an anonymous (to the policymaker) intelligence analyst; but his critics are likely to assert that he is behaving as irrationally and illegitimately as Cleopatra. What may increase the tension is the typical failure of the intelligence product to make clear the kind of evidence on which it is based. (Except for the highest officials, policymakers may not learn very much about the sources for the written materials they receive.) The policymaker may come to believe that this lack of information about sources masks the fact that the main intelligence judgments are just speculative judgments that are not based on hard data.

In any case, the possibility that the policymaker is right—that his judgment will be superior to that of the intelligence analyst—is not so small. It is true that, in the United States at least, the policy-making community is often characterized by a high turnover rate among top officials, giving rise to a certain amateurism. It may well be that, as an article by a U.S. intelligence official put it, "after a few months on the job [new intelligence analysts] are among the most knowledgeable people in the government on a particular issue, . . . [F]or the first time in their lives, they are writing for an audience that knows less than they do."[11]

However, this is not necessarily the case, and policymakers who do have some expertise in the area would likely dismiss an intelligence report that reflects this view of their abilities. Furthermore, the "policymaker may have direct access to information unavailable to the analyst (confidential conversations with foreign officials, for example) and, in any case, knows U.S. policy—often a key piece of the puzzle—far better than the analyst."[12] Thus, in the absence of particularly secret information, or of a specialized method of analysis, the intelligence analyst's judgment often does not have any special character that entitles it to be accepted over the judgment of anyone else. As Charles Fairbanks has pointed out with respect to a controversy over Soviet intentions toward Iran in 1985 (whether there was a Soviet threat to Iran was a major question affecting U.S. policy toward that country):

> As for the means of analysis the Intelligence Community uses, these are not anything arcane: the means is *thinking*, of the same kind that an official outside the Intelligence Community or a reporter or a citizen would use in trying to interpret similar facts. The composition of a Special National Intelligence Estimate on [such] an issue . . . is essentially the same exercise as the one the members of the [National Security Council] staff engaged in, well or badly, when they decided to sell arms to Iran. It is an exercise in policy reasoning.[13]

It is only when the result of such a reasoning process receives the label of "intelligence" (and a classification stamp) that it becomes possible to pretend that what is involved "is some hard nugget of fact that transcends the dubious or self-interested policy arguments of other agencies and will serve as a neutral test to evaluate them."[14]

This same situation may arise even when there is a hard fact available to the intelligence analyst, because very rarely will this fact speak for itself. It must be interpreted in some context, and this context is supplied, first of all, by the intelligence analyst. Yet understanding the context requires making the speculative judgments I have been discussing.

These arguments go against the mainstream of current opinion on this topic, which emphasizes the importance of maintaining the independence of intelligence from policy and of forcing policy to listen to it. The consonance of a policy with the intelligence view is often taken as a measure of its reasonableness. What is lost is any sense of the solidity of the intelligence view itself—is it based on incontrovertible fact or quite controvertible speculation?

This point may be seen with respect to the circumstances surrounding the Fairbanks article excerpted above. The conclusion of the SNIE to which he refers—that the likelihood of a Soviet invasion of Iran was relatively small—had been leaked to the press evidently to criticize "the secret sale of U.S. arms to Iran, which President Reagan ordered in January 1986 partly to assist Iran against 'intervention by the Soviet Union.' "[15]

This motivation may also be seen in the article in which the leak appeared that claims "Casey's amended analysis appears to have called into question a primary White House rationale."[16] In other words, the intelligence judgment is used as the touchstone of the reasonableness of a policy, regardless of the "hardness" of the evidence on which it is based.

The Independence of Intelligence

Given these potential sources of friction in the intelligence-policy relation, the question of how independent of policy intelligence should be is bound to be a complicated one. In a military command, for instance, the chief intelligence officer is as much a part of the commander's staff (and hence as much under his command) as any other aide; there is no question of any independence. Indeed, the very meaning of the demand that an intelligence agency be "independent" is not clear. In principle, nobody would advocate an intelligence service be independent from the head of government. Nevertheless, as the above discussion indicates, people often want to use intelligence as a neutral arbiter of policy fights—not only among government officials but between government officials and their legislative and extragovernmental critics. This implies independence from *all* government officials, and a corresponding direct responsibility to some other group, either a legislative body (as a representative of the public) or the public itself.

As previously discussed, the main argument for independence derives from the "killing the messenger" syndrome: intelligence must be independent to enable analysts to tell the truth as they see it. In this context, independence means the ability to shield individual analysts from any pressures or threats that might induce them to make their conclusions more palatable to the product's consumer. To some extent, this sort of independence can be achieved by the creation of a central intelligence agency, one that is subordinate to the head of government, but not to the major intelligence consumers such as the foreign affairs or defense ministries or departments. However, heads of government are themselves intelligence consumers who may have invested a great deal of personal prestige in a policy. In this case, the problem reappears at a higher level. Ultimately, as long as the intelligence service is a part of the government, the only safeguards are the backbones of the chiefs of the intelligence services and their willingness and ability to protect analysts from outside pressure.

Independence is particularly important when it is necessary to abandon policies that are not working or that changed circumstances have rendered obsolete or counterproductive. For this to take place, some mechanism must ensure that all relevant information, positive and negative, is available for reviewing the policy. As the Johnson quote suggests, policymakers must devote most of their energy to implementing policies with some consistency in the face of constant crosscurrents, doubts, political attacks—not necessarily motivated by a sincere belief in the superiority of some other policy— and so forth. Under these conditions, it is particularly difficult for such officials to change gears and conduct a fully open-minded policy review.

In this situation, intelligence takes on an adversarial posture, since its most important function will be to point out areas in which the policy is not working or has become inappropriate. It must counteract, in other words, the political pressure on bureaucrats to be good team players and cheerleaders for current policies. Therefore, the intelligence service presenting information that suggests the policy is obsolete or wrong-headed must have enough independence to withstand the pressures such a situation generates.

One such situation that has attracted public attention is the intelligence role in verifying compliance with arms control agreements. An accusation that a party to an arms control agreement has violated it calls into question the wisdom of having made the agreement in the first place or, at any rate, of continuing to adhere to it. The desire to maintain the agreement (or to maintain or improve relations generally with the party in question) provides a strong incentive to ignore or hide the disturbing evidence. In any case, the difficulty of forcing the party to comply with the agreement or doing anything else about a violation is a strong inducement for denying that one exists.

In addition, an intelligence service must be sufficiently independent to take the initiative in looking at issues or areas of the world without policy community support. An intelligence service should scan the horizon, as it were, for potential issues and problems in areas that are not attracting the policymakers' attention. This warning function inevitably involves giving the policymakers information that they have not requested and do not particularly want because they do not know its value.

Independence carries some disadvantages as well. Perhaps the greatest is the risk that the intelligence work will become, or will be perceived as, irrelevant to the policy process. This can occur because the intelligence analyst does not know what problems appear most important to the policymakers or what options are being considered for dealing with them.

More than mere organizational or physical distance from the policymakers leads to this problem. Intelligence analysts occasionally refuse to cooperate in implementing a policy they do not support. Former Deputy Director of Central Intelligence Robert Gates provides an example of this problem:

> When Secretary of State Alexander Haig asserted that the Soviets were behind international terrorism, intelligence analysts initially set out, not to address the issue in all its aspects, but rather to prove the secretary wrong—to prove simply that the Soviets do not orchestrate all international terrorism. But in so doing they went too far themselves and failed in early drafts to describe extensive and well-documented indirect Soviet support for terrorist groups and their sponsors.[17]

In other words, a policy to address the problem of international terrorism that would have pressured the Soviet Union to reduce its support (whether direct or indirect) of terrorist groups was thwarted by the unwillingness of the intelligence analysts to cooperate, based on their view that such Soviet involvement was a relatively small part of terrorism. Their view may have been true, but that does not imply that the policy was incorrect: it might be, for example, that the major psychological, sociological, or even political causes of terrorism simply cannot be addressed by U.S. policy, or that addressing them would conflict with other foreign policy goals.

If intelligence concentrates too much on its (admittedly necessary) adversarial role (such as would be involved in reviewing ongoing policies), it makes it all the more difficult for it to support the actual implementation of policy. In a supportive role, intelligence must concentrate its efforts on finding and analyzing information relevant to implementing the policy. In the above example, it might have meant discovering the mechanisms by which an international terrorist group receives financial and logistic support from its patrons. In supporting policy implementation, the agency should be willing not to insist on its view—that patron state support is not a major cause of international terrorism—of why the policy is misguided or wrong.

Intelligence and Democracy

Democracy and Secrecy

Secrecy, as already noted, raises a potential problem for the control of intelligence agencies by their nonintelligence superiors. The legitimate need to keep many details of their operations within the smallest possible circle may facilitate a cover-up of unauthorized actions, thereby preventing higher, nonintelligence authorities from finding out about them.

In a democracy, however, secrecy may pose an additional problem: it has the potential to call into question the political legitimacy, as opposed to the actual control, of an intelligence service. If democracy is government not only for the people, but of and by them as well, it is not surprising that institutions that rely so heavily on secrecy can easily become the objects of popular mistrust. This suspicion is not limited to intelligence services: President Woodrow Wilson's promise that the international issues of the post–World War I period would be resolved by "open covenants, openly arrived at" reflected public suspicion of prewar secret diplomacy as well as of secrecy generally.

Legislative and Public Oversight

This skepticism concerning governmental secrecy, which is probably endemic in democratic societies, has led, in the United States and to a much lesser extent in other democratic countries, to calls for oversight of intelligence agencies by a part of the government that enjoys some independence from the head of state. In the United States, a system of congressional oversight by means of two committees created for that purpose (the House of Representatives Permanent Select Committee on Intelligence and the Senate Select Committee on Intelligence) was established in the mid-1970s.

The cornerstone of this oversight system is the committees' statutory right to be "fully and currently informed of all intelligence activities" by the director of central intelligence and the heads of other intelligence entities.[18] This right to be informed is particularly significant in light of the congressional power of the purse—its power to appropriate, or refuse to appropriate, funds for any governmental activity. The result, according to former Deputy Director of Central Intelligence Robert Gates, has been that the oversight process has . . . given Congress—especially the two intelligence committees—far greater knowledge of and influence over the way the CIA and other intelligence agencies spend their money than anyone in the executive branch would dream of exercising, from expenditures in the billions of dollars to line items in the thousands. . . . Congress may actually have more influence today over the CIA's priorities and its allocation of resources than the executive branch.[19]

The congressional oversight system may be viewed as a compromise between the requirement for secrecy and the desire to bring public opinion to bear on the intelligence agencies to make sure that their secret activities neither use means nor seek ends public opinion would condemn. Congressional oversight allows the intelligence committees to serve as a sounding board, a surrogate for the much wider debate (intra-executive branch, congressional, and public) that might otherwise accompany a governmental policy or initiative.

The ambiguities created by using the intelligence committees as a surrogate for public opinion are most readily seen regarding covert action, concerns about which led to the introduction of congressional oversight in the first place. The legal basis of the committees' role is the requirement that they be notified each time the president orders a covert action. While in principle the notification requirement does not imply that the committees possess a veto power over covert action programs, strong objections from committee members can cause revision or even cancellation of a proposal, if the political cost looks like it will be greater than the program's expected results.[20] Thus, one purpose of prior notification might be described as to test a proposal against a (somewhat restricted) cross section of political opinion, represented by individuals independent of the president, to see if it is out of line with fundamental beliefs or values.

Beyond this sounding board function, spreading the knowledge of covert action to members of Congress creates the opportunity for bringing into play the congressional power of the purse. This power can be exercised by the intelligence committees themselves, or it can involve full-scale debate on the floor of the Senate and House of Representatives, as in the case of the various Boland amendments restricting or prohibiting aid to the Nicaraguan resistance in the 1980s.

The fundamental claim on behalf of congressional oversight of covert action is that it succeeds in combining the advantages of checks and balances on the one hand with those of secrecy on the other. Committee consideration serves as a surrogate for the full-scale public debate and democratic decision-making process that is of course incompatible with secrecy.

The validity of this claim has been attacked in both practical and theoretical terms. Practically, the issue is whether congressional oversight does not inevitably lead to public revelation of the information, regardless of what the rules say. In fact, there is little hard information about the source of the numerous leaks that occur with respect to covert action, and investigations of particular leaks almost never produce results. Given the importance journalists place on not revealing their sources, this is not surprising.[21]

Furthermore, even the information available may be misleading. A reference in a news report to a "congressional source" or an "administration official" may not indicate who first tipped the journalist off; the original source may have spoken on "deep background," precluding any reference to him at all.[22] Thus, the reference in the article could refer to a source who confirmed the story, not to the one who originally leaked it.[23]

In any case, there is no doubt that congressional oversight broadens the number of people who are given access to information about covert action. In general, the risk of a leak varies with the number of people with access to the information. Furthermore, the congressmen and their staff aides typically are less used to dealing with classified information and work in a more political setting than the average intelligence official. The requirement to brief Congress probably leads to the involvement of additional people within the executive branch itself, since some of those who handle congressional relations have to be informed as well. In most cases, enough executive branch employees have access that the expansion due to congressional oversight probably does not significantly increase the risk of a leak; in special cases, where access is strictly limited within the executive branch, the increase would be relatively greater, as would the risk of a leak.

While much of the public debate about congressional oversight concerns leaks, the more theoretical challenge to congressional oversight of covert action deals with the propriety and effectiveness of Congress adopting secret procedures as a routine matter.

Thus, before the Church Committee, Morton Halperin argued against the concept as follows:

> [Better forms of control] cannot succeed in curing the evils inherent in having a covert capability. The only weapon that opponents of a Presidential policy, inside or outside the executive branch, have is public debate. If a policy can be debated openly, then Congress may be persuaded to constrain the President and public pressure may force a change in policy. But if secrecy is accepted as the norm and as legitimate, then the checks put on covert operations can easily be ignored.[24]

While this prediction has proved excessively dismissive of what congressional committees can achieve in quiet negotiation with the executive branch (the threat to "go public" remaining in the background), it does contain a kernel of truth: in major disagreements, such as "covert" aid to the Nicaraguan resistance, the norm of secrecy was abandoned, and the issue received full-scale and public congressional debate.

Thus, the notion of congressional oversight conducted secretly contains a self-contradiction: one wants to obtain the benefits of legislative deliberation on intelligence matters, but one rules out from the start the major method of such deliberation—full and open public debate.

These issues of intelligence secrecy and oversight often become confused with what is properly a separate issue: to what extent does the fact that a nation is a democracy affect the kind of foreign policy it ought to adopt? This is particularly true with respect to covert action, which is the element of intelligence that in the United States has attracted the most criticism as being antidemocratic. However, much of the criticism directed against the CIA for its covert action programs would have been more properly directed against the foreign policy those programs served.

In the United States, the main complaint against covert action has been that it interferes in another country's internal affairs. It seems to be a secondary question whether that interference is secret or overt. The argument is sometimes made that such activity is undemocratic in the sense that it is carried on covertly because domestic public opposition to it would be overwhelming if it were known. This situation, however, is not so clearly the case as those who make this argument claim: for example, the various covert actions directed against Fidel Castro, including the assassination attempts, might have received public support at the time they were under way. When the Church Committee complained that these actions went counter to American public opinion, it was judging the CIA's past covert actions not by contemporaneous public opinion, but by the post-Vietnam public opinion of the mid-1970s.

Since the mid-1970s, when the congressional intelligence oversight committees were created in the United States, other democratic countries have considered establishing some form of independent oversight of intelligence activities. For example, in 1984, the Canadian Parliament created the Security Intelligence Review Committee (SIRC) to exercise oversight of the country's domestic intelligence apparatus, which was at the same time separated from the Royal Canadian Mounted Police and made into a new civilian agency, the Canadian Security Intelligence Service.

Unlike the American oversight committees, the SIRC is not a committee of Parliament but is composed of privy councillors appointed by the prime minister after consultation with the opposition party leaders. (The Privy Council is a group whose members, usually former cabinet members, have been officially recognized by the Canadian government as senior advisers.) The SIRC reports to Parliament annually, but itself has no legislative or budgetary powers. The differences between the Canadian and U.S. oversight mechanisms reflect the differences in the two political systems: the main tension within the U.S. system is between the executive and legislative branches of the government, which is not the case in Canada's parliamentary system with strong party discipline. Instead, in Canada, the necessary independence from the executive branch is obtained by relying on eminent senior statesmen.[25]

Democracy, Counterintelligence, and Domestic Intelligence

Rather than covert action, counterintelligence is the element of intelligence most fundamentally affected by the democratic nature of the regime it serves; the greatest number of difficulties in the relationship between democracy and intelligence concern counterintelligence. In particular, these difficulties involve defining the circumstances under which a government agency may legitimately conduct surveillance of a citizen and determining the limits, if any, on the amount and kind of such surveillance.

In the United States, this discussion tends to be conducted in terms of constitutional law. For example, questions arise as to how the prohibition, contained in the Fourth Amendment to the U.S. Constitution, against unreasonable searches and seizures should be interpreted with respect to national security cases.[26] One such question involved the legitimacy of wiretaps (which are considered a form of search) for such cases. It was resolved by the Foreign Intelligence Surveillance Act of 1978, which created a special court to grant warrants permitting wiretaps in national security cases.[27] Other proposals, which did not become law, would have established similar procedures for other forms of surveillance.[28]

This focus on the admissibility or inadmissibility of *means* (which will not be discussed in detail here) has been accompanied by a neglect of the more fundamental questions concerning the proper *ends* of counterintelligence or domestic intelligence in a democracy.[29] What kind of information, in other words, is needed? What purpose is such information supposed to serve? What kinds of threats give rise to domestic intelligence requirements?

These questions are very difficult to answer with respect to a democratic state, as opposed to a totalitarian or authoritarian one. In the latter kinds of states, any opposition to the current leadership of the state is, in principle, of intelligence interest. By constantly monitoring dissent, the government strives to be in a position to take whatever steps necessary, either through the ordinary law enforcement system or outside of it, to maintain its power.

In a democratic state, on the other hand, mere opposition to the government of the day is not, and should not be treated as, a threat to the country. The country's national security interests (as opposed to the government's political interests) are not threatened by opposition as such, and domestic intelligence collection about it is not needed. The question is, then, What forms of activities are potentially threatening to national security such that intelligence should be collected about them?

In particular, where is the line to be drawn between activities that are legitimately of intelligence interest and those that are not? Should intelligence ever be interested in someone's opinions, in and of themselves, or only when they are accompanied by activities? Should the criterion be the legality or illegality of the activity, or are there activities that, although legal, the government nevertheless has a legitimate need to know about and hence may keep under some form of surveillance?

The Criminal Standard

Because of the focus on domestic intelligence means (especially in terms of their constitutionality or lack of it) rather than ends, these questions have not been addressed explicitly in public debates on intelligence. However, an answer of sorts was suggested in the mid-1970s in the United States (at the time of the Church Committee's intelligence investigations and those of its counterpart in the House of Representatives, chaired by Representative Otis Pike), when an attempt was made to apply what was called the "criminal standard" to domestic intelligence. In other words, domestic intelligence investigations would be strictly limited to situations where a violation of the law has occurred or is about to occur. The implication is that the proper scope of domestic intelligence is delimited by the law; an illegal action may be a proper subject of domestic intelligence, but a legal one cannot be.[30]

While this principle was never promulgated in so many words, it set the tone for the guidelines in which the attorney general in 1976 first set down both the conditions under which the FBI could conduct investigations and the techniques it could use in carrying them out. Its impact also can be seen in the Foreign Intelligence Surveillance Act of 1978, the sole piece of congressional legislation in this area in that period.[31]

The guidelines were established by then–Attorney General Edward Levi to specify the circumstances under which the FBI could use various surveillance and investigatory techniques. For the purposes of these guidelines, domestic intelligence was divided into two parts—domestic security on the one hand and foreign intelligence and counterintelligence on the other—and separate guidelines were established for investigations in each category.

The guidelines governing foreign intelligence and counterintelligence investigations were issued on a classified basis and have never been made public in their totality.[32] It is therefore difficult to know to what extent they embody the criminal standard with respect to the investigations they govern. The vast majority of the investigations conducted under these guidelines would deal with detecting and preventing espionage. Thus, they focus on potential criminal activity. The same holds for the detection and prevention of terrorist activities carried out under foreign direction, which is probably the FBI's second most important task to be accomplished in accordance with these guidelines.

It is not clear to what extent the guidelines envisage the investigation of legal political activities carried out on behalf of a foreign government, that is, cooperation with the covert action or active measures conducted by a foreign government and targeted against the United States. It is true that, according to the guidelines,

> the FBI is, *under standards and procedures authorized in these guidelines*, authorized to detect and prevent espionage, sabotage and *other clandestine intelligence activities*, by or pursuant to the direction of foreign powers through such lawful foreign counterintelligence operations within the United States and its territories, including electronic surveillance, as are necessary or useful for such purposes.[33]

This implies that generally legal activities such as political propaganda, organizational work, and fund-raising are subject to surveillance when carried out pursuant to the direction of a foreign power. Furthermore, theoretically at least, anyone engaged in such activity on behalf of a foreign government is obliged to register as a foreign agent under the Foreign Agent Registration Act (FARA), and failure to register would itself constitute a crime.[34]

On the other hand, failure to register is rarely used as the sole basis for a foreign counterintelligence investigation or for prosecution.[35] One such investigation that has come to light involved the Committee in Solidarity with the People of El Salvador (CISPES), which was the subject of a three-month FBI investigation in 1981. The investigation was conducted at the request of the Criminal Division of the Department of Justice, "to determine whether CISPES is required to register under" FARA as an agent of the Salvadoran Frente Democratica Revolucionario, the political arm of the Salvadoran guerrilla movement.[36] However, it is not publicly known to what extent the standards and procedures authorized in these guidelines would permit any effective investigation of clandestine intelligence activities that did not involve violence or the violation of any law (other than FARA).

As opposed to the foreign counterintelligence guidelines, the domestic security ones (called the Levi guidelines) have been made public.[37] They deal primarily with investigations of groups once called subversive or un-American. While these are vague terms, they generally include groups (1) that are hostile not merely to the government of the day and its policies but to the constitutional structure and its fundamental principles, (2) that seek to deprive some class of persons (such as a racial, ethnic, or religious group) of their civil rights, or (3) more generally, that seek to bring about political change by violent means.

The key point in the Levi guidelines is that investigation of such groups is permitted only when a group (or an individual) is or may be engaged in activities "which involve or will involve the use of force or violence and which involve or will involve the violation of federal law, . . ."[38] This is the essence of the criminal standard that effectively defines the government's interest in the domestic security area.

The most important motive for adopting this standard has been to ensure that no surveillance takes place just because an individual or group is exercising its rights of freedom of speech, of the press, or of association, as protected by the First Amendment to the U.S. Constitution.[39] Two general lines of argument support this goal. First, there is the view that government investigation of an individual or a group is itself a kind of punishment from which those who have done nothing illegal should be exempt. The second argument holds that this type of investigation, either because of its intrinsic unpleasantness for the target or because it seems to threaten future punishment, inevitably "chills" the activity (the exercise of the right) that forms the basis of the surveillance. These reasons have some plausibility but are not as compelling as is sometimes claimed. In constitutional terms, the questions would be whether surveillance under these conditions would amount to an abridgement of the freedoms of the First Amendment.

This issue cannot be dealt with here at length. A few points, however, illustrate the cases for and against the criminal standard. On the one hand, the violation of privacy involved in the notion that the government is keeping tabs on an individual is indeed distasteful. This is true of all law enforcement investigations that target individuals who have not been convicted of any crime and who, indeed, may well not be charged with any. An income tax audit, a customs inspection, and any number of other law enforcement actions are invasions of privacy, which the government may and does undertake without probable cause to believe that the target has committed a crime.

Similarly, the possibility of government surveillance might scare people away from controversial political activity, because they fear the inclusion of their names in a file might lead to unpleasant consequences or for some other reason. Nevertheless, the chilling effect of a secret investigation that leads to no government activity can only be minimal, if anything. The effect seems more equivalent to the social obloquy one might earn by espousing unpopular opinions than to an abridgement of First Amendment freedoms. As a matter of constitutional law, the Supreme Court has rejected the contention that an individual suffered any harm from "the mere existence, without more, of a governmental investigative and data-gathering activity. . . ." It ruled that, as far as achieving the legal status ("standing") to contest a governmental investigation in court is concerned, "allegations of a subjective 'chill' [resulting from the secret government investigation] are not an adequate substitute for a claim of specific present objective harm or a threat of specific future harm."[40]

As has been noted by Kenneth Robertson, this issue is typically discussed in terms of constitutional law prohibitions against certain types of governmental activity. The question also must be faced of whether these standards allow the government to meet its legitimate needs for information about what is going on in its own society.[41] In at least two areas of interest an argument can be made that, theoretically at least, these standards do not allow the government enough leeway.

The Criminal Standard and Personnel Security

The first area has to do with the government's personnel security program for screening applicants for government positions and current employees before giving them access to classified information. For such purposes, it is legitimate for the government to want to know if the applicants have any affiliations or loyalties that might lead them to disclose classified information to representatives of foreign powers or otherwise act against the country's interests. In general, it is difficult to determine this information during the screening, for all the reasons noted in chapter 5. The only way the government can have some confidence that the applicant is disclosing any such affiliation is if the government possesses other sources of information, derived from surveillance of the organizations in question.

In this regard, it is important to understand how far the First Amendment's protection extends. According to the Supreme Court's decision in the case of

Brandenburg v. *Ohio,* what may be called abstract advocacy of the overthrow of the U.S. government is protected. Advocacy can be forbidden only when ''such advocacy is directed to inciting or producing *imminent* lawless action and is likely to incite or produce such action.''[42] Thus, under the criminal standard, an organization that openly called for the violent overthrow of the U.S. government could not be subject to surveillance unless and until its advocacy passed from the abstract to the concrete, as defined above.

Furthermore, membership in such an organization can be considered criminal only if it is active rather than nominal membership and involves ''knowledge of the [organization's] illegal advocacy and a specific intent to bring about violent overthrow [of the U.S. government] 'as speedily as circumstances would permit.' ''[43] This implies that, under a criminal standard, it would be impossible to conduct surveillance of such an organization for the purpose of compiling a complete list of its members, since there would not be evidence that each member met the standard for criminal membership, even if the organization as a whole met the Brandenburg test.

To some extent, this was an intended result of the adoption of the criminal standard. As John Elliff has noted, in describing the initial policy decisions taken by Attorney General Edward Levi:

> Levi rejected the federal employee security program as a basis for FBI intelligence investigations. As Levi saw it, the Executive Order [on the personnel security program] authorized the Bureau only to investigate Executive Branch employees and applicants. It could not supply a basis for the FBI's authority to conduct domestic intelligence investigations in general.[44]

In other words, investigations cannot start with a group's public words or actions. They have to start from the individual applicant for government employment, whose affiliation with the group might be well hidden.

Without surveillance of such groups for the purpose of compiling a list of their members, the federal government cannot, in principle, guard against granting access to confidential information to, or placing in sensitive positions, individuals who are members of a political party loyal to a hostile foreign power, of various cult groups fanatically devoted to a leader whose ultimate aims may not be compatible with constitutional government, or of hate groups that want to expel part of the American people from the body politic. This may or may not pose a problem at any given time, depending on whether such groups exist and whether they are sophisticated enough to develop a strategy of placing their members in sensitive positions in the federal government (penetrating it.)

The Criminal Standard and Counterterrorism

A somewhat different issue arises in the case of terrorist groups. While an active terrorist group would meet any conceivable criminal standard for surveillance, it can be extremely difficult to establish such surveillance if the group is as sophisticated as the major terrorist groups of the past decades in the Middle East and Western Europe. Given the rarity of known fixed facilities and means of communication, which might be covered by technical collection means, the most fruitful investigative technique, and often the only useful one, is to penetrate the group with one's own agent.

However, a sophisticated group will be suspicious of outsiders and will take into its confidence only individuals with whom current members have long personal associations or who have proved their loyalty to the group by committing serious crimes. Absent a lucky break, it is difficult or even impossible for an intelligence service, starting from scratch, to penetrate a terrorist group once it is organized and in operation.

Intelligence agencies have to fall back on other strategies to deal with this problem. First, they must be able to collect information about support groups, which are groups of sympathizers who provide various kinds of support—financial, logistic, political, and legal support—but do not take part in the actual terrorist activities. They, of course, present themselves to the public as solely political organizations engaged in legitimate political or charitable activities.

Penetrating a support group, while much easier to accomplish, is not as valuable as penetrating the terrorist group itself. Nevertheless, it can be very useful: the kind of aid provided may make it possible to deduce the timing and nature of future terrorist acts. Furthermore, a support group member, through personal ties or actual recruitment by the terrorist group, may work his way into a position to provide much more precise information. Finally, an agent within a support group might be able to foil a terrorist act, either by providing the police with a key piece of information (such as the description of the rental car to be used in a terrorist act) or by directly sabotaging a bomb (for example, by replacing the gunpowder with sawdust) or other equipment.

As explained by Shlomo Gazit, former director of Israeli Military Intelligence,

> Very few [terrorist] organizations can operate in a complete or full compartmentalization and do not depend on networks of local supporters. Such supporters help the terrorist organization, either because of ideological motivation or through fear and blackmail, without being directly involved in terrorist operations. The importance of penetrating the sympathizers' or supporters' system lies in the fact that it is easier to penetrate

it than the more highly closed terrorist organizations. By penetrating this supportive system it may be possible to penetrate the organization itself or obtain indirect information about it.[45]

The criminal standard inhibits the penetration of support groups since they typically present themselves to the public as political or charitable groups. One group may describe itself as being engaged in political propaganda in favor of various causes, which just happen to be the same as those espoused by the terrorist group. Similarly, another will characterize its activity as the charitable support of the wives and children of alleged terrorists who have been imprisoned or killed. A third group may claim to limit its activities to providing lawyers and funds for the accused terrorists' legal defense.

Without getting an informer into the support group, it may not be possible to establish the exact nature of the group's additional (and not so innocent) efforts on behalf of the terrorist group. But the use of this or other intrusive techniques is permitted only if evidence is already available that the group is involved in violent, criminal activities.[46] In this respect, the criminal standard is something of a catch-22: one cannot know about the support group's additional activities because one may not look, and one may not look as long as one does not know.

A second way of overcoming the difficulty of conducting surveillance against terrorist groups relies on the fact that terrorist groups are typically offshoots of politically extremist, nationalist, or separatist groups; they are usually composed of members of such groups who become frustrated with the failure of less violent means to accomplish the groups' goals. By having informers in the groups from which terrorist groups are likely to form, one would know about a terrorist group as soon as it formed. Having agents in the original group would increase the possibility that a penetration agent could be placed in the terrorist group from its beginning. A criminal standard, on the other hand, makes it impossible to maintain the initial surveillance that could provide the first indication of a new terrorist group.

A particular circumstance that comes under the rubric of counterterrorism involves the responsibility of the U.S. Secret Service to protect the president, other senior government officials, and foreign dignitaries. As with counterterrorism in general, the goal here is to prevent the criminal act from taking place, rather than to react to it by punishing the perpetrator to deter future attacks. The Secret Service's responsibility requires advance intelligence on assassination attempts against its protectees. A criminal standard for investigating groups that might engage in assassination may mean the Secret Service does not receive warnings about assassination attempts until after the group has engaged in illegal violence, which might be too late.

In 1982, the Treasury Department official responsible for the Secret Service explained the problem this way:

Today, the [Secret S]ervice has to be . . . concerned about the terrorist. . . . The Secret Service needs to know . . . about the intentions and activities of terrorists or other extremist groups. Further, we need to know about this kind of threat before it materializes, not after.[47]

This official also noted that a reasonable allocation of the Secret Service's resources would require that it "know, for example, that an organization using extreme rhetoric is either disinclined to put words into action or incapable of launching dangerous activities." In his view, the current

problem is that the FBI is not . . . able to collect enough intelligence. This partly because [of] . . . Attorney General Levi's Domestic Security Guidelines. . . . Prior to the Levi Guidelines, the Secret Service received from the FBI a vast amount of intelligence information on individuals and potentially violent groups. . . . Although it has been claimed that this resulted in the Secret Service being overinformed—the service obviously had to sift through an awful lot of information and sort out the wheat from the chaff . . . the situation was ideal as far as the Secret Service was concerned.

The problem now is that investigations in important areas are simply not being pursued. The result is a lack of information about the location, structure, plans, and activities of groups that may not be labelled terrorist as such, but that certainly are radical, . . . that support terrorist causes and are potentially terroristic or violent.

Of course, this general point would apply to all law enforcement; in general, very little law enforcement activity is devoted to preventing crime (except by deterrence) as opposed to detecting it afterward and apprehending the perpetrators. Certainly, it would be impossible for ordinary law enforcement organizations to set themselves the goal of preventing crime by establishing an intelligence network that would warn them of planned criminal activity. In counterterrorism and executive protection, however, because of the potential seriousness of a single incident, there is a strong desire to prevent crime and not merely to punish it; this implies a requirement to collect intelligence about individuals or groups who, although they have not yet done so, are likely either to engage in such activities or to maintain close ties with those that do.

The Case for the Criminal Standard

Taking note of the theoretical argument against the criminal standard for domestic security investigations is much easier than determining what could replace it. The criminal standard was adopted after the Church Committee documented many cases in which the FBI had conducted investigations that represented both a waste of resources and unwarranted intrusion into political activities that posed no domestic security threat. This "overbreadth," as the Church Committee termed it, argued for a relatively clear-cut standard that would limit investigations to those undeniably necessary. Necessary investigations were defined as being targeted against specific acts of criminal violence that had already occurred or were about to occur.

The examples of this overbreadth in domestic security investigations fall under various headings. Perhaps the most glaring were those cases in which, at White House direction, the FBI undertook investigations against the president's partisan opponents, apparently for purely political purposes. Judge and former Deputy Attorney General Laurence Silberman testified in 1978 that

> of all the abuses of various agencies of Government over the last 20 years, I think the single most egregious abuse was President Johnson's direction to the FBI to see if they could find any dirt on [Senator Goldwater's] staff 2 weeks before the [1964 presidential] election.[48]

There are other similar examples of the use of the FBI against political opponents in Congress, the media, or elsewhere.

In many other cases, investigations were directed against activist political groups targeted under vague labels, such as

- "rightist" or "extremist" groups in the "anticommunist field,"
- "anarchistic or revolutionary beliefs,"
- "black nationalists" and "extremists,"
- "white supremacists," and
- "agitators."[49]

In these cases, while there might have been some nexus between the organization being investigated and potential violence or links to foreign intelligence services, clearly the investigations were indeed overbroad in terms of the individuals and groups involved, the extraneous information collected about them, and the time unpromising investigations were allowed to continue. The extraneous information that was collected was not only retained in investigatory files, but freely disseminated within the government; thus, information about legitimate political activities was made available for the administration's partisan political use.[50]

From the history the Church Committee compiled, it seems clear that excesses were facilitated by the absence of clear standards for domestic intelligence investigations. Thus, it is easy to see how a criminal standard would be an attractive, clear-cut option. If that limitation is too narrow, then one must search for a broader one that still would protect against the sorts of abuses that have occurred.

This task cannot be accomplished quickly. To approach it in a responsible manner, one would have to start by considering what domestic political or other activities a democratic government legitimately needs to know about to protect against threats to the country. In the United States, the legislation, executive orders, and guidelines dealing with domestic intelligence have been cast in terms of the conditions that must be met before various investigative techniques may be employed. There is, on the other hand, no formal statement of what the purpose of domestic intelligence is, or of what type of information it is supposed to provide. Such a statement would have to be elaborated before one could develop guidelines that focus on the goal (what information is necessary) rather than on the means (which investigative technique may be used).

By contrast, Canadian law defines the threats with which the domestic intelligence agency, the Canadian Security Intelligence Service (CSIS), should be concerned. The CSIS is authorized to collect information regarding activities ''that may on reasonable grounds be suspected of constituting threats to the security of Canada.'' These are defined as:

- espionage or sabotage, or activities directed toward or in support of espionage or sabotage,
- foreign-influenced activities that are detrimental to Canadian interests and are clandestine or deceptive or involve a threat to any person,
- activities directed toward or in support of the threat or use of serious violence to achieve a political purpose, and
- activities directed toward or intended ultimately to lead to the destruction or violent overthrow of the Canadian government.[51]

Even with an adequate definition of the scope of domestic intelligence, questions will arise as to whether a given group constitutes a threat or is simply engaging in hyperbolic rhetoric, and as to the amount and type of evidence required for a group to be considered a threat that should be investigated. But without an understanding of what domestic security information is required, it is impossible to judge whether specific restrictions on investigative means are reasonable.

7

TWO VIEWS OF INTELLIGENCE

In the five preceding chapters I have discussed the four elements of intelligence—the four general headings under which intelligence activities may be categorized—as well as some of the issues concerning the relationship between intelligence and the rest of the government and society of which it is a part. I now return to the more general issue of the nature of intelligence as a whole. I first compare what may be called the "traditional" view of intelligence, which emphasizes obtaining, protecting, and exploiting secret information relevant to the struggle among nations, with a newer, characteristically American view of intelligence that has evolved since World War II.

To some extent, the "traditional" view as developed here is my invention—hence the quotation marks. While it reflects traditional concepts of intelligence, those concepts were not typically articulated in this manner. (It should be remembered that public writings about intelligence were rare in the past.) I use it here primarily as a foil to highlight the distinctive aspects of the American view of intelligence that has arisen since World War II.

The "traditional" view can be traced back to one of the oldest known thematic discussions of intelligence, which is found in a Chinese classic entitled *The Art of War*, commonly attributed to a sixth century B.C. general and military thinker named Sun Tzu. He explains the importance of intelligence as follows:

Now the reason the enlightened prince and the wise general conquer the enemy whenever they move and their achievements surpass those of ordinary men is foreknowledge.

What is called "foreknowledge" cannot be elicited from spirits, nor from the gods, nor by analogy with past events, nor from calculations. It must be obtained from men who know the enemy situation [directly, i.e., men with access to the enemy camp].[1]

Espionage is at the center of this understanding of intelligence. Given the close connection between learning the enemy's secrets and achieving victory over him, it would follow that the protection of one's own secrets (counterintelligence) must be as important as the obtaining of the adversary's. Sun Tzu mentions two methods of achieving this:

- doubling enemy agents, presumably by making them a better offer, and
- sending into the enemy camp spies who have been deceived as to one's own situation, so that, once captured by the enemy and forced to talk, they will unwittingly deceive him.[2]

The ultimate goal of this espionage is to elucidate the adversary's strategy so well that one can devise means of circumventing and defeating it at the lowest possible cost. Indeed, from the point of view of Sun Tzu, for whom defeating an enemy's strategy is more important than defeating his army, the intelligence component of international struggle is as vital as the armed component:

Thus, what is of supreme importance in war is to attack the enemy's strategy;
Next best is to disrupt his alliances;
The next best is to attack his army.[3]

Intelligence is as much a struggle with an enemy as is armed combat; the difference lies in the means employed.

In an article that calls for the "growth of a truly American intelligence system," former Director of Central Intelligence William Colby distinguishes such a system from traditional intelligence systems, which he describes and dismisses, as follows:

For centuries, intelligence was the small, private preserve of monarchs and generals. Governmental and military espionage ferreted out the secrets of other powers in order to provide its sponsors with advantage in their dealings. Secret agents intrigued and subverted in order to discredit an opponent or support their [*sic*] adversaries within his own camp. The spy was the prototype of this traditional "intelligence" discipline.[4]

Elsewhere, Colby defines the "traditional concept of intelligence" as a "secret service which ferrets out an enemy's secret plan and shares it with a monarch so that he can win a battle."[5] He claims that the American experience during World War II saw the rise of a new view of intelligence that challenged the "traditional" one in major respects. In the postwar period, this view had continued to develop both within U.S. intelligence and among academic students of the subject. This chapter discusses that new view and compares it with the "traditional" one.

Historical Development of the American View

The unsettled conditions brought about by the beginning of World War II, and America's subsequent entry into it, led to massive increases in resources the United States devoted to intelligence. It also led to a new bureaucratic development, the creation of a central intelligence service (known first as the Office of the Coordinator of Information and then as the Office of Strategic Services, or OSS) whose purposes included the collection, analysis, and correlation of national security information and data.[6] Despite President Franklin Roosevelt's decision in July 1941 to create a central capability to correlate information, none was in place by December 1941, when the failure to foresee the Japanese attack on Pearl Harbor highlighted the lack of intelligence correlation and analysis, since many relevant bits and pieces of information were available.

The Centrality of Analysis

The OSS set up a research and analysis branch that was to analyze "all the relevant information, that was overtly available as well as that secretly obtained."[7] Although this goal was not fulfilled during World War II, it remained the ideal situation, which was essentially realized with the creation of the Central Intelligence Agency in 1947.[8]

This emphasis on intelligence analysis, the intellectual work of piecing together disparate bits of information to develop an accurate picture, suggests a view of intelligence different from the "traditional" one. This newer view pays less attention to secrecy and the means of overcoming it and more attention to the analytic function, an activity that comes to resemble social science research more than it does traditional espionage.

This view was most influentially put forward immediately after World War II by Sherman Kent, former OSS officer and future head of the Office of National Estimates, the Central Intelligency Agency office then in charge of producing overall assessments of the world situation. His well-known book, *Strategic Intelligence for American World Policy*, argued the case for understanding intelligence as the scientific method (in its social science variant) applied to strategic matters:

> Research is the only process which we of the liberal tradition are willing to admit is capable of giving us the truth, or a closer approximation to truth, than we now enjoy. . . . we insist, and have insisted for generations, that truth is to be approached, if not attained, through research guided by a systematic method. In the social sciences which very largely constitute the subject matter of strategic intelligence, there is such a method. It is much like the method of physical sciences. It is not the same method but it is a method none the less.[9]

Of course, this social science method cannot be the whole of intelligence, even if it is its heart. There must, after all, be data upon which it can work. While recognizing that some of the data must be gathered by clandestine means, Kent insists that the popular view of intelligence as dealing primarily with secrets is a myth. Instead, in his view, intelligence analysis can rely on nonsecret, openly available information, with only a small number of clandestinely gathered secrets added as seasoning. Referring to the knowledge necessary to conduct foreign policy—the content of the strategic intelligence about which he is writing—he says: "Some of this knowledge may be acquired through clandestine means, but *the bulk of it must be had through unromantic open-and-above-board observation and research.*"[10]

In its most extreme form, this new view equates intelligence with a sort of universal, predictive social science. This social science was described by former DCI Colby in 1981, as follows:

> A new discipline specifically designed for intelligence analysis must be refined, and the process of research and development has already begun. It will step beyond academic analysis through new techniques to project future probabilities rather than explain the past. Experiments in this new discipline are by no means limited to the official intelligence community, as they also take place in information science research centers, among political risk analysts, and in the projections of the Club of Rome, the Global 2000 study, and others.[11]

The central importance of analysis is a major distinguishing characteristic of the new view of intelligence. To understand this view better, I examine the argument that a proponent might use to convince a "traditionalist" of its truth. I'll start by observing that, whatever one's view of intelligence, one must recognize an important role for at least some kinds of analysis.

First of all, collection activity immediately generates the need for some analysis, either technical (such as decoding coded messages) or more general (such as comparing reports from two different sources to determine whether they support or contradict one another). Some evaluation of the information received is needed to determine, for example, whether it should be accepted as genuine or whether it should be regarded as a deliberate attempt by the adversary to mislead.[12]

More significantly, it often may be too difficult to ferret out the relevant secret information directly. As a result, the only alternative is to try to deduce it from whatever data is available. This could include information that the adversary does not consider, in itself, to be sensitive and so does not keep secret.

For example, the most direct and reliable warning of imminent attack would probably come from an agent within the enemy's General Staff. Failing this, one would have to attempt to deduce the enemy's intention from various pieces of information concerning the deployment of his armed forces, their readiness, the status of his reserves, and so forth. In addition, public information might be useful as well; before Pearl Harbor, for example, the United States paid attention to the locations and planned itineraries of Japanese merchant ships on the grounds that, were Japan planning to go to war, it would make sure that its merchant fleet had been recalled to relatively safe waters.

Thus far, those holding the "traditional" view would not argue with the necessity of such activities, despite their view that intelligence deals primarily with secrets. The questions come as the sphere of intelligence concerns expands to the dimensions of Colby's "new discipline . . . [of] intelligence analysis," a universal, predictive social science covering all aspects of society.

Obviously, to manage military affairs and to conduct foreign policy, a country's governmental officials must know more about its potential adversaries than merely their military or diplomatic secrets. Other factors, such as the potential adversary's economic activity and potential, its demographic trends, and its internal political forces and concerns, also must be considered. With respect to these factors, the difficulty is likely to lie not so much in gathering the raw data (although in the case of a closed society with an idiosyncratic political system, this may present many challenges) as in evaluating the information correctly.

For example, despite the openness of the American political process, an observer, whether American or not, has difficulty understanding, let alone predicting, the course of a major political event such as a congressional vote or a presidential campaign. Yet, clearly, to conduct its policy toward the United States, another country would find that a good understanding of such matters could be as important as obtaining U.S. national security secrets. As Eliot Cohen has pointed out, the openness of American political life in the 1930s did not by itself enable its future opponents to understand it:

> Although the United States . . . was nothing if not accessible to foreign agents, both legal and covert, it was in another sense impenetrable to the Axis powers because of their own failure to comprehend the workings of democratic states. Both the Germans and the Japanese repeatedly underestimated the American polity—its tenacity and ingenuity, as well as its ability to organize, improvise, and produce. And these colossal failures of intelligence helped doom both states to ruinous defeat.[13]

In other cases, the bit of information most important for a nation to have cannot be considered a secret because, when the information is most needed, it does not even yet exist. Sherman Kent gives as an example of this the intelligence problem the Soviet Union faced when it sought to determine whether the United States would resist the 1950 North Korean invasion of the South. Had Soviet agents been looking in U.S. files for documents containing the U.S. decision whether to fight, they could not have found any, since the decision was made by President Truman only after the invasion began: "Thus, if knowledge of the other man's intentions is to be divined through the reading of his intimate papers and one's own policy is to be set on the basis of what one discovers, here is a case where policy was on the rocks almost by definition."[14] Instead, Kent argues that such information can only be had through research and analysis:

> I have urged that if you have knowledge of Great Frusina's [Kent's hypothetical great power] strategic stature [Kent's term for the totality of a nation's capabilities—military, political and economic—to act on the international scene], knowledge of her specific vulnerabilities, and how she may view these, and knowledge of the stature and vulnerabilities of other states party to the situation, you are in a fair way to be able to predict her *probable courses of action*.

> To strengthen the reliability of your prediction you should possess two additional packages of knowledge. First, you should know about the courses of action which Great Frusina has followed in the past. . . . Second: you should know, as closely as such things may be known, how Great Frusinans are estimating their own stature in the situation.[15]

There can be no doubt that such information, and the thought processes that lead to it, is a vital part of strategic thinking in general and high-level foreign policy-making in particular. No policies can be adopted or implemented without some view of the potential actions of other countries. Nevertheless, it is not clear why it should be considered "intelligence" and why it should be located in the intelligence agencies. This issue, which involves important questions concerning the relationship between intelligence and the policymakers it serves, has already been discussed in the previous chapter.

For present purposes, it is sufficient to observe two connected consequences of this view of intelligence, which emphasizes the centrality of analysis. The first consequence is that a good deal of the thinking that goes into policy analysis can be, and ought to be, carried out within the intelligence agencies themselves. In intelligence agencies this work can then be done according to some kind of scientific method. In other words, the social sciences can, or should be able to, provide methods of approaching these problems that deserve some of the respect and authority routinely granted to science. As a result, in this view, a superior wisdom may be attributed to intelligence results, even when these conclusions reflect not covertly obtained and jealously guarded hard data, but speculation based on facts generally available to the policy community. In this view, it becomes possible to use intelligence to "grade," or judge the correctness of, policy.

A second consequence is that intelligence analysis can be divorced from the policy process and, indeed, be apolitical in nature. Intelligence is less a specific aid to policy-making than it is a kind of living encyclopedia or reference service whose information should be made available not only to the policymakers' political opponents in the legislature, but also to the domestic public and the world at large.[16] For example, Colby foresees an era of free trade in intelligence, in which nations recognize the

> mutual benefit from the free flow and exchange of information, in the fashion that the SALT agreements recognize that both sides can benefit from pledges against concealment and interference with the other's national technical means of verification.[17]

However fantastic this may sound, it illustrates the power of the view that intelligence is, at bottom, an endeavor similar to social science, if not equivalent to it.

Espionage vs. Technical Intelligence
Collection

No matter how central to intelligence the analytic process is considered to be, the raw data to be analyzed must come from somewhere. While it is true that some of it can be found in open sources (publications, radio and television broadcasts, and so forth), the fact remains that some nations—in particular, the Soviet Union (even in the era of *glasnost*)—do not make public even basic facts about their military forces and the economic resources that support them. Thus, even if Kent's view of the relative importance of open and secret sources were true for more ordinary states, it is clearly not true of a state that conceals almost all the details of the composition of its military forces.

The Soviet Union's particularly strong security measures made it very difficult, in the post–World War II period, for the United States and other Western countries to use espionage to obtain the missing basic data about Soviet military forces. The problem was solved primarily by the development of technical intelligence collection platforms that could pass above Soviet territory—at first, the U-2 plane and then reconnaissance satellites.

These technical means not only leapfrogged over Soviet security precautions, but appeared to be free of espionage's other problems as well. The whole problem of determining whether a human source was trustworthy seemed to have been avoided by relying instead on machines, which could not lie or be suborned. At the same time, access to a particular location could be assured (although the ability to photograph it required the absence of cloud cover). In this way, too, technical intelligence seemed more reliable than humint.

The result was an exaggeration of the importance of techint at the expense of humint, a tendency that has been characteristic of the post–World War II American view of intelligence. This made intelligence seem a more scientific undertaking, not only because it required the latest and most sophisticated technology, but also because it appeared that the uncertainty associated with human agents could be overcome by technical collectors that provided broad coverage of the adversary's territory and enabled one to see what was there for oneself.

The Depreciation of Counterintelligence

Another characteristic of the new view of intelligence is its tendency to depreciate the importance of counterintelligence in general, and deception and counterdeception in particular. This is closely related to the notion that intelligence is a variety of social science dealing with foreign countries. Even though intelligence work obviously differs in some respects from social science, the two endeavors, according to this view, remain similar.

For example, Kent notes that strategic intelligence is, in his terminology, an "extension," in several senses, of the search for knowledge in general.

One of these extensions is that "difficult barriers," which "are put there on purpose by other nations," often stand in the way. Nevertheless,

> important as they are, these extensions, as I have called them, are *external* to the heart of the matter: intelligence work remains the simple, natural endeavor to get the sort of knowledge upon which a successful course of action can be rested. And strategic intelligence, we might call the knowledge upon which our nation's foreign relations, in war and peace, must rest.[18]

For the "traditional" view, on the other hand, the fact that an adversary is trying to keep vital information secret is the very essence of the matter; if an adversary were not trying to hide his intentions, there would be no need for complicated analyses of the situation in the first place.

These different stances toward the importance of secrecy reflect basic differences with respect to what intelligence is. If, according to the "traditional" view, intelligence is part of the real struggle with human adversaries, we might say that in the new view intelligence, like science in general, is a process of discovering truths about the world (or nature) that can be only metaphorically called a struggle. In other words, while there are secrets of nature, they are not pieces of information being jealously guarded from our view; they are simply truths we have not yet discovered. The paradigmatic intelligence problem is not so much ferreting out the adversary's secret intention (as the Korean War example shows, the adversary himself may not know how he will react to future events) as it is of predicting his behavior through social science methodology. This is particularly true the more the emphasis in intelligence analysis shifts to research on long-term trends, often societal and economic in nature. With respect to future social or economic conditions, no real secret can be obtained, because the adversary himself is uncertain what will happen.

The same tendency to say counterintelligence occupies a marginal place in intelligence also affects the importance accorded to deception and counterdeception. By categorizing intelligence as social science endeavor, the new view ignores the possibility of deception. Nature, while it may hide its secrets from scientific investigators, does not actively try to deceive them.

The Audience for Intelligence

The two views of intelligence differ also regarding who the recipients of intelligence information, the consumers, are. In Colby's formulation, the "traditional" view sees the head of state as the prime, and perhaps the only, recipient of intelligence. This view was also reflected in the National Security Act of 1947, which established the Central Intelligence Agency and placed it under the authority of the National Security Council and the president, rather than under the Department of State or Defense. The implication of this bureaucratic arrangement seems to be that the CIA would remain close to high-level policymakers and would monitor and coordinate the work of the other, departmental, intelligence agencies on their behalf.

Since the new view, as advocated by former DCIs Colby and Turner, tends to depreciate secrecy, it is not surprising that it also seeks to widen the audience for intelligence as far as possible. For example, Turner envisages the creation of an international satellite agency to conduct technical intelligence collection on behalf of the United Nations, with the information being made available to the whole world.[19] Similarly, Colby argues that we are, or should be, entering a period of free trade with respect to intelligence, in which the large volume of information available because of modern technology "can be seen to provide mutual rather than one-sided benefits."[20] A philosophy to guide this new era is needed; such a philosophy "must insist on the recognition of mutual benefit from the free flow and exchange of information."

Intelligence and Moral Issues

It may seem strange, when writing on a topic in the usually hardheaded field of national security studies, to discuss moral issues explicitly. Certainly, one risks being accused of naïveté for doing so. Yet, those who reflect on the subject of intelligence have often had to deal with the question of its morality or, more precisely, the difficult relationship between, for example, the seeming immorality of inducing people to commit treason, on the one hand, and its great usefulness and even necessity, on the other.[21] In Sun Tzu's view, the key to success in intelligence lies in one's ability to suborn officials in the enemy's camp. Sun Tzu realizes that this is a questionable business, especially for someone who regards loyalty as an important virtue. He regards "moral influence"—by which he means "that which causes the people to be in harmony with their leaders"—as the first fundamental factor determining success or failure in war.[22] He certainly seems aware that the necessity of corrupting officials and subjects of other states can hardly be squared with the ideal of harmony between subjects and rulers.

Even so, in a manner we might anachronistically refer to as Machiavellian, he exhorts his reader to employ espionage. He argues that the opposite course—which he expects his readers would regard as more "honorable"—is in fact inhumane. After noting the great burden that war places on the people and the disruption it causes to their lives, he admonishes in strident tones:

One who confronts his enemy for many years in order to struggle for victory in a decisive battle yet who, because he begrudges rank, honors and a few hundred pieces of gold, remains ignorant of his enemy's situation, is completely devoid of humanity. Such a man is no general; no support to his sovereign; no master of victory.[23]

The fact that Sun Tzu makes a moral, and not only a practical, argument for espionage indicates that he feels it necessary to overcome his readers' moral qualms against it.

Despite the antiquity of this illustration, the moral question should not be regarded as a mere curiosity. It has practical effects in modern times. For example, in 1929, U.S. Secretary of State Henry L. Stimson, newly appointed by President Hoover, closed down the Black Chamber, the State Department's cryptographic bureau that had been reading foreign diplomatic and other coded messages for more than a decade. He is said to have acted on the grounds that "gentlemen do not read each other's mail."[24] From the point of view of U.S. success in World War II, it was fortunate that a cryptographic capability was maintained in the Army and Navy, paving the way for the major successes of the war in breaking the Japanese diplomatic and naval codes.

The moral issue concerning intelligence resides in the fact that it is a devious or underhanded form of struggle between nations, as compared with armed combat, traditionally seen as more open (and hence more honorable). In its very essence, it involves deception and depends heavily on inducing the adversary's citizens to commit treason. As the Stimson example illustrates, this type of activity was hardly congenial to the typical (and recurring) American optimism toward placing international relations on a higher moral plane. (That communications intelligence is now often regarded as "clean" compared to the "messy" business of espionage may only demonstrate the extent to which our standards of international morality have been diluted.[25])

Needless to say, Stimson's view did not survive the unsettled international conditions of the 1930s, let alone World War II itself. However, the new view of intelligence, as sketched out above, has many characteristics that make it seem more moral than the "traditional" one in the eyes of its proponents:

- the centrality of analysis (understood as a variant of science, and thus partaking of its prestige) as opposed to espionage,
- the primacy of "clean" technical intelligence over "messy" espionage,
- the depreciation of counterintelligence and deception, diminishing the awareness that intelligence involves a struggle between nations,

- the expansion of intelligence to include areas (societal changes, demography, narcotics trafficking, and so on) more remote from the political and military core of the struggle among nations, and

- the widening of the intelligence audience, tending to convert a handmaiden of policy (which is used to enhance national interests, often at the expense of others) into a morally neutral provider of information for the government, its opponents, and eventually the domestic and world public.

Thus, this new view of intelligence can be understood as a reassertion of America's optimistic outlook after the harsh realities of international relations during and after World War II.

8

TOWARD A THEORY OF INTELLIGENCE

In this concluding chapter, I return to the original question, What is intelligence? On the basis of discussion of the elements of intelligence, we are now better able to evaluate the various extant views of intelligence, particularly that presented in the preceding chapter as the "new American view," and to attempt a more general definition.

The word "intelligence" is used to refer to a certain kind of knowledge, to the activity of obtaining knowledge of this kind (and thwarting the similar activity of others), and to the organizations whose function is to obtain (or deny) it.[1] Of these three categories (knowledge, activity, and organization), the first is the most basic, since the other two are defined in terms of it. Thus, the first problem in defining intelligence is to determine the scope of the knowledge with which it is concerned.

Kent provides a definition of what he calls "high-level foreign positive intelligence": the adjectives are meant to exclude intelligence that is operational or tactical intelligence (not "high-level"), domestic intelligence (not "foreign"), or counterintelligence (not "positive"). According to Kent:

> What is left is the knowledge indispensable to our welfare and security. It is both the constructive knowledge with which we can work toward peace and freedom throughout the world, and the knowledge necessary to the defense of our country and its ideals.[2]

Thus, the knowledge involved is that necessary for conducting foreign policy and making the major decisions concerning the development and de-

171

ployment of military forces in peacetime. It is the knowledge, according to Kent, on which national security policy may be based.

Its very title (*Strategic Intelligence for American World Policy*) makes clear that Kent's book is a discussion of U.S. intelligence rather than intelligence generally. Accordingly, his definition of intelligence is couched in terms of the information the U.S. government requires. Nevertheless, there does not seem to be anything about the definition or about the book as a whole that would limit the applicability of the propositions to the United States alone. The basic principles are all general, and, indeed, in considering what one wishes to know about a foreign country, Kent does not look at America's potential adversaries, but rather invents the country of "Great Frusina" to serve as the generic intelligence target. In this discussion, I therefore take Kent's statements as applying to intelligence generally.

As Kent implies (by his use of the qualifiers "high-level," "foreign," and "positive"), his description is too narrow to define intelligence altogether. One would have to take account, somehow, of what he calls "operational/tactical intelligence," "domestic intelligence," and "counter-intelligence." But the most important point to note is that Kent's description of "high-level foreign positive intelligence," as given above, implies that these other kinds of intelligence are not necessary for "our welfare and security."

It seems fair to assume that Kent's definition is focused only on peacetime intelligence requirements. In time of war, intelligence would have to support not only strategic military decisions, but also the operations of military forces in the field. Thus, the operational/tactical level of intelligence ought to be included in any overall discussion of intelligence, and it is hard to believe that Kent would disagree.

The situation may be different with respect to the other two limitations. First, limiting intelligence to foreign subjects seems arbitrary, at least in theory. Threats to the country and its ideals may be domestic as well as foreign, or they may involve domestic groups with foreign ties. As we have seen, defining the scope of domestic intelligence is a very difficult task.

Although we typically speak of national security, a nation acts in these matters through its government, which generally regards the survival of its form of government as a vital interest. Note that, in the definition above, Kent refers to "the defense of [the United States] and *its ideals*." This recognizes that American democracy could be threatened by something that did not threaten the country in a physical sense. Be this as it may, domestic intelligence, in the sense of the information necessary for the regime to protect itself against violent or revolutionary change, also seems to be a necessary part of intelligence. Of course, what the proper subjects of that information are, and how much of it is required, depends heavily on the nature of the government (the regime).

In addition, the defense of the country may depend on thwarting an adversary's intelligence activities, as well as his military operations; counterintelligence as well as positive intelligence must be regarded as necessary for the "defense of [the] country." As compared with the previous example (operational or tactical intelligence), it is less clear that Kent would agree to these additions.

In any case, the scope of intelligence must be broadened to include these areas as well. If intelligence is to provide the knowledge needed to conduct national security policy, it must include the knowledge to support the actual use of military forces to pursue national goals and the knowledge that enables one to frustrate other countries' intelligence activities. Thus, Kent's definition of intelligence must be significantly broadened if it is truly to be "the knowledge indispensable to [a country's] welfare and security."

At the same time, however, that we have to broaden Kent's definition to include knowledge relevant to conducting national security policy, in other respects, the definition is already too broad. A great deal of information (for example, technical knowledge in physics or engineering) may be needed to make informed decisions on some military development questions, but such information would not ordinarily be considered intelligence. Similarly, a general understanding of meteorological phenomena is necessary to plan military actions, but again this type of knowledge would not be considered intelligence.[3] In other words, even when some branch of natural science makes a major contribution to a nation's pursuit of its security interests, it does not automatically become a part of intelligence.

The situation is less clear when it comes to the social sciences. The subject matter of an intelligence analysis (for example, the political situation of a foreign country and how it is likely to evolve) may be similar to the work done in the social sciences. Even so, the two kinds of analysis exhibit important differences that suggest that different approaches may be necessary even if the substantive content is similar.

To be useful, an intelligence analysis ought, in discussing the determinants of the political situation in a foreign country, to emphasize those factors that can be manipulated or changed; the consumer of the analysis is, after all, typically interested in affecting that political situation and not just knowing about it. An academic analysis, on the other hand, will be most interested in discovering the most fundamental causes of a given situation, even if, or especially if, they are immune to change. To the extent that social science can predict the future course of events (which is, according to Kent, why it is useful for intelligence), it must regard the future as already determined.[4]

Thus, the relationship between intelligence and social science is complex. The nature of this relationship can be better addressed in the context of another major difference between intelligence and science—the close connection between intelligence and secrecy, on the one hand, and science and the free exchange of ideas, on the other.

From the point of view of the traditional understanding of intelligence (to say nothing of the popular understanding), what seems to be most glaringly missing from the definition of intelligence as a kind of knowledge is the element of secrecy. For Kent, indeed, a concern with secrets is not an inherent part of intelligence; while noting that one's adversary may attempt to deny one access to the information one requires, he regards this as an incidental problem, akin to the organizational problems that derive from the large size of a modern state's intelligence establishment:

> Important as they are, these extensions, as I have called them, [i.e., subtlety, expertise, *clandestinity* and size] are *external* to the heart of the matter: intelligence work remains the simple, natural endeavor to get the sort of knowledge upon which a successful course of action can be rested.[5]

However, the connection between intelligence and secrecy is central to most of what distinguishes intelligence from other intellectual activities. By depreciating its importance, Kent can maintain the position that there is no fundamental difference between intelligence and social science; the Colby article discussed earlier only takes this view to its logical conclusion when it puts forward futurology of the "Club of Rome" variety as the model for intelligence to imitate.[6]

The connection between intelligence and secrecy in turn reflects the fundamental issue of the relationship between intelligence and science. Whatever similarities might emerge, there is a fundamental difference in the ultimate goals of the two enterprises. The goal of science is knowledge, either for its own sake or to further the conquest of nature—the ability to manipulate natural forces according to man's will in the interests of his comfort, health, longevity, and so forth. However, the concept of a struggle with nature is only a metaphor. In fact, nature, although sometimes complicated and difficult to understand, is indifferent to human efforts to conquer it and is not purposefully acting to obstruct them.

Intelligence, on the other hand, involves a real struggle with human opponents, carried on to gain some advantage over them. It is not surprising, therefore, that these opponents often are trying not only to obstruct one's efforts to learn about them, but also to mislead and deceive one. One side's intelligence failure is likely to be another side's counterintelligence success. Conversely, an intelligence coup by one country implies a counterintelligence or security failure on the part of its opponent.

Once we understand that intelligence is part of a struggle between two countries, we see why counterintelligence is not an afterthought but is rather a part of it. Not only is it important to limit or distort what one's adversary can learn about one, but one cannot even be sure of what one knows about an adversary without counterintelligence capability to detect any deception effort he might have undertaken.

One objection often made to this approach is that it ignores the important role that open-source information can play in the intelligence process. This objection is, however, based on a misunderstanding. Open-source information is vital for both intelligence and social science; the important distinction is that, in its intelligence role, it is primarily a means to get around the barriers that obstruct direct access to the information being sought.[7]

Fundamentally, intelligence seeks access to information some other party is trying to deny. Obtaining that information directly means breaching the security barriers that the other party has placed around the information, by intercepting communications, stealing documents, overflying restricted areas and taking photographs, suborning officials with authorized access to the information, or some other means. But in the absence of direct access to the information, it may be possible to deduce it from other data—open-source as well as whatever secret data is available—that can be analyzed.

In the context of this discussion it may appear that the difference between the view of intelligence emphasizing the importance of secrecy and Kent's is mainly a matter of emphasis. The former view stresses the fact that the adversary is keeping the desired information secret, while Kent stresses the usefulness of open-source information in finding out what one needs to know. To some extent, Kent's emphasis on open sources reflects his view that secret sources are often unreliable. Perhaps one's agent on the enemy's general staff is really a double agent who is providing deceptive information; perhaps he is an imaginative swindler (the operator of a paper mill) who is clever enough to forge plausible war plans to sell at a high price; perhaps the agent is genuine but his involvement in espionage is already known to the enemy, who will arrest him just as he is about to relay a critical message.

While this is true, open-source data also can be manipulated to deceive. Take for example the Arab deception measures designed to convince the Israelis that no attack was imminent in the fall of 1973. They "ranged from welcoming Dr. Kissinger's peace initiatives in September 1973 to planting news items in a Lebanese newspaper about the neglect and deterioration of the Soviet equipment in the Suez Canal zone."[8] The point is that any type of intelligence data is subject to distortion, and analysis of it must take this possibility into account. Indeed, this is a fundamental difference between intelligence analysis and social science: no one falsifies election returns for the purpose of confusing the social scientist who is analyzing them (someone might, of course, do so for other reasons); the intelligence analyst is not so fortunate. In the intelligence context, even open-source information is not as innocent as it appears.

However, Kent's depreciation of secret sources has a deeper motive. Espionage is obviously limited to obtaining information the adversary already has. It is incapable of predicting the enemy's behavior when he has not yet made a decision and hence does not know what he will do. Kent, on the other hand, believes that such prediction is a feasible intelligence task, provided that intelligence learns to use the methods being developed in the social sciences.

It is not only that this method is useful for statesmen. Their use of it is, Kent implies, almost mandatory—anyone rejecting it can be accused of relying on a crystal ball or, to put it more politely, intuition:

> When the findings of the intelligence arm are regularly ignored by the consumer, and this because of consumer intuition, he should recognize that he is turning his back on the two instruments by which western man has, since Aristotle, steadily enlarged his horizon of knowledge—the instruments of reason and scientific method.[9]

Thus, whatever insight into the political situation a statesman may possess is treated as intuition, as opposed to the "reason and scientific method" of the "intelligence arm."

If intelligence could reliably make the predictions implied in Kent's discussion, the policymakers would indeed be foolish to ignore them, and their jobs would be made much easier. Kent's optimism on this point reflects the general optimism of the social sciences in the 1940s and 1950s. This optimism held that adopting a scientific method (such as quantitative methods) and a scientific outlook (such as behaviorism) would enable the social sciences to understand social and political phenomena in much the same way (and ultimately with the same success) as physics understands the atom. In particular, this understanding would be precise enough to support the predictive capability Kent attributes to intelligence.

In general, these prospects for the social sciences have not been realized in recent decades, and they have little chance of realization. The predictive abilities of intelligence are likely to remain much less than Kent envisaged.

This raises a much more difficult question about the proper relationship between intelligence and policy.

Everyone would agree that intelligence is subordinate to policy, in the sense that intelligence activities are directed toward serving the policymaker (although, as already noted, this subordination would be trivial if the predictive capability of social science–based intelligence could be perfected). The range of this service can be quite broad. At one extreme, intelligence is sometimes used as a reference service, a source of answers to very specific questions.[10] At the other, it prepares extensive analyses, complete with predictions, of major issues. In either case, however, it supports policymakers who must make the actual decision.

The belief in the availability (if not in the present, then in the near future) of a social science method that would be as rigorous and fruitful as the scientific method is with respect to the physical world naturally suggests that those who are expert in it deserve to be heeded regarding subjects with which the method deals. Thus, policy should not only accept the facts provided by intelligence (if relevant facts are available, it would be madness to ignore them), but its assessments as well.

Unfortunately, such a social science method does not exist. In that case, intelligence assessments that attempt to make predictions (especially contingent predictions) do not differ from the conclusions that policymakers might draw about the same situations. Other factors would determine the relative status to be granted the two estimates.

The intelligence analyst probably has a greater background in the area and almost certainly can devote greater resources (such as time and access to data) to the effort. The policymaker is likely to know more about his government's own policies in the area and other countries' diplomatic reactions to them, is more likely to focus on the possible actions to influence the situation, and is, in any case, responsible for the outcome. The most comprehensive and policy-relevant assessment of the situation is likely to result from a joint effort between the two groups.

The Dual Nature of Intelligence

Intelligence is concerned with that component of the struggle among nations that deals with information. As such, it has a dual nature, one part governed by the fact that it deals with information, the other part by the fact that it is part of the conflict among nations. The first part, taken to its logical extreme, gives rise to the notion of intelligence as a universal, predictive social science that completely meets the needs of policymakers for information about other countries, including about their futures. Furthermore, like scientific information, intelligence of this sort would be intrinsically capable of being shared; it would not lose the characteristic of being intelligence by being disseminated widely.

The second part, that concerned with the struggle among nations, leads in another direction. Because intelligence is part of a struggle, the obstacles to understanding do not simply arise from the difficulties of the subject matter; the more important of them, and those that are potentially the most dangerous, are put there by one's adversary, either in the form of information denial or deliberate deception. Thus, whatever else one wishes to know, one has to pay attention to the adversary's intelligence services as well; indeed, those services become a prime intelligence target since the reward for penetrating and, at best, being able to manipulate them is so high. In this respect, intelligence has an internal dynamic that tends to transform it into a counterintelligence duel, in which each nation's intelligence service seeks, most of all, to penetrate and manipulate the intelligence service of its adversary.

In his memoir, former DCI Colby makes the following complaint about the way that James J. Angleton, the long-time head of the CIA's counterintelligence staff, conducted the operations of his division: "Indeed, we seemed to be putting more emphasis on the KGB as the CIA's adversary than on the Soviet Union as the United States' adversary."[11] Obviously, an intelligence service exists to serve the interests of its nation with respect to the nation's adversaries. But to do this, it often must focus particularly on the adversary's intelligence service.

When an intelligence service focuses primarily on the activities of the adversary service, it runs the risk of descending into a "wilderness of mirrors," in which nothing and nobody can be trusted and in which everything may be the opposite of how it appears. If it constantly doubts the validity of all available evidence, it cannot make much progress in understanding the outside world. Intelligence would be analogous to a science of physics that concentrated on questions of epistemology to the exclusion of experimentation.

If an intelligence service ignores its adversaries, however, it runs the risk of being completely deceived and of completely misinterpreting the world it is trying to understand. In intelligence matters, analysts can rarely be completely confident of the solidity of the foundations on which they are building; they must remain open to the possibility that their evidence is misleading.

Intelligence is thus caught in a dilemma that reflects its dual nature. Intelligence seeks to learn all it can about the world and its goal may be characterized by the bibilical verse that Allen Dulles, President Eisenhower's director of central intelligence, adopted as the CIA's motto: "And ye shall know the truth and the truth shall make you free."[12] But intelligence can never forget that the attainment of the truth involves a struggle with a human enemy who is fighting back and that truth is not the goal but rather only a means toward victory.

NOTES

Introduction: Writing About Intelligence

1. Sherman Kent, a former intelligence officer, is the best-known and most important representative of this school of thought. The argument was first expressed in his book, *Strategic Intelligence for American World Policy* (Princeton, N.J.: Princeton University Press, 1949; reprint, 1966) and is discussed in detail in chapter 7.

2. Victor Marchetti and John D. Marks, *The CIA and the Cult of Intelligence* (New York: Alfred A. Knopf, 1974), pp. 4, 12.

3. Jeffrey Richelson, *The U.S. Intelligence Community* (Cambridge, Mass.: Ballinger, 1985) is a good example of this genre. In the footnotes, "private information" is occasionally cited as a source; one should probably assume this refers to leaked information, that is, unauthorized disclosures of information by government officials.

4. It should be noted for the record that, prior to its publication, this book was submitted to the Central Intelligence Agency and the Select Committee on Intelligence of the U.S. Senate for security review. In agreeing that *Silent Warfare* does not contain classified information, those organizations are not, of course, endorsing its contents in any way.

5. Kenneth G. Robertson has noted that intelligence studies in the United Kingdom tend to be more historical in nature than in the United States. See his "Editorial Comment: An Agenda for Intelligence Research," *Defense Analysis* 3, no. 2 (June 1987):95–101. This is due in part to the much stricter control the British government exercises over information concerning intelligence in the present and the

recent past. In the United States the focus has tended to be more on current public policy issues involving intelligence. Many issues of this sort were publicly debated at the time of the mid-1970s congressional investigations of intelligence.

1. What Is Intelligence?

1. Following Sherman Kent, whose book, *Strategic Intelligence for American World Policy* (Princeton, N.J.: Princeton University Press, 1949; reprint, 1966), is organized according to this three-part description of intelligence.

2. The term "adversary" is used here in a broad sense. A friendly government, with which one is negotiating a treaty, is in this sense an adversary in the context of the negotiation; each side is presumably seeking to maximize the benefits the agreement affords it, at least partially at the expense of the other.

3. Herbert E. Meyer, *Real-World Intelligence* (New York: Weidenfeld & Nicolson, 1987), p. 6. Meyer is former vice-chairman of the National Intelligence Council, the body responsible for producing the most comprehensive and authoritative U.S. intelligence analyses.

4. A more detailed discussion of this point may be found in Roy Godson, "Intelligence: an American View," in *British and American Approaches to Intelligence,* ed. K. G. Robertson (London: Macmillan Press Ltd., RUSI Defence Studies Series, 1987), pp. 5–16.

5. The Attorney General's Guidelines on General Crimes, Racketeering Enterprise and Domestic Security/Terrorism Investigations, 1983, part III. The text of the guidelines may be found in Roy Godson, ed., *Intelligence Requirements for the 1980's: Domestic Intelligence* (Lexington, Mass.: Lexington Books, 1986), pp. 245–64; the discussion of criminal intelligence investigations appears on page 254.

6. In addition, an intelligence service has many opportunities to make money to fund its own operations or to remit to its government: the clandestine operational capability of a service could be used to conduct such profitable activities as drug trafficking and other kinds of smuggling, and the clandestine collection capability could obtain valuable insider-type information to support speculation on financial and commodity markets. It is not clear to what extent nations have used their intelligence services like this.

7. U.S. Commission on the Organization of the Government for the Conduct of Foreign Policy (Murphy Commission), *Report* (Washington, D.C.: Government Printing Office, 1975), p. 100.

8. See John Ranelagh, *The Agency: The Rise and Decline of the CIA* (New York: Simon & Schuster, 1986), pp. 199–200, for a discussion of the conflicts between the Office of Policy Coordination (the U.S. government's covert action agency) and the Office of Special Operations (the CIA's espionage arm.) See Christopher An-

drew, *Her Majesty's Secret Service: The Making of the British Intelligence Community* (New York: Viking, 1986), pp. 476–77, for a discussion of the rivalry between the British Secret Intelligence Service and its Special Operations Executive, which was established to carry out sabotage activities and support partisan forces in Nazi-occupied Europe during World War II.

2. Spies, Machines, and Libraries: Collecting the Data

1. This categorization lists the most commonly used collection methods but is not meant to be complete. For instance, intelligence information can also be collected by stealing documents or codes from an adversary's embassy. Such theft may be considered humint, but it differs greatly from espionage as described in the text.

2. The term "agent" is ambiguous: it usually refers to the source, although it sometimes, as in the lexicon of the U.S. FBI, refers to the intelligence officer instead.

3. For the sake of simplicity, the discussion in the text is phrased in terms of intelligence officers tasked with spying on the country to which they are posted. This is not necessarily the case: officers may be posted to Fredonia to recruit Ruritanians (such as foreign service, intelligence, or military officers) who are also stationed there. In this case, the officers may be declared (their intelligence connection revealed) to the Fredonian authorities; the purpose of their cover would be to avoid arousing Ruritanian suspicions. Also, intelligence officers may work in their own country to recruit foreign diplomats stationed there.

4. Despite the risks of having Soviet nationals working in the U.S. Embassy in Moscow, reportedly as, among other things, telephone receptionists and operators, the State Department for many years resisted efforts by other parts of the U.S. government to force it to end this practice. Eventually, a decision was reached to reduce dependence on foreign nationals almost to zero. Before it was implemented, the situation was resolved when, in response to the expulsion of a large number of Soviet "diplomats" from Washington in October 1986, the Soviets withdrew the Soviet work force from the embassy. Presumably they believed that their nationals would soon be expelled in any case; withdrawing them suddenly disrupted the embassy's functioning and let the Soviets respond to the American step without escalating the conflict and inviting a further response.

5. Given that this claim was made by opponents of a proposed law, since enacted, to prohibit the disclosure of the identities of intelligence officers, one must take it with a grain of salt. Nevertheless, there seems to be a good deal of truth behind it. Clearly certain practices, such as the extensive use of the (otherwise rare) Foreign Service Reserve (FSR) status for intelligence officers, did help identify them.

6. Cover may also be provided by a business established, owned, and run by an intelligence service; such an organization is known as a proprietary. A proprietary

may also serve as an agent for the intelligence service that owns it in executing tasks other than the collection of intelligence and hence can be useful for covert action purposes.

7. This account is based on John Barron, *KGB Today: The Hidden Hand* (New York: Reader's Digest Press, 1983; New York: Berkley Publishing Group, 1985), pp. 247–314.

8. Frank Gibney, comp., *The Penkovskiy Papers* (New York: Doubleday & Company, 1965; New York: Ballantine Books, 1982), pp. 57, 87–88.

9. Burgess and Maclean both served at the Foreign Office, while Philby joined the British Secret Service (MI6) and rose to be head of its counterintelligence section and its Washington-based liaison officer with the CIA and FBI. See Andrew Boyle, *The Fourth Man* (New York: Dial Press, 1979) for an exhaustive account of the Soviet spy ring that had its roots in 1930s' Cambridge.

10. See U.S. Senate, Select Committee on Intelligence, *Meeting the Espionage Challenge: A Review of United States Counterintelligence and Security Programs,* 99th Cong., 2d sess., 1986, S. Rept. 99-522, pp. 13–15, for a survey of the major cases of espionage against the United States that came to light in 1981–86.

11. See David Wise, *The Spy Who Got Away* (New York: Random House, 1988) for a detailed account of the Howard case.

12. This account is based on Thierry Wolton, *Le KGB en France* (Paris: Bernard Grasset, 1986), pp. 71–73.

13. Allan Dulles, *The Craft of Intelligence* (New York: Harper & Row, 1963; Boulder, Colo.: Westview, 1985), p. 216.

14. Christopher Andrew, *Her Majesty's Secret Service: The Making of the British Intelligence Community* (New York: Viking, 1986), p. 488.

15. *U.S. News & World Report,* March 19, 1954, p. 62, as cited in Harry Howe Ransom, *Central Intelligence and National Security* (Cambridge, Mass.: Harvard University Press, 1959), p. 23.

16. The story is told in David C. Martin, *Wilderness of Mirrors* (New York: Harper & Row, 1980). As the title suggests, Martin's view is that the conflicting stories can never be resolved, and he recommends abandoning the effort to determine which defectors were genuine and which were "plants."

17. Even earlier, balloons were used as aerial observation posts by the first French Republic in 1794 and by the Union Army in the American Civil War. In neither case was great success achieved; both armies later disbanded their fledgling "air forces." See William E. Burrows, *Deep Black: Space Espionage and National Security* (New York: Random House, 1987; New York: Berkley Publishing Group, 1988), pp. 26–28.

18. Andrew, *Her Majesty's Secret Service,* p. 133.

19. William Mitchell, *Memoirs of World War I: "From Start to Finish of Our Greatest War"* (New York: Random House, 1960), p. 59, as cited in Russell F. Weigley, *The American Way of War* (Bloomington, Ind.: Indiana University Press, 1977), p. 224.

20. Andrew, *Her Majesty's Secret Service,* p. 136. At the same time (1915), the appearance of the German Fokker monoplane fighter meant that aerial reconnaissance could be a dangerous business.

21. For a masterful discussion of British scientific intelligence in World War II by one of its greatest practitioners, see R. V. Jones, *The Wizard War: British Scientific Intelligence, 1939-1945* (New York: Coward, McCann & Geoghegan, 1978). The book was first published in Great Britain as *Most Secret War* (London: Hamish Hamilton, 1978).

22. John Prados, *The Soviet Estimate: U.S. Intelligence Analysis and Russian Military Strength* (New York: Dial Press, 1982), pp. 29-30.

23. Stephen E. Ambrose, *Eisenhower: The President,* vol. 2 of *Eisenhower* (New York: Simon & Schuster, 1984), pp. 264-65.

24. Ibid., p. 228.

25. Testimony of Major General B. L. Schriever, *Inquiry into Satellite and Missile Programs,* Hearings before the Preparedness Investigating Subcommittee of the Committee on Armed Services, U.S. Senate, 85th Cong., 2d sess., January 6-22, 1958, part 2, pp. 1633-35, as cited in Amrom Katz, "Technical Collection in the 1980s," in *Intelligence Requirements for the 1980's: Clandestine Collection,* ed. Roy Godson (Washington, D.C.: National Strategy Information Center, 1982), p. 116.

26. G. Zhukov, "Space Espionage Plans and International Law," *International Affairs* (Moscow) (October 1960), as reprinted in U.S. Senate, Committee on Aeronautical and Space Sciences, *Legal Problems of Space Exploration,* 87th Cong., 1st sess., 1961, S. Doc. 26, p. 1100.

27. Burrows, *Deep Black,* p. 107.

28. Katz, "Technical Collection," p. 102.

29. The detection and analysis of electromagnetic radiations emanating from radioactive sources or nuclear detonations (*nucint*) are not considered a part of elint. See, for example, the definition of electronics intelligence in U.S. Joint Chiefs of Staff, *Dictionary of Military and Associated Terms,* JCS Publication 1 (Washington, D.C.: Joint Chiefs of Staff, 1986), p. 126.

30. Thus, electromagnetic waves given off by electric typewriters, word processors, or computers can be intercepted and analyzed; in this manner, the texts or data

prepared on these machines might be recovered. To avoid this danger, the United States has established a set of standards called "Tempest." These standards require that machines of this sort be used to process secret information only if they are surrounded by shielding that reduces the emanations and impedes any attempt to intercept them.

31. The practice of intercepting messages predates the use of radio as a means of communication: couriers were captured and letters opened long before radio existed. In addition, telegraph cables may be tapped if physical access to them is available. Before and during World War I, the British gained a special advantage from the fact that their companies owned and operated the major international cable lines.

32. Precisely because radio messages might be intercepted, important messages are likely to be sent in encrypted form. Thus comint and cryptanalysis, the breaking of codes and ciphers, are intimately related, although cryptanalysis is probably more reasonably seen as a branch of intelligence analysis than of intelligence collection.

33. For a full discussion of British naval comint during World War I, see Patrick Beesley, *Room 40: British Naval Intelligence 1914–18* (New York: Harcourt Brace Jovanovich, 1982).

34. An account of this operation may be found in CIA Clandestine Services Historical Paper, "The Berlin Tunnel Operation," June 1968. (This paper was released by the CIA to me in sanitized form in accordance with the Freedom of Information Act.) The possibility that the Soviets knew about the Berlin operation and used it to pass misleading information is discussed in the section on deception in chapter 5.

35. In his memoir, Herbert O. Yardley, the head of the Black Chamber, is uncharacteristically coy on the subject of how he obtained the encrypted cables. He does note, however, that the censorship imposed during World War I had been lifted and that "supervision of messages [had been] restored to the private cable companies." *The American Black Chamber* (Indianapolis: The Bobbs-Merrill Co., 1931; reprint, New York: Ballantine Books, 1981), pp. 156–57.

36. Jones, *The Wizard War*, p. 198.

37. For a fictional account of intelligence collection through sonar, see Tom Clancy, *The Hunt for Red October* (Annapolis, Md.: Naval Institute Press, 1984). Nonfictional accounts are somewhat harder to come by in the open literature.

38. Minor but unpredictable changes in orbit can be accomplished by firing small rockets on the satellite; the number and magnitude of such maneuvers is limited by the fuel capacity of the satellite, which is typically small.

39. ABM Treaty, art. XII, para. 1; Interim Agreement on the Limitation of Strategic Offensive Arms (SALT I), art. V, para. 1; and SALT II, art. XV, para. 1.

40. Since the provision recognizes the right to do only those things allowed by international law, one might wonder why it is included at all. The answer appears to be that the Soviets wished to make sure that the United States could not claim, in order to provide itself with "assurance of [Soviet] compliance," a right to conduct inspections on Soviet territory. In fact, the provision, as written, does not confer a *right* to do anything; rather, it imposes a *duty* to use NTM in accordance with international law. The next paragraph, which likewise appears in all three agreements, prohibits interference with NTM when they are "operating in accordance with [international law]."

41. See, for example, A.S. Piradov, ed., *International Space Law*, Boris Belitsky trans. (Moscow: Progress Publishers, 1976), pp. 192, 218. This work notes the fear, which it considers well grounded, that "the use of satellites for the study of natural resources in other countries might become a form of legalized economic espionage . . ." (p. 216). The same views are expressed more recently in Gennady Zhukov and Yuri Kolosov, *International Space Law*, Boris Belitsky trans. (New York: Praeger, 1984), pp. 133, 143.

42. Piradov, *International Space Law*, p. 136.

43. Stansfield Turner, *Secrecy and Democracy: The CIA in Transition* (Boston: Houghton Mifflin, 1985; New York: Harper & Row, 1986), p. 92.

44. Jozef Garlinski, *The Enigma War* (New York: Charles Scribner's Sons, 1979), p. 16.

45. Sherman Kent, *Strategic Intelligence for American World Policy* (Princeton, N.J.: Princeton University Press, 1949; reprint, 1966), pp. 3–4. Kent—a veteran of the Office of Strategic Services (OSS), the U.S. intelligence service of the World War II era—provided a peculiarly American theory of intelligence right after World War II.

46. V. Zaykin, " 'Secret' Classification Removed," *Izvestiya*, Sept. 3, 1988, p. 2, reprinted and trans. in Federal Broadcast Information Service (FBIS), *Soviet Report*, September 8, 1988 (FBIS-SOV-88-174), pp. 53–54.

47. One might wonder why such an operation should be conducted by an intelligence agency at all, given its total reliance on open-source materials and on methodologies developed in the academic world that are familiar to the Soviets. Obviously, it need not be, but whether placing it in a nonclassified research center would be a good idea depends on a balance of several factors. On the one hand, it might be easier to attract personnel to such an open center, and its product would be more easily shared with the academic community. On the other hand, special, potentially cumbersome procedures would be needed to integrate this open-source material with secret information or to use this information to support secret intelligence activities. For example, a request for information needed to recruit a Soviet

official to do espionage would have to be camouflaged to conceal the reason for the request.

48. Donald E. Queller, *The Office of Ambassador in the Middle Ages* (Princeton, N.J.: Princeton University Press, 1967), p. 90.

49. What is described in the text is the ordinary activity of a military attaché, which is essentially overt, although there may be cases where he attempts to travel in or near restricted areas to observe objects the host country would prefer he did not. At the same time, however, the position of military attaché (like any diplomatic position) could be used by an intelligence officer as cover.

50. For a discussion of the possibilities opened up by the relaxation in Soviet travel regulations, see R. Keeler and E. Miriam Steiner, "Collection," in *Intelligence Requirements for the 1990's: Collection, Analysis, Counterintelligence and Covert Action,* Roy Godson ed. (Lexington, Mass.: D.C. Heath & Co., Lexington Books, 1989), pp. 42–57.

3. What Does It All Mean? Intelligence Analysis and Production

1. See David Kahn, *The Codebreakers: The Story of Secret Writing* (New York: Macmillan, 1967) for the most complete public treatment of the history of cryptography. Since his book was published, however, revelations about the British success in breaking German ciphers in World War II have added a new and most important chapter to that history.

2. See Patrick Beesly, *Room 40: British Naval Intelligence 1914–18* (New York: Harcourt Brace Jovanovich, 1982), pp. 3–7, 22–33.

3. See Barbara Tuchman, *The Zimmermann Telegram* (New York: Macmillan, 1958, 1966) for a full account of this incident.

4. See Herbert O. Yardley, *The American Black Chamber* (Indianapolis: The Bobbs-Merrill Co., 1931; reprint, New York: Ballantine Books, 1981), p. 4.

5. Kahn, *The Codebreakers,* p. 348.

6. The official Japanese name for the machine American cryptanalysts called "Purple" was Alphabetical Typewriter 97.

7. Such a mathematical theory was developed at the beginning of the 1930s by the Polish mathematician-cryptographers who laid the groundwork for the early Polish successes and the later Allied wartime successes against the German Enigma machine. See, for example, Jozef Garlinski, *The Enigma War* (New York: Charles Scribner's Sons, 1979), pp. 25, 196–204.

8. For example, there is now an academic-style journal called *Cryptologia* devoted to these topics. In addition, the U.S. government's National Bureau of Stan-

dards has developed a data encryption standard (in the form of an enciphering algorithm) for the electronic transmission and computer storage of unclassified government data; it would also be available for businesses, such as banks, that might want to encrypt their electronic transmissions.

9. More speculatively, it might be noted that on the basis of British World War II experience skill in chess seems to be positively correlated with cryptologic ability. If so, the Soviet Union would not suffer from a lack of potential cryptanalysts. Similarly, the British cryptanalysts tended to be musical, as well.

10. Many possible mistakes in using a cipher can help the cryptanalyst. For example, the German World War II procedure of repeating, at the beginning of each message, a three-letter key was particularly damaging: simply knowing that the first and fourth letters of the plaintext were the same (as were the second and fifth, and the third and sixth) was a tremendous help to British cryptanalysts. Similarly, routine message formats, standard salutations, or other stock phrases may provide important clues for cryptanalysts.

11. Kahn, *The Codebreakers*, p. 603. Ronald Lewin, *The American Magic: Codes, Ciphers and the Defeat of Japan* (New York: Farrar Straus Giroux, 1982), p. 113.

12. Kahn, *The Codebreakers*, p. 604.

13. Lewin, *The American Magic*, pp. 116–17. See also Edwin T. Layton, *"And I Was There": Pearl Harbor and Midway—Breaking the Secrets* (New York: William Morrow and Company, Inc., 1985), pp. 453–56, for a discussion of this incident.

14. Lewin, *The American Magic*, p. 117.

15. Summary of Magic intelligence (derived from intercepted Japanese diplomatic cable traffic) dated September 11, 1942, cited in B. Nelson Macpherson, "The Compromise of U.S. Navy Cryptanalysis After the Battle of Midway," *Intelligence and National Security* 2, no. 2 (April 1987):321. The summary does not indicate the date of the message from Japan to Lisbon.

16. See Christopher Andrew, *Her Majesty's Secret Service: The Making of the British Intelligence Community* (New York: Viking, 1986), pp. 331–32, for a description of this incident.

17. Bob Woodward and Patrick E. Tyler, "Libyan Cables Intercepted and Decoded," *Washington Post*, April 15, 1986, p. A1.

18. Stephen Engleberg, "U.S. Aides Worried over Libya Cables," *New York Times*, April 17, 1986, p. A24.

19. See Ronald Lewin, *Ultra Goes to War* (London: Hutchinson & Co., 1978; New York: McGraw Hill Book Co., 1987), pp. 99–103, for an account of Ultra intelligence with respect to the raid.

20. For a rough analogy, one might imagine being confronted with a set of graphs, lacking both labels and scales for the x and y axes, and being told only the general

nature of the phenomenon of which the graphs describe various aspects. One would then be asked to figure out what each graph means and to describe the phenomenon in detail.

21. The Second Common Understanding to article XV, paragraph 3, of the SALT II Treaty states:

> Each Party is free to use various methods of transmitting telemetric information during testing, including its encryption, except that, in accordance with the provisions of paragraph 3 or article XV of the Treaty, neither Party shall engage in deliberate denial of telemetric information, such as through the use of telemetry encryption, whenever such denial impedes verification of compliance with the provisions of the Treaty.

22. Some have argued that U.S. insistence on including an antiencryption clause in the SALT II Treaty backfired by alerting the Soviets to the fact that the United States was successfully intercepting and using Soviet missile telemetry. On the other hand, Senator Gordon J. Humphrey, basing his discussion on news reports, has suggested that Soviet espionage success against a U.S. sigint-collecting satellite "may have contributed to the Soviet decision to encrypt telemetry . . ." ("Analysis and Compliance Enforcement," in *Verification and SALT: The Challenge of Strategic Deception,* ed. William C. Potter [Boulder, Colo.: Westview Press, 1980], p. 112.

23. The President's Unclassified Report to the Congress on Soviet Noncompliance with Arms Control Agreements, February 1, 1985. This report reaffirms the finding of the president's earlier Report to the Congress of January 23, 1984.

24. Amrom Katz, a key figure in the development of aerial photography and photo interpretation in the United States during and after World War II, has noted that, despite the fact that PIs were able to identify the Cuban sites for Soviet intermediate-range ballistic missiles on photographs taken from high altitudes, the U.S. Air Force and Navy conducted low-level reconnaissance flights during the missile crisis to get detailed photography that would be more convincing to the policymakers. "Technical Collection," in *Intelligence Requirements for the 1980's: Clandestine Collection,* ed. Roy Godson (Washington, D.C.: National Strategy Information Center, 1982), p. 107.

25. "Ground resolution" refers to the ability of a photograph to render barely distinguishable a standard pattern consisting of parallel black-and-white lines (i.e., lines and spaces) of equal width. A ground resolution distance of, say, one foot would describe a photograph in which the pattern whose line-plus-space width is one foot would be rendered barely recognizable as such. In a finer pattern—one with a smaller line-plus-space width—the lines would not be distinguishable at all. (This definition, and the citation in the text, are from Amrom Katz, "Observation Satellites: Problems and Prospects," *Astronautics* [April 1960]:5–6; "essentially identical" to Amrom Katz, *Observation Satellites: Problems, Possibilities and Prospects,* RAND Paper P-1707, May 25, 1959.)

26. For a discussion of crateology, see Robert S. Greenberger, "Can CIA Cratology Ultimately Outsmart Kremlin's Shellology?" *Wall Street Journal,* January 10, 1985, p. A1.

27. See William E. Burrows, *Deep Black: Space Espionage and National Security* (New York: Random House, 1987; New York: Berkley Publishing Group, 1988), pp. 108–11, for a discussion of this point. Burrows claims that an intelligence analyst at the Defense Intelligence Agency made this connection, although it is not clear whether the inference was accepted elsewhere in the intelligence community before the discovery of the IRBM launch sites. DCI John McCone did expect the Soviet missile deployments, but it appears that his prediction was based more on political judgments about Nikita Khrushchev than on evidence of this sort. See John Ranelagh, *The Agency: The Rise and Decline of the CIA* (New York: Simon & Schuster, 1986), pp. 394–96.

28. The reason for the emplacement pattern in the first place was presumably that it maximized the antiaircraft missiles' effectiveness. Nevertheless, given the high premium the Soviets placed on secrecy as an ingredient of the deployment plan, a degradation in the SA-2s' effectiveness would have been a small price to pay for not letting the cat out of the bag.

29. Sherman Kent, *Strategic Intelligence for American World Policy* (Princeton, N.J.: Princeton University Press, 1949; reprint, 1966), pp. 12–13, gives the table of contents of one such book about a country of interest prepared in Germany for use during World War II:

  I. *General Background.* Location. Frontiers. Area. History. Governmental and Administrative Structure.
  II. *Character of the Country.* Surface Forms. Soils. Ground Cover. Climate. Water Supply.
  III. *People.* Nationalities, Language, Attitudes. Population Distribution. Settlement. Health. Structure of Society.
  IV. *Economic.* Agriculture. Industry. Trade and Commerce. Mining. Fisheries.
  V. *Transportation.* Railroads. Roads. Ports. Airfields. Inland Waterways.
  VI. *Military Geography.* [Detailed regional breakdown].
  VII. *Military Establishment in Being.* Army: Order of Battle, Fixed Defenses, Military Installations, Supply. Navy: Order of Battle, the Fleet, Naval Shore Installations, Naval Air, Supply. Air: Order of Battle, Military Aircraft, Air Installations, Lighter than Air, Supply.
  VIII. *Special Appendixes.* Biographical data on key figures of government. Local geographical terminology. Description of rivers, lakes, canals. List and specifications of electric power plants. Description of roads. List of airdromes and most important landing grounds. List of main telephone and telegraph lines. Money, weights, and measures. Beaches [as for amphibious military operations].

30. House of Representatives, Committee on the Armed Services, *Lessons Learned as a Result of the U.S. Military Operations in Grenada: Hearing,* 98th Cong., 2d

sess., 1984, H. Rept. 98-43, p. 24. Given the Reagan administration's concern with the Marxist-Leninist regime of Grenadian leader Maurice Bishop (whose arrest and execution by his colleagues set in motion the events that led to the invasion), this lack of maps and other basic data provides an illustration of a failure to anticipate U.S. policy.

31. For a full discussion of this task, described as the avoidance of technological surprise, see Michael I. Handel, "Technological Surprise in War," *Intelligence and National Security* 2, no. 1 (January 1987):1–53. Handel characterizes the importance of scientific and technical intelligence as follows:

> More than any other type of war in the past, modern warfare, based on the continuous development of new weapons systems at an ever-accelerating pace, depends on intelligence. . . . Victory or defeat [in the Battle of Britain] was often decided by the "battle of intelligence" before combat had even begun. The role played by scientific technological intelligence in war will increase in proportion to the technological advancement of the adversaries and the use they make of state-of-the-art weaponry (p. 40).

32. R. V. Jones, *The Wizard War: British Scientific Intelligence, 1939–45* (New York: Coward, McCann & Geoghegan, 1978), p. 104. The Knickbein system involved two unidirectional radio beams transmitted from different antennae that intersected over the bombers' target; the bombers would fly along one beam and would drop their bombs when they crossed the other.

33. Eliot Cohen, "Analysis," in *Intelligence Requirements for the 1990s: Collection, Analysis, Counterintelligence and Covert Action,* ed. Roy Godson (Lexington, Mass.: D. C. Heath & Co., Lexington Books, 1989), p. 82. Emphasis supplied.

34. Even in the case of Soviet economics, where the intelligence analyst's access to data the Soviets do not publicly release might give the intelligence analyst an advantage over other experts, this has not necessarily been the case. In 1977, for example, the CIA produced several studies of the Soviet oil industry that predicted that production would have fallen to 8 million to 10 million barrels per day (mb/d) by 1985 and that the Soviet Union would import (for its own use and for reexport to Eastern Europe) between 3.5 and 4.5 mb/d. Academic and business exports were skeptical of these results, and indeed they have turned out to be wide of the mark. Soviet oil production stayed at or near the 12 mb/d level through the 1980s, and the Soviet Union has continued to be an exporter, rather than an importer, of oil. For a review of this issue generally sympathetic to the CIA, see U.S. Senate, Select Committee on Intelligence, *The Soviet Oil Situation: An Evaluation of CIA Analyses of Soviet Oil Production: Staff Report,* 95th Cong., 2d sess., 1978, Committee Print.

35. Kent, *Strategic Intelligence,* pp. 7–8.

36. Intelligence agencies are sometimes regarded as competitors of the news media, often to the agencies' disadvantage. For example, news reports that U.S. officials followed the failed Panamanian coup d'état of October 1989 on the Cable

News Network insinuated that this was evidence of a failure of American intelligence. But it is an unfair comparison, since the CIA is not designed to provide up-to-the-minute reporting.

37. Kent, *Strategic Intelligence*, p. 38.

38. Cord Meyer, *Facing Reality: From World Federalism to the CIA* (New York: Harper & Row, 1980), p. 352.

39. U.S. Senate, Select Committee to Study Governmental Operations with Respect to Intelligence Activities ("Church Committee"), *Final Report, Book I: Foreign and Military Intelligence*, 94th Cong., 2d sess., 1976, S. Rept. 94-755, pp. 272–73.

40. Consider the following reported remark of a high official of the U.S. State Department: "I had a friend of mine from the CIA come down yesterday to give me a briefing on East Germany. He told me that he revised his paper three times on the drive from the CIA to the State Department just because of things he was hearing on the radio" (Thomas L. Friedman, "In Quest of a Post–Cold War Plan," *New York Times,* November 17, 1989, p. A22). The remark was meant to illustrate how quickly Eastern Europe was changing in November 1989; it also indicates that the analyst's briefing was concerned more with the latest events than with a deeper understanding of the political dynamics of East Germany.

41. See Timothy M. Laur, "Principles of Warning Intelligence," in *The Military Intelligence Community,* ed. Gerald W. Hopple and Bruce W. Watson (Boulder, Colo.: Westview Press, 1986), pp. 149–68, for a fuller description of warning analysis.

42. Gordon Brook-Shepherd, *The Storm Birds: Soviet Postwar Defectors* (New York: Weidenfeld & Nicolson, 1989), pp. 330–31.

43. According to the most recent Executive Order on United States Intelligence Activities (EO 12333, December 4, 1981), the intelligence community is defined as the CIA, the National Security Agency, the Defense Intelligence Agency, "offices within the Department of Defense for the collection of specialized national foreign intelligence through reconnaissance programs," the State Department's INR, and the intelligence elements of the armed services, the FBI, and the Departments of the Treasury and of Energy. Para. 3.4(f). The text of the executive order appears as Appendix II in *Intelligence Requirements for the 1980's: Elements of Intelligence,* rev. ed., ed. Roy Godson (Washington, D.C.: National Strategy Information Center, 1983), pp. 117–37.

44. Avi Shlaim, "Failures in National Estimates: The Case of the Yom Kippur War," *World Politics* 28, no. 3 (April 1976):368–69.

45. Alexander Orlov, *Handbook of Intelligence and Guerrilla Warfare* (Ann Arbor: University of Michigan Press, 1965), p. 10.

46. Barton Whaley, *Codeword Barbarossa* (Cambridge: MIT Press, 1973); Shlaim, "Failures in National Intelligence Estimates," pp. 348–80; Michael I. Handel, *Perception, Deception and Surprise: The Case of the Yom Kippur War* (Jerusalem: Leonard Davis Institute of International Relations, Jerusalem Paper No. 19, 1976); Roberta Wohlstetter, *Pearl Harbor: Warning and Decision* (Stanford, Calif.: Stanford University Press, 1962); Edwin T. Layton, *"And I Was There: Pearl Harbor and Midway—Breaking the Secrets* (New York: William Morrow and Company, Inc., 1985); Gordon W. Prange et al., *At Dawn We Slept: The Untold Story of Pearl Harbor* (New York: McGraw-Hill Book Co., 1981); Harvey de Weerd, "Strategic Surprise in the Korean War," *Orbis* 6, no. 3 (Fall 1962):435–52.

47. See Cohen, "Analysis," in *Intelligence Requirements for the 1990s,* pp. 84–87, for a discussion of the latter event. Cohen argues that although the political leadership in Washington may have been surprised by the Chinese attack, General MacArthur, the U.S. and U.N. commander, was well aware of the massive infiltration of Chinese troops into Korea; the disaster was caused not so much by surprise as by the use of inappropriate tactics against the Chinese Army. This will be discussed in note 52 to this chapter.

48. Lewin, *Ultra Goes to War,* pp. 317–18.

49. Stansfield Turner, *Secrecy and Democracy: The CIA in Transition* (Boston: Houghton Mifflin, 1985; New York: Harper & Row, 1986), p. 113. Turner received the note on November 11, 1978.

50. A report by the staff of the U.S. Senate Intelligence Committee contends that "the question of oil price levels was analyzed in the context of a narrow supply-and-demand framework, which tended to overlook both political influences and such economic factors as elasticities of supply and demand." It also claims that "political aspects of relationships among OPEC nations and the internal dynamics of the Saudi Government . . . were not consistently integrated into the community's economic analysis" (Select Committee on Intelligence, Subcommittee on Collection, Production, and Quality, *U.S. Intelligence Analysis and the Oil Issue, 1973–1974: Staff Report,* 95th Cong., 1st sess., 1977, Committee Print, pp. 4, 5). This suggests that the intelligence analysts involved practiced economic analysis that was too theoretical and hence apolitical.

51. There were elements of tactical surprise, for example, with respect to using artificial harbors to supply the Allied forces until major harbors such as Cherbourg could be captured. See Handel, "Technological Surprise in War," pp. 14–15, for a discussion of the problem these artificial harbors posed for German intelligence.

52. See Cohen, "Analysis," in *Intelligence Requirements for the 1990s,* pp. 84–87. General MacArthur's command believed that U.S. supremacy in the air could be used as effectively against the Chinese People's Liberation Army (PLA) as it had

been against the North Korean People's Army (NKPA). Ultimately, this mistaken judgment reflected a failure to assess the significance of the differences between the heavily mechanized and hence road-bound NKPA (formed on the Soviet model) and the unmechanized and nonroad-bound PLA, whose more dispersed infantry hordes presented less lucrative targets for aerial attack.

53. Lewin, *Ultra Goes to War,* pp. 347–51.

54. Albert Wohlstetter, "Is There a Strategic Arms Race?" *Foreign Policy,* no. 15 (Summer 1974):3–20, and "Rivals, But No Race," *Foreign Policy,* no. 16 (Fall 1974):48–81.

55. This is similar to the question of "paradigm shift" discussed in the philosophy of science—the way in which one organizing framework, such as Newtonian physics, gives way to another, for example, relativity. However, two important differences, both of which suggest that paradigm shift can occur more easily with respect to scientific theory than to intelligence analysis, should be noted: (1) the pioneers of the new framework do not need the tolerance, let alone the agreement, of the upholders of the old framework to publish their views, and (2) it is possible to conceive and carry out experiments specifically designed to decide between the two frameworks. Even so, it has been claimed that shifts are due not so much to the conversion of existing scientists to the new framework as to its adoption by new entrants into the discipline.

56. This is sometimes referred to by the psychological term "projection," which means, more technically, the psychological mechanism by which one attributes to others the feelings or characteristics (such as hostility or dishonesty) that one dislikes about oneself and wishes to disown. While this mechanism may be a psychological basis of mirror-imaging in some cases, the two concepts, which operate at different levels, are not identical; for example, projection could not be the cause of mistakenly attributing to an adversary a characteristic (such as peacefulness or satisfaction with the status quo) that one possesses and with which one is comfortable.

57. The failure of Israeli intelligence in this case is discussed in Shlaim, "Failures in National Intelligence Estimates." A key cause of the failure was the continued adherence by Israeli intelligence, in the face of accumulating evidence of a possible attack, to the "conception," or the view, that Egypt would not attack until it was able to stage deep air strikes to destroy the Israeli Air Force and that Syria would not attack without Egypt. The first and crucial part of the conception reflects, on the military level, the same mirror-imaging that existed on the political level—the belief that Egypt would not start a war it did not stand a good chance of winning.

58. *Al-Hamishmar,* September 14, 1975, as cited in Shlaim, "Failures in National Intelligence Estimates," p. 362.

59. This passage was deleted from the final version of the NIE but survived as a dissenting footnote expressing the separate views of the director of the INR of the

Department of State (U.S. Senate, Church Committee, Final Report, Book I: Foreign and Military Intelligence, 94th Cong., 2d sess., 1976, S. Rept. 94-755, p. 78).

60. Jones, *The Wizard War,* p. 457.

61. Ibid., p. 458.

62. In principle, one could speak of failures of intelligence collection; however, one rarely does so. Part of the reason may be that the most interesting cases of intelligence failure are those for which relevant information was in fact available.

63. It may be noted that, to the extent that intelligence shifts its focus from political and military matters to economic and social ones (as suggested by, for example, former Director of Central Intelligence William Colby, and discussed in chapter 7), this assertion becomes less convincing. An intelligence service concerned primarily with forecasting socioeconomic trends might find that its adversaries were unconcerned about its progress and not interested in impeding it. (But not necessarily: a major Soviet deception effort of the 1920s tried to convince Western intelligence services that communism in the Soviet Union was fading and that its leaders were moving toward an unthreatening nationalism. John J. Dziak, *Chekisty: A History of the KGB* [Lexington, Mass.: D.C. Heath and Co., Lexington Books, 1988], p. 48.)

Similarly, sometimes one wants one's adversary to understand the situation correctly. For example, a strategy of nuclear deterrence (assuming one possesses adequate forces to carry it out and is not bluffing) depends on the other government's correctly assessing that one's forces, even after an initial attack, would still be capable of wreaking unacceptable damage on its country.

64. See U.S. Senate, Select Committee on Intelligence, Subcommittee on Collection, Production and Quality, *The National Intelligence Estimates A-B Team Episode Concerning Soviet Strategic Capability and Objectives,* 95th Cong., 2d sess., 1978, Committee Print.

65. Richard K. Betts, "Analysis, War, and Decision: Why Intelligence Failures Are Inevitable," *World Politics* 31, no. 1 (October 1978):61–89.

66. In the early 1980s, the CIA's Intelligence Directorate was reorganized along geographical lines, that is, the political, economic, and (for the most part) military analysis with respect to a given country or region were combined in the same division. (Previously, it had been organized functionally; for example, all the economic analysis was in one office.) Although undertaken mainly to improve interaction with the policy community, which itself tends to be organized geographically, this was a helpful step from the point of view of the problem discussed in the text.

4. Working Behind the Scenes: Covert Action

1. Paragraph 3.4(h) of Executive Order 12333 of December 4, 1981, United States Intelligence Activities [48 Fed. Reg. 58847 (1981)], reprinted in *Intelligence*

Requirements for the 1980's: Elements of Intelligence, rev. ed., ed. Roy Godson (Washington, D.C.: National Strategy Information Center, 1983), p. 137.

2. Section 662 of the Foreign Assistance Act of 1961, as amended (22, U.S.C. 2242), known as the Hughes-Ryan Amendment. The amendment itself does not name the set of activities defined in this way, but they are commonly called covert action.

The two definitions substantially overlap but do not coincide. Secret foreign influence activities undertaken by a government agency other than the CIA would be considered covert action under the executive order but not under Hughes-Ryan. Secret CIA operations (other than intelligence gathering) in support of a hostage rescue mission would be covert action under Hughes-Ryan but arguably not under the executive order, if the purpose were solely humanitarian and not to advance any foreign policy objectives. (The latter point is admittedly unclear, since it could be said that obtaining the release of hostages is itself a foreign policy objective.) See Americo R. Cinquegrana, "Dancing in the Dark: Accepting the Invitation to Struggle in the Context of 'Covert Action,' The Iran-Contra Affair and the Intelligence Oversight Process," *Houston Journal of International Law* 11, no. 1 (Fall 1988):177–209, for a complete discussion of the various definitions of covert action.

3. Donald E. Queller, *The Office of Ambassador in the Middle Ages* (Princeton, N.J.: Princeton University Press, 1967), p. 93. Queller notes that "[t]he line between legitimate gathering of information and espionage is difficult to draw, ..." (p. 93). He also gives examples of ambassadorial involvement in bribery, subversion, and assassination (pp. 93–95). We are somewhat relieved to read that, despite their bad reputation, "it does not seem that [Renaissance] ambassadors [, even those from Venice,] commonly participated in assassinations" (p. 93).

4. See U.S. Congress, *Report of the Congressional Committees Investigating the Iran-Contra Affair,* 100th Cong., 1st sess., 1987, H. Rept. 433, S. Rept. 216, pp. 37–45, 67–69, 504, and passim for a discussion of this activity.

5. John Bruce Lockhart, a former officer of Britain's Foreign Office with practical experience in intelligence, uses the term "special political action" as a synonym for covert action; this presumably reflects British usage ("Intelligence: A British View" in K. G. Robertson, ed., *British and American Approaches to Intelligence* [London: Macmillan Press, 1987], pp. 37, 46).

6. This definition of active measures is taken from Richard H. Shultz and Roy Godson, *Dezinformatsia: Active Measures in Soviet Strategy* (McLean, Va.: Pergamon-Brassey's, 1984), p. 193.

7. The United States has invented a term, "public diplomacy," that would cover some of the overt active measures techniques but has not created the organizational structures to implement it. National Security Decision Directive 77 (NSDD-77), January 14, 1983, defines public diplomacy very broadly as "those actions of the

U.S. Government designed to generate support for our national security objectives.''

8. In their exposé of the CIA, Victor Marchetti and John D. Marks mention critically a police-training program in South Vietnam; however, their main complaint is directed against the involvement of an academic institution (Michigan State University in this case) in a covert program (*The CIA and the Cult of Intelligence* [New York: Alfred A. Knopf, 1974], p. 234).

9. Section 660 of the Foreign Assistance Act of 1961, as amended in 1974 by P.L. 93-559 [22 U.S.C. 2420]. This provision was watered down in 1985 by the enactment of exemptions for Costa Rica, El Salvador, and Honduras.

10. See Shultz and Godson, *Dezinformatsia,* pp. 133–49, for a discussion of the case and a detailed analysis of the contents of the newsletter.

11. Shultz and Godson, *Dezinformatsia,* p. 38.

12. The quoted material is from Bob Woodward, "CIA Curried Favor With Khomeini, Exiles," *Washington Post,* November 19, 1986, pp. A1, 28. The defection was reported in "Soviet Diplomat in Iran Defects and Flees to Britain," *New York Times,* October 24, 1982, p. A14.

13. Churchill relates the story of this attempt in his history of World War II. He tried to get around Stalin's suspicions by sending a "short and cryptic" message that did not warn of the German attack but merely discussed some German troop movements that pointed in that direction; he hoped that such a message "would arrest [Stalin's] attention and make him ponder," thereby leading him to draw the desired conclusion on his own. Unfortunately, the implementation of Churchill's tactic was somewhat botched by the British ambassador in Moscow (*The Grand Alliance,* vol. 3 of *The Second World War* [Boston: Houghton Mifflin Company, 1951], pp. 357–61).

14. Ladislav Bittman, *The KGB and Soviet Disinformation: An Insider's View* (McLean, Va.: Pergamon-Brassey's, 1985), pp. 112–13.

15. See John Barron, *KGB Today: The Hidden Hand* (New York: Reader's Digest Press, 1983; New York: Berkley Publishing Group, 1985), pp. 32–159, for Levchenko's account, as told to Barron, of his intelligence career and eventual defection.

16. Ibid., pp. 76–81, 85–90, and 93–94. The article, by suggesting that the double-agent operation was an American provocation, was aimed at reducing public support for a tough stand by the Japanese government against Soviet diplomatic pressure; the GRU agent was in fact released. The purpose of the letter—to create public pressure on the Japanese government to accede to the Soviet demand that the pilot be returned—was not achieved.

17. Total concealment may not be possible, depending on the case. Thus, a foreign intelligence service can determine the location from which a "black" radio station

NOTES TO PAGES 83-85 199

is broadcasting by using direction-finding equipment. This information, however, will not typically be available to the average listener.

18. The National Voice of Iran (NVOI) and its inflammatory anti-American rhetoric are discussed in a CIA study, "Soviet Covert Action and Propaganda," presented to the Oversight Subcommittee, Permanent Select Committee on Intelligence, House of Representatives, February 6, 1980, by the deputy director for operations, Central Intelligence Agency. The study is reproduced in U.S. House of Representatives, Permanent Select Committee on Intelligence, Subcommittee on Oversight, *Soviet Covert Action (The Forgery Offensive): Hearings,* 96th Cong., 2d sess., 1980. The discussion of the NVOI appears on pages 78–79.

19. Ray S. Cline, *The CIA: Reality vs. Myth,* rev. ed. (Washington, D.C.: Acropolis Books, 1982), p. 151.

20. Cord Meyer, *Facing Reality: From World Federalism to the CIA* (New York: Harper & Row, 1980), pp. 110–13.

21. Novosti is not an acknowledged voice of the Soviet government or the Soviet Communist party; instead, it is supposed to be an organ of public opinion as represented by such associations as the Union of Journalists and the Union of Writers (Shultz and Godson, *Dezinformatsia,* p. 28).

22. The version provided to foreign media included thirty-four paragraphs on Soviet foreign policy that were absent from the *New York Times* version. In 1977, the *Times* claimed that these paragraphs had been forged by the CIA (John M. Crewsdon, "The CIA's 3-Decade Effort to Mold the World's Views," *New York Times,* December 25, 1977, p. A1).

Crewsdon reported that the CIA had obtained "an expurgated version" of Khrushchev's original speech, a version that had been "prepared for delivery to the nations of Eastern Europe, from which some 34 paragraphs of material concerning future Soviet foreign policy had been deleted"; the extra thirty-four paragraphs made available to foreign media were written by CIA counterintelligence experts in Khrushchev's style and presumably designed to cause confusion in the Soviet bloc countries. Crewsdon does not explain why the additional paragraphs were omitted from the domestic version—the one plausible explanation, that the CIA withheld the forged material from the *Times* to reduce the possibility that U.S. public opinion would be misled, would have been at odds with the article's general tenor.

John Ranelagh concludes, from the fact that the Soviets never disputed their authenticity, that the additional paragraphs were genuine (*The Agency: The Rise and Decline of the CIA* [New York: Simon & Schuster, 1986], p. 287n). According to him, the CIA received two copies of the text, a complete version (presumably from a source in the Soviet Union) as well as the expurgated (Eastern European) version. However, he does not explain why the CIA gave only the expurgated version to the *Times.* He would, it seems, have to argue that domestic publication would have placed the Soviet source in greater jeopardy than foreign publication.

23. U.S. Senate, Select Committee to Study Governmental Operations with Respect to Intelligence Activities ("Church Committee"), *Final Report, Book I: Foreign and Military Intelligence*, 94th Cong., 2d. sess., 1976, S. Rept. 94-755, p. 194.

24. See House Permanent Select Committee on Intelligence, *Soviet Covert Action (The Forgery Offensive)*, for a discussion of this phenomenon in the 1960s and 1970s. Soviet use of this technique has continued into the 1980s; for recent examples, see U.S. Department of State, *Soviet Influence Activities: A Report on Active Measures and Propaganda, 1986–87*, August 1987, pp. 29–32 and 79–80. A question relating to a possible U.S. use of this technique has arisen with respect to the CIA's dissemination of Khrushchev's "secret speech" on Stalin. See note 22 to this chapter.

25. See Shultz and Godson, *Dezinformatsia*, pp. 194–95.

26. The additional paragraphs—the authenticity of which has been disputed—dealt only with foreign policy issues. See note 22 to this chapter.

27. Cline, *The CIA*, pp. 123–24.

28. NSC directive 10/2 (June 1948), as cited in ibid., p. 126.

29. Church Committee, *Final Report, Book I*, p. 145.

30. Cline, *The CIA*, pp. 150–51.

31. Church Committee, *Staff Report: Covert Action in Chile: 1963–1973*, 94th Cong., 1st sess., 1975, Committee Print, pp. 29, 45.

32. Ibid., p. 49. Emphasis in original.

33. Gregory F. Treverton, *Covert Action: The Limits of Intervention in the Postwar World* (New York: Basic Books, 1987), p. 142.

34. Ibid., p. 143.

35. See Church Committee, *Alleged Assassination Plots Involving Foreign Leaders: Interim Report*, 94th Cong., 1st sess., 1975, S. Rept. 94-465, for the committee's investigation of these issues.

36. Executive Order 11905, "United States Foreign Intelligence Activities," February 18, 1976, sect. 5(g) [41 Fed. Reg. 7733 (1976)].

37. Executive Order 12036, January 24, 1978, sect. 2-305 [43 Fed. Reg. 3687 (1978)] and Executive Order 12333, December 4, 1981, sect. 2.11 [48 Fed. Reg. 59947 (1981)]. Both provisions drop the adjective "political," but the meaning is presumably unchanged.

38. Turner's testimony may be found in U.S. House of Representatives, Permanent Select Committee on Intelligence, Subcommittee on Legislation, *H.R. 1013, H.R. 1371, and Other Proposals Which Address the Issue of Affording Prior Notice of*

Covert Actions to the Congress: Hearings, 100th Cong., 1st sess., 1987, pp. 44–49. One might argue that such a rescue mission was humanitarian and not undertaken to influence foreign conditions, events, or behavior and hence not a covert action at all. However, Admiral Turner had no choice but to describe it as such. First, it met the relevant legal tests: it was an activity engaged in by the CIA for a purpose other than the collection of intelligence (the Hughes-Ryan standard), and given that a great deal of the U.S. government's foreign policy activity was devoted to freeing the hostages, it may be said to have been an activity "conducted abroad in support of national foreign policy objectives . . . planned and executed so that the role of the U.S. Government is not apparent or acknowledged publicly" (the definition contained in President Carter's Executive Order 12036 on United States Intelligence Activities, which was then in effect). Second, whatever its motive, the rescue attempt had a significant effect on international relations, since it resulted in the closing of the Canadian Embassy in Teheran.

39. Sefton Delmer, *Black Boomerang* (New York: Viking Press, 1962), p. 120.

40. Note that the Executive Order 12333 definition of covert action cited above refers to activities "which are planned and executed so that the role of the United States Government is not apparent or *acknowledged publicly,* . ." (emphasis supplied). This would appear to envisage cases where the government's role, though apparent to an observer of international affairs, or even reported in the press, is still not publicly acknowledged.

41. Nikita S. Khrushchev, *Khrushchev Remembers: The Last Testament* (Boston: Little, Brown and Company, 1974), pp. 447–48.

42. See John Dyson, *Sink the Rainbow! An Enquiry into the 'Greenpeace Affair'* (London: Victor Gollancz Ltd., 1986), pp. 157–86, for an account of the French government's handling of the affair.

43. Section 662(a) of the Foreign Assistance Act of 1961, as amended. This text was itself amended in 1980 by the intelligence oversight provisions of the Intelligence Authorization Act for Fiscal Year 1981 (P.L. 96-450).

44. In its *Final Report,* the Church Committee ignored the issue of plausible denial in discussing the amendment's effects. Instead, it describes the two results of the amendments as (1) a statutory responsibility of the executive branch to inform Congress about covert actions and (2) inclusion of the Senate Foreign Relations and House Foreign Affairs among the committees to be informed (*Book I: Foreign and Military Intelligence,* p. 151).

45. *Report of the Congressional Committees Investigating the Iran-Contra Affair,* 100th Cong., 1st sess., 1987, H. Rept. 100-433, S. Rept. 100-216, p. 271.

46. See Christopher Andrew, *Her Majesty's Secret Service: The Making of the British Intelligence Community* (New York: Viking, 1986), pp. 476–77. It has been suggested that SOE's existence as an agency separate from the MI6 was due in part

to domestic political considerations: by placing SOE under the minister of economic warfare, a member of the Labour party, Churchill met the demands of his coalition partners for a share of control of the intelligence services. See M. R. D. Foot, *SOE, An Outline History of the Special Operations Executive, 1940–46,* rev. ed. (n.p.: University Publications of America, 1986), pp. 19–20.

47. Church Committee, *Final Report, Book I,* p. 106.

48. The name was later changed to the Directorate of Operations (DDO).

49. Church Committee, *Final Report, Book I,* pp. 107–8.

50. For a critique of the concept of the elements of intelligence, see Kenneth G. Robertson, "The Study of Intelligence in the United States," in *Comparing Foreign Intelligence: The U.S., the USSR, the U.K. and the Third World,* ed. Roy Godson (McLean, Va.: Pergamon-Brassey's, 1988), pp. 26–28.

5. *Spy vs. Spy: Counterintelligence*

1. The term "counterintelligence" is sometimes defined to include protection against "sabotage, or assassinations conducted for or on behalf of foreign powers, organizations or persons, or international terrorist activities, . . ." (The quoted words are from the definition of counterintelligence in President Reagan's Executive Order 12333 of December 4, 1981, on United States Intelligence Activities, para. 3.4[a].) This is a reasonable development, since these activities are identical with or similar to the kinds of covert action a hostile intelligence service might carry out; protecting against them, therefore, is likely to involve many of the same skills and methods as protecting against hostile intelligence activities.

2. The executive order definition of counterintelligence referred to in note 1, above, specifically excludes "personnel, physical, document or communications security programs." This reflects the bureaucratic fact that, in general, U.S. departments and agencies that deal with secret information are responsible for the security programs to protect that information, while the FBI and CIA have primary responsibility for counterintelligence (as defined in the executive order) at home and abroad, respectively. For our (theoretical) purposes, however, security should be considered as a part of counterintelligence since it serves the same function.

3. Harold C. Relyea, "The Presidency and the People's Right to Know," in Harold C. Relyea, ed., *The Presidency and Information Policy* (New York: Center for the Study of the Presidency, 1981), pp. 11–19.

4. Executive Order 10290, September 24, 1951.

5. Executive Order 12356 on National Security Information, April 1, 1982.

6. Ibid., sect. 1.1(a).

7. National Security Act of 1947, sect. 102(d) (3) [50 U.S.C. 403 (d) (3)].

8. *Keeping the Nation's Secrets,* A Report to the Secretary of Defense by the Commission to Review DoD Security Policies and Practices, November 1985, p. 23, cited in U.S. Senate, Select Committee on Intelligence, *Meeting the Espionage Challenge: A Review of United States Counterintelligence and Security Programs,* 99th Cong., 2d sess., 1986, S. Rept. 99-522, p. 66.

9. The current Soviet policy of *glasnost* might be viewed in this light, as a policy established by the top leader (Gorbachev) to advance his political goals and weaken his potential opponents in the party and state bureaucracies by allowing the news media to publicize their faults and mistakes. This is, of course, not to say that *glasnost* cannot develop, and has not already developed, into something more deeply rooted in Soviet society that the top leadership might find difficult to do away with in the future.

10. Until 1989, the Soviet government published only a single number that it described as its defense budget. However, the number was patently too small to include all Soviet military expenditures. In 1989, along with the disclosure of a much higher total defense expenditure, the Soviets explained that the previously published budget figure included only the salaries and upkeep of the members of the armed forces.

11. Similarly, the Soviet decision in 1989 to publish a more (but not completely) plausible figure for its defense expenditures may have resulted from an internal political factor—a desire to increase the new Supreme Soviet's control over military matters. Alternatively, the Soviets may have recognized that the secrecy surrounding the defense budget increased Western distrust and, for that reason, was an obstacle to achieving more important foreign policy goals.

12. *Keeping the Nation's Secrets,* p. 49.

13. Bob Woodward, "CIA Paid Millions to Jordan's King Hussein," *Washington Post,* February 18, 1977, p. A1.

14. Atomic Energy Act of 1954 Sec. 11y [42 U.S.C. 2014y].

15. Sec. 148 [42 U.S.C. 2168].

16. Adm. B. R. Inman, "National Security and Technical Information," paper presented to the annual meeting of the American Association for the Advancement of Science, January 1982, mimeo (Washington, D.C.: The American Association for the Advancement of Science, 1982).

17. The general export controls are contained in the International Trade in Arms Regulations 22 CFR chapter I, subchapter M, part 125. These regulations explicitly address the issue of the export of unclassified technical data; in general, an export license is required except when the data are in the public domain, that is, readily accessible to the public.

18. In the United States, at least theoretically, lack of loyalty to the government disqualified a person from any federal civil service position; however, this criterion

has been in effect dropped with respect to jobs that do not require access to classified information. See Guenter Lewy, "The Federal Loyalty-Security Program," in *Intelligence Requirements for the 1980's: Domestic Intelligence,* ed. Roy Godson (Lexington, Mass.: Lexington Books, 1986), p. 147 and passim, for a discussion of this development. The loyalty requirement is contained in President Truman's Executive Order 10450, Security Requirements for Government Employment, April 27, 1953.

19. Provided that no violent, criminal action had been taken based on this belief. Even then, it would not be permissible to compile a complete membership list of the organization unless it could be shown that the membership at large was involved in the organization's violent activities. These issues are discussed further in the next chapter.

20. U.S. Senate, Subcommittee on Criminal Laws and Procedures, Committee on the Judiciary, *Hearings on the Erosion of Law Enforcement Intelligence and Its Impact on the Public Security,* part 8, 95th Cong., 2d sess., 1978, as cited in Guenter Lewy, "The Federal Loyalty-Security Program," p. 152.

21. In 1983, the Office of Technology Assessment (OTA) of the U.S. Congress produced a study generally critical of the claims made on behalf of the polygraph. *Scientific Validity of Polygraph Testing: A Research Review and Evaluation— Technical Memorandum,* OTA-TM-H-15 (Washington, D.C.: Government Printing Office, 1983). The following year, the Defense Department, whose National Security Agency makes widespread use of the polygraph, published a rebuttal. U.S. Department of Defense, *The Accuracy and Utility of Polygraph Testing* (Washington, D.C.: Government Printing Office, 1984).

22. See the discussion, later in this chapter, of the Cuban double-cross operation run against the United States. Presumably, at least some of these double agents, whom the CIA accepted as genuine, had been subjected to polygraph tests.

23. See U.S. Senate, Select Committee on Intelligence, *Meeting the Espionage Challenge: A Review of United States Counterintelligence and Security Programs,* 99th Cong., 2d sess., 1986, S. Rept. 99-522, pp. 12–15, for a summary of the major cases between 1980 and 1986.

24. Testimony of James Schlesinger before the Senate Budget Committee, as cited in "For the Record," *Washington Post,* July 1, 1987, p. A18.

25. Howard evaded FBI surveillance and turned up several months later in Moscow. Yurchenko redefected to the Soviet Union, which suggests that his original defection might have been bogus and that he might have been dispatched by the Soviets to mislead U.S. intelligence or for some other reason. If so, giving up Pelton and Howard—no longer employed by the United States, they were presumably of no further use to the Soviets in any case—was intended to bolster Yurchenko's authenticity or bona fides. See David Wise, *The Spy Who Got Away* (New York: Random House, 1988), pp. 17–21 and passim.

26. A particularly dramatic case (not, however, involving a double agent) is the famous Japanese bomb-plot message of September 1941. In this message, the Japanese consulate in Honolulu was instructed to provide the precise berths of the U.S. Navy ships at Pearl Harbor. The United States decoded the message but did not figure out why Japan wanted such detailed information. See Gordon W. Prange, *At Dawn We Slept: The Untold Story of Pearl Harbor* (New York: McGraw-Hill, 1981), pp. 248–52.

27. John C. Masterman, *The Double-Cross System in the War of 1939 to 1945* (New Haven: Yale University Press, 1972), p. 3 (emphasis in the original). This work, by the man who managed the system, is the source of the account in the text; further citations are from pp. 30–31, 38–40, 41, 49, and 58.

28. The original agent had worked for the German Abwehr (military intelligence) in the late 1930s; the British, aware of his existence, allowed him to continue operating in part because he had also had some dealings with British MI6 that would have complicated any attempt to prosecute him.

29. Masterman, *The Double-Cross System.*

30. Ibid.

31. Michael Wines and Ronald J. Ostrow, "Cuban Defector Claims Double Agents Duped U.S.," *Washington Post,* August 12, 1987, p. A8.

32. Formally, the All-Russian Extraordinary Commission to Combat Counterrevolution and Sabotage; "Cheka" is an acronym based on the second and third words of the formal name.

33. For a discussion of the Trust, see John J. Dziak, *Chekisty: A History of the KGB* (Lexington, Mass.: D.C. Heath and Co., Lexington Books, 1988), pp. 47–50.

34. John Prados, *The Soviet Estimate: U.S. Intelligence Analysis and Russian Military Strength* (New York: Dial Press, 1982), pp. 42–43.

35. See Arnold L. Horelick and Myron Rush, *Strategic Power and Soviet Foreign Policy* (Chicago: University of Chicago Press, 1966), pp. 42–116, for a full discussion of these exaggerated claims and the purposes they served.

36. See Horelick and Rush, *Strategic Power,* pp. 117–40.

37. Prange, *At Dawn We Slept,* pp. 338, 353.

38. One would also want to know how the adversary processes the information. If, for instance, because of the time pressure of combat, he will not have the opportunity to analyze the photographs fully before having to take action, it may be possible to fool him with an inferior imitation. By the time detailed analysis reveals to him that the object was a dummy, he has already acted on the basis of his mistaken first impression. This is another reason successful deception operations are more to be expected in wartime than in peacetime.

39. See M. R. D. Foot, *SOE, An Outline of the Special Operations Executive, 1940–46*, rev. ed. (n.p.: University Publications of America, 1986), pp. 130–34. For a more complete account, see the memoir of the German counterintelligence officer who ran the operation, H. J. Giskes, *London Calling North Pole* (London: William Kimber and Co., 1953). It does not appear that the Germans used this channel to deceive the British on matters other than the operations of their supposed SOE agents in the Netherlands.

40. This incident is recounted in H. M. G. Lauwers, "Epilogue," in Giskes, *London Calling North Pole*, p. 194. Lauwers, a Dutch SOE agent captured by the Germans, tried unsuccessfully to alert London to the deception operation by transmitting messages without the proper security checks. Unfortunately, headquarters ignored their absence and treated the messages as genuine.

41. Stansfield Turner, *Secrecy and Democracy: The CIA in Transition* (Boston: Houghton Mifflin, 1985; Harper & Row, 1986), p. 65.

42. As with everything else, a trade-off is involved here. Varying the orbit means that some satellites follow one that is less than optimal in its coverage; what is required is a balance between the ordinary measures of cost effectiveness and the more subtle (and less measurable) requirement to counter the adversary's concealment and deception operations.

43. David Kahn, an expert on cryptology, makes these points in "Discussion," in *Intelligence Requirements for the 1980's: Clandestine Collection*, ed. Roy Godson (Washington, D.C.: National Strategy Information Center, 1982), p. 119.

44. The CIA had noticed that one type of U.S. electric cipher machine transmitted an electrical signal representing the plaintext character (the machine's input) along with the enciphered character (its intended output); this electrical signal, although faint compared to the enciphered character, could be picked up from the transmission wire far away from the cipher machine. It turned out that Soviet cipher machines suffered from the same defect, enabling the United States to recover the plaintext messages along with their encrypted versions (John Ranelagh, *The Agency: The Rise and Decline of the CIA* [New York: Simon & Schuster, 1986], p. 140).

45. Ibid., p. 289.

46. Ibid., p. 295.

47. Why would the Soviets would want to close down the operation if they were using it to pass deceptive information? They might have done so to harm CIA and MI6 morale, or because they believed that the Western powers would soon discover that the Soviets knew about the operation anyway, or because the cost in chicken feed (legitimate information deliberately given away to bolster confidence in the operation) was higher than they wished to pay. The discovery may have been accidental in the sense that the repair party was not in the know and stumbled across the tunnel because no one who was had thought to prevent it from working in the

tunnel area (if the Soviets were running a deception operation, knowledge of it would have been kept within a small circle). Once the United States and Britain became aware of the discovery, they would have become suspicious had the Soviet continued to use the cable without removing the taps.

48. Charles Cruickshank, *Deception in World War II* (Oxford: Oxford University Press, 1979), p. 182.

49. This entire controversy has been called the "wilderness of mirrors" and is the subject of a book with that title by David Martin (New York: Harper & Row, 1980).

6. Guarding the Guardians: The Management of Intelligence

1. Loch Johnson, *A Season of Inquiry: The Senate Intelligence Investigation* (Lexington, Ky.: University Press of Kentucky, 1985), pp. 224, 268.

2. U.S. Senate, Select Committee to Study Governmental Operations with Respect to Intelligence Activities ("Church Committee"), *Alleged Assassination Plots Involving Foreign Leaders: Interim Report,* 94th Cong., 1st sess., 1975, S. Rept 94-495, p. 263.

3. On May 7, 1962, Attorney General Robert F. Kennedy was officially informed of actions taken during 1960 and 1961 in connection with attempts to assassinate Castro, specifically the CIA's involvement in this connection with two Mafia figures, John Roselli and Sam Giancana. The formal necessity for the briefing arose from the fact that the FBI wanted to prosecute Robert Maheu, the CIA's go-between with the Mafia figures, for installing an illegal wiretap, and the CIA wanted to forestall this prosecution to prevent the revelation of the entire story. Kennedy is reported to have been very angry about the Mafia involvement, which would have complicated prosecution of Roselli or Giancana for any involvement they may have had in organized crime; he is not reported as being angry about the assassination attempt itself (ibid., pp. 131–34).

4. The best evidence for this proposition is of the "dog that didn't bark" variety. One would have expected major Kennedy administration figures, such as former Defense Secretary Robert McNamara, to express some outrage had they believed that the CIA had undertaken such an action without approval by higher authority; instead, McNamara emphasized, in testifying before the Church Committee, his belief that "the CIA was a highly disciplined organization, fully under the control of senior officials of the government" (ibid., p. 158, citing McNamara's testimony of July 11, 1975). Robert Kennedy's reaction in 1962 is reported to have been similar; see the preceding note.

5. Christopher Andrew, *Her Majesty's Secret Service: The Making of the British Intelligence Community* (New York: Viking, 1986), p. 1.

6. See Winston S. Churchill, *Marlborough: His Life and Times,* vol. 6 (New York: Charles Scribner's Sons, 1938), pp. 482–84 and 526–29. Marlborough's

opponents claimed that these monies were public funds and should have been accounted for as such; since he spent the funds to pay his secret agents for information, this would have been impossible. Churchill makes a strong case that his illustrious ancestor behaved properly in using traditional sources of money to finance intelligence operations, which were not otherwise funded by the government.

7. These provisions originally appeared in the resolutions that established the Senate and House intelligence committees and were enacted into law in 1980. The National Security Act of 1947, as amended, sect. 501.

8. Robert M. Gates, "The CIA and American Foreign Policy," *Foreign Affairs* 66, no. 2 (Winter 1987/88):225.

9. *Antony and Cleopatra*, Act II, scene 5, lines 85–88.

10. Henry Brandon, *The Retreat of American Power* (New York: Doubleday & Co., 1973), p. 103. President Johnson is said to have made this remark at a White House dinner in the presence of Director of Central Intelligence Richard Helms.

11. "Managing/Teaching New Analysts," *Studies in Intelligence* 30, no. 3 (Fall 1986):3–4. The name of the author (apparently a manager in the Directorate of Intelligence, CIA) was deleted when the article was released in response to a Freedom of Information Act request. I am grateful to Eliot Cohen for calling my attention to this article. He discusses it in "Analysis," in *Intelligence Requirements for the 1990s: Collection, Analysis, Counterintelligence and Covert Action,* ed. Roy Godson (Lexington, Mass.: D.C. Heath & Co., Lexington Books, 1989), pp. 71–96.

12. Cohen, "Analysis," p. 76.

13. Charles H. Fairbanks, Jr., "Where Is the Secret?" *Washington Post,* February 25, 1987, p. A23. Emphasis in original.

14. Ibid.

15. Bob Woodward and Dan Morgan, "Soviet Threat Toward Iran Overstated, Casey Concluded," *Washington Post,* January 13, 1987, p. A1. It was this newspaper article that contained the original leak of the SNIE.

16. Ibid.

17. Robert M. Gates, "The CIA and Foreign Policy," *Foreign Affairs* 66, no. 2 (Winter 1987/88):221.

18. The National Security Act of 1947, sect. 501, as amended [50 U.S.C. 413].

19. Gates, "The CIA and Foreign Policy," p. 225.

20. The 1980 intelligence oversight legislation explicitly provided that "the foregoing [notification] provision shall not require approval of the intelligence committees as a condition precedent to the initiation of any such anticipated intelligence

activity [i.e., covert action]." The National Security Act of 1947, as amended, sect. 501(a)(1)(A) [50 U.S.C. 413(a)(1)(A)].

21. Jim Lehrer, of the Public Broadcasting System's "McNeil/Lehrer News Hour," was quoted by Radio TV Reports in March 1987, as follows: "I think the House and Senate Intelligence Committees are colanders of leaks, and it comes from the staff. It doesn't come from the principals . . . let me tell you, when you're 30 years old or 34 and you're carrying all that wisdom and heavy stuff in your head, they [sic] are going to go tell it." Coming from someone presumably in a position to know, such a comment about sources, even in generalized form, is very rare.

22. Leon V. Sigal, *Reporters and Officials: The Organization and Politics of Newsmaking* (Lexington, Mass.: D.C. Heath & Company, 1973), pp. 113–14, discusses the use of deep background to help an official "establish an alibi."

23. Once a reporter has the original lead, he can often force other officials to comment by threatening to run the story anyway; thus, the official faces the choice of having the story appear in print or on the air in a version that reflects the view of the original leaker (who may be a bureaucratic rival) or of providing additional information or another interpretation (confirming the basic facts in the process) in an attempt to make sure the published story is more balanced from his point of view.

24. U.S. Senate, Select Committee to Study Governmental Operations with Respect to Intelligence Activities ("Church Committee"), *Final Report: Book I: Foreign and Military Intelligence,* 94th Cong. 2d sess., 1976, S. Rept. 94-755, p. 522. Halperin, an official of the American Civil Liberties Union, was arguing at this point for the abolition of the capacity for carrying out covert operations.

25. This account is taken from a paper by the chairman of the SIRC, Ronald G. Atkey, "Security Intelligence Review Committee: Legislative Oversight and Government Policy in Canada," prepared for the Conference on Intelligence and Policy, sponsored by the Defense Intelligence College, Washington, D.C., August 26–28, 1986.

26. "The right of the people to be secure . . . against unreasonable searches and seizures, shall not be violated, and no warrants shall issue, but upon probable cause, . . ." U.S. Constitution, Fourth Amendment.

27. P.L. 95-511 [50 U.S.C. 1801-11].

28. See, for example, the proposal to require warrants for "unconsented physical searches" in national security cases in the proposed National Intelligence Reorganization and Reform Act of 1978 (S. 2525, 95th Cong., 2d sess., informally known as the intelligence charter), sect. 341.

29. In a thorough survey entitled "The Study of Intelligence in the United States," Kenneth G. Robinson notes: "So far there has been little work on the nature of internal threats and how these can be linked to intelligence requirements for domestic intelligence." *Comparing Foreign Intelligence: The U.S., the USSR, the*

U.K. and the Third World, ed. Roy Godson (McLean, Va.: Pergamon-Brassey's, 1988), p. 19.

30. Of course, not all illegal actions are of interest from the point of view of domestic intelligence; the criminal standard does not indicate what domestic intelligence should do, only what it should not do.

31. Surveillance of U.S. persons (citizens and legal aliens) is permitted only if there is probable cause to believe that the individual knowingly engages, for or on behalf of a foreign power, in sabotage, international terrorism, or other clandestine intelligence activities that involve or are about to involve a violation of criminal law.

32. A sanitized version of these guidelines was released in connection with a Freedom of Information Act request and appears in U.S. Senate, Select Committee on Intelligence, *National Intelligence Reorganizataion and Reform Act of 1978: Hearings,* 95th Cong., 2d sess., 1978, Committee Print, pp. 774–90. According to the guidelines, foreign intelligence (as opposed to counterintelligence) may "be collected only with the express approval of the Attorney General or his designee" (para. VI.B.3, ibid., p. 782). This requirement would seem to imply that the collection of foreign intelligence information was viewed as an exceptional activity.

33. Para. II.A, ibid., p. 775. Emphasis supplied.

34. The Foreign Agents Registration Act of 1938, as amended, requires "public disclosure by persons engaging in propaganda activities and other activities for or on behalf of . . . foreign principals so that the government and people of the United States may be informed of the identity of such persons and may appraise their statements and actions in the light of their associations and activities." (The citation is from the act's statement of "Policy and Purpose." The act itself, less this statement, is codified at 22 U.S.C. 611-21.)

35. On February 7, 1989, Alan Thomson, director of the National Council of American-Soviet Friendship, was arrested in connection with a bank deposit of $17,000 in cash. The money was allegedly provided by the Soviet Society for Friendship and Cultural Relations with Foreign Countries, which, according to an FBI report, is directed by the International Department of the Central Committee of the Communist party of the Soviet Union. While this may be the first arrest in the United States connected with a Soviet active measures or covert action operation, the actual charge centered on illegal avoidance of the requirement to report large cash transactions rather than failure to register as a foreign agent. (Associated Press story, February 8, 1989; *Washington Post,* February 8, 1989, p. A4.)

36. U.S. Senate, Select Committee on Intelligence, *The FBI and CISPES: Report,* 101st Cong., 1st sess., 1989, S. Rept. 101-46, p. 21. A longer investigation of CISPES was subsequently undertaken by the FBI on other grounds.

37. In 1983, the Levi domestic security guidelines were superseded by new "Guidelines on General Crimes, Racketeering Enterprise and Domestic Security/

Terrorism Investigations" promulgated by Attorney General William French Smith. The text of both guidelines may be found in Roy Godson, ed., *Intelligence Requirements for the 1980's: Domestic Intelligence* (Lexington, Mass.: D.C. Heath and Co., 1986), pp. 225–64.

38. Levi, Domestic security guidelines, para. I.A., ibid., p. 225.

39. The Levi domestic security guidelines do not say precisely this; rather, they state that "all investigations undertaken through these guidelines shall be designed and conducted so as not to limit the full exercise of rights protected by the Constitution and laws of the United States" (para. II.B). This leaves open whether the mere act of investigation is regarded as limiting free speech by chilling it; if so, then an investigation based only on the individual's or group's protected speech would violate this provision. A proposed charter for the intelligence agencies, introduced in 1978, but not enacted, would have spelled this out specifically: "No intelligence activity may be directed against any United States person solely on the basis of such person's exercise of any right protected by the Constitution or laws of the United States" (S. 2525, 95th Cong., 2d sess., the National Intelligence Reorganization and Reform Act of 1978, sect. 241. The context, however, is the regulation of the collection of foreign intelligence and counterintelligence information, rather than domestic security information, with which this legislation did not deal).

40. *Laird* v. *Tatum,* 408 U.S. 1 at 10, 13–14.

41. Robertson, "The Study of Intelligence in the United States," p. 18.

42. *Brandenburg* v. *Ohio,* 395 U.S. 444 at 447 (1969). Emphasis supplied. *Brandenburg* may be viewed as the culmination of a series of cases, *Dennis* v. *United States,* 341 U.S. 494 (1951), *Yates* v. *United States,* 354 U.S. 298 (1957), *Scales* v. *United States,* 367 U.S. 203 (1961), and *Noto* v. *United States,* 367 U.S. 290 (1961), in which the Supreme Court evolved this rule and endowed it with constitutional authority.

43. *Scales* v. *United States,* 367 U.S. 203 at 220 (1961). The Supreme Court is paraphrasing and (with respect to the material inside the quotation marks) citing the trial judge's instructions to the jury; the Supreme Court later goes on to uphold these instructions and state that the "statute was correctly interpreted by the two lower courts" (ibid. at 224).

44. John T. Elliff, *The Reform of FBI Intelligence Operations* (Princeton, N.J.: Princeton University Press, 1979), p. 57.

45. Shlomo Gazit and Michael Handel, "Insurgency, Terrorism and Intelligence" in *Intelligence Requirements for the 1980's: Domestic Intelligence,* p. 134.

46. The precise standard (the "threshold") varies in the different guidelines. Under the Levi domestic security guidelines, the FBI could not use an informer unless it already possessed "specific articulable facts giving reasons to believe that . . . a group is or may be engaged in activities which involve the use of force or violence

and which involve or will involve the violation of federal law" (sec. II[I], pp. 227–28).

47. This, and the two subsequent, citations are from John M. Walker, Jr., "Discussion," in *Intelligence Requirements for the 1980's: Domestic Intelligence,* pp. 194–96.

48. Testimony of Laurence H. Silberman, July 18, 1978, in U.S. Senate, Select Committee on Intelligence, *National Intelligence Reorganization and Reform Act of 1978: Hearings,* 95th Cong., 2d sess., 1978, Committee Print, p. 616.

49. U.S. Senate, Select Committee to Study Governmental Operations with Respect to Intelligence Activities ("Church Committee"), *Final Report, Book II: Intelligence Activities and the Rights of Americans,* 94th Cong., 2d sess., 1976, S. Rept. 94-755, p. 166.

50. See ibid., pp. 225–40, for cases in which purely political information was collected and disseminated to administration political operatives.

51. *Canadian Security Intelligence Act.* Assented to June 28, 1984, Ottawa: Acts of the Parliament of Canada, 2d session, 32d Parliament, 32-33, Elizabeth II, 1983-84, sects. 2, 12, as cited in Atkey, "Security Intelligence Review Committee," pp. 10–12.

7 Two Views of Intelligence

1. Sun Tzu, *The Art of War,* trans. Samuel B. Griffith (Oxford: Oxford University Press, 1963), pp. 144–45 (chap. 8, paras 3–4).

2. Ibid., p. 146 (chap. 8, paras. 9–10).

3. Ibid., pp. 77–78 (chap. 3, paras. 4–6). This view may be contrasted with that of Carl von Clausewitz, for whom the destruction of the enemy's fighting forces is crucial. *On War,* ed. and trans. by Michael Howard and Peter Paret (Princeton, N.J.: Princeton University Press, 1976), p. 90 (bk. 1, chap. ii).

4. William E. Colby, "Intelligence in the 1980s," *The Information Society* 1, no. 1 (1981):53–54.

5. Ibid., p. 65.

6. On July 11, 1941, President Roosevelt ordered the establishment of "the position of Coordinator of Intelligence, with authority to collect and analyze all information and data, which may bear upon national security; to correlate such information and data, and to make [it] available to the President and to such departments and officials . . . as the President may determine, . ." (Presidential Order, "Designating a Coordinator of Information," para. 1). The order is reprinted in Thomas F. Troy, *Donovan and the CIA* (Washington, D.C.: CIA Center for the Study of Intelligence, 1981), p. 423.

7. Colby, "Intelligence in the 1980s," p. 54.

8. See Ray S. Cline, *The CIA: Reality vs. Myth,* rev. ed. (Washington, D.C.: Acropolis Books, 1982), pp. 78, 80–81, for a discussion of the inability of the research and analysis branch of the OSS to fulfill the analytic function of a central intelligence operation. Cline states that "[no] component of the OSS ever used signals intelligence in its reporting" (p. 78). Thus, it lacked access to the major intelligence sources (Ultra and Magic) available to the U.S. government.

9. Sherman Kent, *Strategic Intelligence for American World Policy* (Princeton, N.J.: Princeton University Press, 1949; reprint with a new preface, 1966), p. 155.

10. Ibid., pp. 3–4. Emphasis supplied.

11. Colby, "Intelligence in the 1980s," p. 59. The "Club of Rome" produced a series of studies in the late 1970s that projected demographic, economic, and environmental trends into the twenty-first century.

12. According to Alexander Orlov, a defector from the Soviet NKVD (a predecessor organization of the current KGB), analysis, or evaluation, in the Soviet context "concerns itself more with establishing the authenticity of the stolen documents rather than with the significance of the information. The political significance of the information is evaluated principally by the policymaking members of the government and the Party Presidium [Politburo]." Alexander Orlov, *Handbook of Intelligence and Guerrilla Warfare* (Ann Arbor: University of Michigan Press, 1965), p. 187.

13. Eliot A. Cohen, "Analysis," in *Intelligence Requirements for the 1990s: Collection, Analysis, Counterintelligence and Covert Action,* ed. Roy Godson (Lexington, Mass.: D.C. Heath & Co., Lexington Books, 1989), p. 83.

14. Kent, "Preface to the 1966 Edition," *Strategic Intelligence,* p. xxiv.

15. Ibid., pp. 58–59. Emphasis in original.

16. See, for example, Stansfield Turner's suggestions in his intelligence memoir, *Secrecy and Democracy: The CIA in Transition* (Boston: Houghton Mifflin, 1985; New York: Harper & Row, 1986). After proposing the creation of an Open Skies Agency that would release satellite reconnaissance information to the world at large, he concludes:

Our intelligence capabilities are suited to this special role on behalf of our own security and the welfare of all mankind, because we have reconciled the necessary secrecy of intelligence to the democratic processes on which our government is founded. . . . we have opened vast new opportunities to demonstrate the superiority of our democratic system through the employment of our intelligence capabilities to serve not only our nation, but the rest of the world and all mankind (p. 285).

17. Colby, "Intelligence in the 1980s," p. 69.

18. Kent, *Strategic Intelligence,* p. viii. (Emphasis supplied.)

19. Turner, *Secrecy and Democracy*, pp. 279–85. Turner does not state clearly how far he would go in making U.S. technical collection capabilities, or the information obtained by means of them, available to the entire world. While he notes that we *"might"* (emphasis supplied) begin by providing only "intelligence collected by systems so old that they were no longer a mystery to the Soviets" (p. 282), he also believes that "it will not be long before we reach a point where all satellite photography will be so good that the differences between various models of satellites will be insignificant" (p. 280).

20. This, and the subsequent, citation are from Colby, "Intelligence in the 1980s," p. 69.

21. Of course, committing treason against a tyrannical or aggressive regime is defensible in moral terms. In the case of an Oleg Penkovskiy, the motivation was of such an ideological character, and Western intelligence officers did not have to manipulate or suborn him in any manner. In other cases, however, where the motivation is money or excitement, the intelligence officer often must play on these weaknesses to help the potential spy succumb more fully to them. For a fuller discussion of these issues, see E. Drexel Godfrey, "Ethics and Intelligence," *Foreign Affairs* 56, no. 3 (April 1978):624–42, and a response to it by Arthur L. Jacobs in "Comments and Correspondence," *Foreign Affairs* 56, no. 4 (July 1978):867–75.

22. Sun Tzu, *The Art of War*, pp. 63–64 (chap. 1, paras. 2–4).

23. Ibid., p. 144 (chap. 8, para. 2).

24. Henry L. Stimson and McGeorge Bundy, *On Active Service in Peace and War* (New York: Harper Bros., 1948), p. 188. Stimson probably did not make this famous and oft-quoted remark at the time; he expressed the thought later on, in the course of defending his decision both as appropriate to 1929, when "the world was striving with good will for lasting peace, and in this effort all the nations were parties," and as not inconsistent with his later support (as secretary of war) for cryptanalytic efforts (ibid). However, it is unlikely that the World War II successes could have been achieved without an ongoing effort. For example, the successful U.S. attack on the Japanese Purple enciphering machine, first used in 1939, depended critically on the fact that the previous Red machine, dating from 1931, had already been mastered. See Ronald Lewin, *American Magic: Codes, Ciphers and the Defeat of Japan* (New York: Farrar Straus Giroux, 1982), pp. 42–43.

25. Consider, for example, David Kahn's discussion of this issue:

> Immanuel Kant, in his book, *Perpetual Peace,* stated that spying is a kind of crime against the international order because if discovered, it causes international difficulties. But this doesn't seem to happen with SIGINT (*Intelligence Requirements for the 1980's: Clandestine Collection,* ed. Roy Godson [Washington, D.C.: National Strategy Information Center, 1982], p. 120).

In fact, however, when, in 1931, Herbert Yardley, the head of the Black Chamber, revealed that the United States had read the encrypted messages between Tokyo and its delegation to the Washington Naval Arms Limitation talks (1921–22), it caused quite a sensation in Japan (*The American Black Chamber* [Indianapolis: The Bobbs-Merrill Co., 1931; reprint, New York: Ballantine Books, 1981], pp. 187–211).

Similarly, E. Drexel Godfrey, Jr., a former CIA officer, argues that "photographic and audio satellites and other interception devices are immensely expensive, but they have the advantage of doing only minimal damage to the ethical standards of the operators and processors" ("Ethics and Intelligence," p. 637).

8. *Toward a Theory of Intelligence*

1. As noted in chapter 1, this threefold description of intelligence as knowledge, activity, and organization is taken from Sherman Kent's *Strategic Intelligence for American World Policy* (Princeton, N.J.: Princeton University Press, 1949; reprint 1966). Kent, however, does not regard the denial of information to others as a major component of intelligence.

2. Kent, *Strategic Intelligence*, pp. 3–4.

3. If during time of war it is necessary to use clandestine or technical means (such as agents' reports or communications intercepts) to learn about weather conditions over enemy territory, then the term "meteorological intelligence" might be used to describe the resulting information. However, the "intelligence" part of the term clearly refers to the methods by which the raw data are obtained, not the meteorological knowledge that allows it to be evaluated or that permits forecasts to be made on the basis of it.

4. As Willmoore Kendall wrote in 1949, in an important review of Kent's book: "The course of events is conceived [by the 'state of mind' reflected in Kent's book] not as something you try to influence but as a tape all printed up inside a machine; and the job of intelligence is to tell the planners how it reads" ("The Function of Intelligence," *World Politics* 1, no. 6 [July 1949]:549).

5. Kent, *Strategic Intelligence*, p. viii. Emphasis supplied.

6. William E. Colby, "Intelligence for the 1980s," *The Information Society* 1, no. 1 (1981):59.

7. For this formulation of the relationship between intelligence and open-source information, I am indebted to Michael Herman of Nuffield College, Oxford, who proposed it at a panel of the 1989 Convention of the International Studies Association.

8. Avi Shlaim, "Failures in National Intelligence Estimates: The Case of the Yom Kippur War," *World Politics* 28, no. 3 (April 1976):355.

9. Kent, *Strategic Intelligence*, pp. 206–7.

10. According to Kent, this is known as "spot intelligence," or, less respectfully, "Information Please" (ibid., pp. 28–29). An intelligence service like the CIA thus serves as a reference service, similar to the function performed for the U.S. Congress by the Congressional Research Service of the Library of Congress.

11. William E. Colby, *Honorable Men: My Life in the CIA* (New York: Simon & Schuster, 1978), p. 245.

12. Ray S. Cline, *The CIA: Reality vs. Myth,* rev. ed. (Washington, D.C.: Acropolis Books Ltd., 1982), p. 175.

INDEX

Allende, Salvador, 87–88
American Association for the Advancement of Science, 105
Analysis of intelligence information, 2, 7, 8, 37–71, 77. *See also* Photo interpretation
  cryptanalysis, 38–45, 186 n32
  forecasting, 8, 37, 196 n63
  National Intelligence Council, 182 n3
  technical analysis, 37
  technical assistance, 76
  telemetry analysis, 45–47
    U.S. access to Soviet telemetric information, 46
Angleton, James J., 178
Assassination. *See* Castro, Fidel; CIA

Bittman, Ladislav, 82
Board for International Broadcasting, 84, 93
Brzezinski, Zbigniew, 60

Canada, 111
  Canadian Security Intelligence Review Committee (SIRC), 147–48
  Canadian Security Intelligence Service (CSIS), 147, 158
  and domestic intelligence activities, 158
  Privy Council, 147–48
  Royal Canadian Mounted Police, 147
Carter, Jimmy, 24, 60, 88–90

Castro, Fidel, 89, 133–34, 147, 207 n3
Church Committee (1975)
  and CIA, 207 n4
  and covert action, 146–47
  and domestic intelligence investigations, 133–34, 155–57
  National Intelligence Estimate on Soviet offensive nuclear forces (1969), 65, 166
  and plausible denial, 201 n44
Churchill, Winston, 81, 95, 198 n13
CIA (Central Intelligence Agency), 36, 55, 95, 128, 179
  analysis of information and covert action, 8, 54, 74, 86, 161–63
  and assassinations, 89–90, 133–34
  assistance to Italy, 75
  and Church Committee, 207 n4
  and Congress, 135–36
  covert funding, 84, 86
  and Cuban double-agent operations, 115
  "current events syndrome," 55, 193 n40
  failures of, xv, 36, 56–57, 59–60, 63, 133–34, 205 n26
  Intelligence Directorate of, 196 n66
  and Soviet forgeries, 82
  submission of this book to, 181 n4
Classification of information, 100–5
  Atomic Energy Act (1954), 104
  communications security, 105, 116–17
  and defense budgets, 101–2

217

Classification of information (*cont.*)
National Security Act (1947), 100, 168
overclassification, 102–3
Patent Secrecy Act (1952), 105
public accountability for actions, 103–4
technological information, 104–5
Cline, Ray, 86–87
Colby, William, 160–63, 165, 167–68, 174, 178
Collection of intelligence information
activities, 7–8, 11, 92, 125
counterespionage, 8, 109–15, 121
covert action, 7, 73
denying certain information to adversaries, 8, 182 n2
implementation of policy, 8
motivations to commit espionage, 16–17, 108
nation's foreign policy, 73, 171
and nature of target, 18
"positive" foreign intelligence, 110–11
Counterdeception, 123–28
German use of against British in Netherlands, 123–24
U.S.-U.K. tunnel operation (Berlin), 126–27, 206–7 n47
Counterespionage, 109–15
Counterintelligence, 7–9, 99–129, 166, 173, 202 n1, 202 n2
Coup d'état. *See* Covert action
Covert action, 3, 8, 73–97
coup d'état, 60, 73, 76, 87, 88
Foreign Assistance Act (1961), 197 n2, 198 n9
forgery, 85, 89, 91
Hughes-Ryan Amendment, 74, 93, 197 n2, 200–1 n38
information and disinformation, 81–83, 85
and plausible denial, 92–94, 132–34
propaganda, 8, 83–85, 91
"special political action," 74, 197 n5
Cryptanalysis, 25–27, 37, 38–42. *See also* Double-Cross System; Germany; Japan; United Kingdom
British skills in WWII, 25, 43–45, 114, 122
fragility of, 42–45
history of, 39–42
mistakes in using cipher, 189 n10
U.S. breaking Libyan codes, 44, 102
Cryptology/cryptography

correlation with skill at chess, 189 n9
history of, 39–42, 169

Deception operations, 2, 8, 82, 118–23. *See also* Propaganda
blocking intelligence-gathering channels, 121
false signals, 120–22
feedback, 121–22
disinformation, 81–82, 85
and intelligence failures, 119–29
and self-deception, 122–23
true signals, 120–22
Domestic intelligence, 4, 148, 172
and constitutional law, 148–52, 209 n26
criminal standard, 149–58
and counterterrorism, 154–56
and personal security, 152–53
support groups, 153–56
Foreign Agent Registration Act (FARA), 150–51, 210 n34, 210 n35
Foreign Intelligence Surveillance Act (1978), 148–49
Levi guidelines, 149–51, 153, 156, 210–11 n37, 211 n39, 211–12 n46
and national security cases, 148, 150, 209 n28
violation of privacy, 151–52
Double agents (of U.S.S.R.)
Blake, George, 126
Burgess, Guy, 17, 184 n9
and defectors, 20
Hermann, Rudolf, 15
Howard, Edward Lee, 17, 111, 204 n25
MacLean, Donald, 17, 184 n9
Pelton, Ronald, 111, 204 n25
Penkovskiy, Oleg, 16, 85, 214 n21
Philby, Harold ("Kim"), 17, 184 n9
Prime, Geoffrey, 107
Double-agent operations, 2, 18, 111–15, 120, 198 n16
Yurchenko, Vitaliy, 111, 204 n25
Double-Cross System (U.K.), 18, 113–15, 119, 120, 122–23, 127. *See also* Cryptanalysis; United Kingdom

Eisenhower, Dwight David, 22–23, 92–93
and Allen Dulles, 18

Elliff, John, 153
Encryption, 2, 38. *See also* Germany;
     Japan; United Kingdom
  cipher, 38, 40, 116
  codebook, 38, 40
  Cryptologia, 188–89 n8
  data encryption standard, 188–89 n8
  fiber-optic transmission, 32, 117
  microwave transmission, 116–17
  scrambling devices, 116
  in World War II, 41–43
  and Zimmerman telegram (1917), 40

Fairbanks, Charles, 140–41
FBI (Federal Bureau of Investigation),
     5–6, 149–50, 156–57
Ford, Gerald, 89–90
France
  DGSE (Direction Générale de la Secu-
     rité Extérieure), 93
  and German Enigma coding machine,
     32
  and *Rainbow Warrior* incident, 89, 90,
     93
  Secret Service (SDECE), 17

Gates, Robert M., 135, 143, 144–45
Gazit, Shlomo, 154–55
Germany (West), 15, 80, 81
  Abwehr, 114
  counterdeception, 123–24
  Enigma coding machine, 32, 41, 42,
     45
  intelligence failures in world wars, 18,
     25, 45, 59, 61, 113–15, 119–20,
     122, 127
  and Soviet targeting, 15, 86
  technical developments, 21, 27, 50
  U.S.-U.K. tunnel (Berlin), 26, 127
  Zimmerman telegram (1917), 40
Grenada, 34, 49
GRU (U.S.S.R. Committee for Military
     Intelligence)
  double agent in, 83, 111
  use of moles, 15–17

Haig, Alexander, 143
Halperin, Morton, 146
Helms, Richard, 65
Human intelligence collection (humint),

11–20, 166. *See also* Intelligence
     officers
  compared to technit, 30–33
  "dead drop," 20, 109
  and deception, 127–28
  defectors, 20, 83, 111, 127–28
  nonofficial cover officials (NOCs), 12–
     14
  official cover, 12–13, 110
  personality reports, 15, 35
  proprietary cover, 183–4 n6
  quality control, 17–18
  "source," 11–12
  Soviet use of against U.S. and U.K.,
     16–17
  surveillance, 109–10
  "tradecraft," 19–20

Influence actions of foreign governments,
     77–80, 82
Inman, Admiral Bobby Ray, 105
Intelligence
  consumers, 165, 173, 176
  definition of, 1, 171
  and economics, 6–7, 53
     Soviet, 192 n34, 203 n11
  development and deployment, 172
  and law enforcement, 4–6
     informers, use of, 5, 33
  military, 51–52
  political, 52
  recruited source of, 15–17, 183 n3
  relationship between intelligence and
     the policymakers, 165, 176
  terrorism, 5, 19, 33, 150, 154–56
  walk-in source of, 15–17
Intelligence activities, 1, 74, 126, 168.
     See also Cryptanalysis; Cryptology/
     cryptography; Encryption
  collection and analysis of information,
     2, 28–29, 177
  counterintelligence analysis, 2, 82,
     128–29, 166
  decryption of coded messages, 2, 32,
     38, 39
  electromechanical cipher machines, 32,
     41, 42, 45, 206 n44, 214 n24
  espionage, 2, 80, 176
  indications and warnings (I&W), 55–
     57
  interception of communications, 2,
     24–27, 116–17

Intelligence activities (*cont.*)
  radio traffic, 27, 41, 74, 116–17, 127
    Knickbein system, 50, 192 n32
  research and analysis, 2, 164
  struggle between adversaries, 2, 161,
    175, 177
Intelligence failures
  causes of failure, 62–67, 191–92 n30,
    195 n57
    improper security checks, 206 n40
    mirror-imaging, 64–67, 71, 195 n56
  and deception operations, 119–29
  solutions to intelligence failure, 67–71
  types of failure, 59–61
Intelligence information
  analysis and assessment of, 1, 2, 161,
    178
  centrality of, 165, 169
  free flow and exchange, 165
  verification, 165
Intelligence officers, 11–12, 110, 183 n2
  Foreign Service Reserve (FSR) sta-
    tus for, 183 n5
  handler, 12
  illegal officers, 14
  "legal" officers, 14
  "mailbox," 12
  "mole," use of, 15
  "station," 13
Intelligence organizations, 1. *See also*
    CIA; FBI; KGB
  British, 95, 113, 123, 126
  characteristics of, 2–3
  clandestine collection capabilities of,
    182 n6
  French, 17, 93
  rivalries between, 183–84 n8
  undercover agents, use of, 3, 15
  variations among, 58–59
Intelligence "product," 2, 37, 49, 53–71
  National Intelligence Daily (NID), 54
  national intelligence estimate (NIE),
    58, 140
  President's Daily Brief, 54–55
  special national intelligence estimate
    (SNIE), 58, 141
International law. *See also* SALT
  ABM Treaty, 29
  and diplomatic immunity, 12
  Intermediate Range Nuclear Forces
    (INF) Treaty, 36
  International Trade in Arms Regula-
    tions, 203 n17

"national technical means" of verifica-
    tion, 29–30, 187 n40
  Outer Space Treaty, 29
  restrictions on overflying another coun-
    try without consent, 22, 29
Iran, 81, 83, 84, 90, 93
  seizure of U.S. Embassy in Tehran, 90
  Soviet intentions toward, 140–41
  U.S. "listening posts" in, 46
"Iron Curtain," 18
Israel, 58, 59, 64–65, 154, 175, 195 n57

Japan, 83, 169
  attack on Pearl Harbor, 59, 63, 121
  cryptanalysis, 42–43
  "Purple" coding machine, 41

Kennedy, John, 24, 134
Kent, Sherman, 54, 162, 164, 181 n1
  *Strategic Intelligence for American
    World Policy,* 172, 191 n29, 215 n1
KGB (U.S.S.R. Committee for State Se-
    curity), 111. *See also* Double agents
    (U.S.S.R.)
  acquisition of Western technology, 6,
    16
  Cheka, 119
  and Iran, 81, 82
  and moles, 15
  NKVD, 59
Khrushchev, Nikita, 24, 85, 93
Korean War (1950), 22, 59, 61
Kremlinology, 35

Levchenko, Stanislav, 83
Levi, Edward, 149–50, 153, 156. *See
    also* Domestic intelligence
Libya, 44, 92, 102

Management of intelligence
  authorization issues, 134–35
  democracy and secrecy, 144–48
  expertise and policy, 136–44
  funding, 134–35, 144
  history of, 134–35
  and independence of intelligence, 136,
    140, 141–44
  paper trail, 133, 135
  plausible denial doctrine, 132–34

and policymakers, 134–35, 137–45
secrecy and control, 131–34
and intelligence, 174
Masterman, John, 113
McDonald, Admiral Wesley, 49
"Meteorologic intelligence," 215 n3
Meyer, Cord, 54–55
Mirror-imaging. See Intelligence failures
Multidisciplinary counterintelligence
(MDCI), 115–18
communications security, 116–17
emanations security, 117–18

National security, and the type of government, 3–4
National Security Agency (NSA), 54.
See also Classification of information
National Security Council (NSC), 75
National Security Decision Directive, 77,
197–98 n7
National technical means (NTM). See
SALT
Nicaragua, 75, 89, 94, 145, 147
Nixon, Richard, 65
Noriega, Manuel, 90

Office of Strategic Services (OSS), 161
OPEC (Organization of Petroleum Exporting Countries), 34
Open sources
collecting and cataloging information
from, 34, 48–49, 175
data banks, 48–49
diplomatic and attaché reporting, 35–
36
and intelligence agencies, 187–88 n47
predictions from, 34, 57–58, 192 n34
publications and broadcasts, 7, 33–35,
166
Organization of East Caribbean States, 49

"Paradigm shift," 195 n55
Pathé, Pierre-Charles, 80, 82
Photographic/imagery intelligence (photint or imint), 21–24, 47–48, 205
n38
aerial photoreconnaissance, 22–24,
28–29, 118, 120–21, 124–25, 133,
190 n24

"Open Skies" plan, Soviet rejection
of, 22–23, 213 n16
Photo interpretation (PI), 21–24, 37, 47–
48, 124–25, 205 n38
ground resolution distance, 47, 124,
190 n25
and "Open Skies" plan, 22
Propaganda, 83–85, 91

Radio Free Europe, 83, 93
Radio Liberty, 83, 93
Radio Moscow, 76, 93
Ranelaugh, John, 126
Reagan, Ronald, 44, 46, 89–90, 94
Iran-Contra affair, 93

SALT (Strategic Arms Limitations Talks)
I/II, 24, 29–30, 46, 57
antiencryption clause in, 190 n22
and national technical means (NTM),
29–30
Second Common Understanding to,
190 n21
violation of, 93
Security, 99, 105–9, 120. See also Counterintelligence
personnel security, 105–8
polygraphs, 107–8, 204 n21, 204
n22
Privacy Act (1974), 107
physical security, 108–9
Shultz, George, 107
Signals intelligence (sigint), 24–27, 213
n8, 214 n25
communications intelligence (comint),
25–27, 125
compromise of, 107
and cryptanalysis, 25–27, 186 n32
electronic intelligence (elint), 25, 27
nucint, 185 n29
telemetry intelligence (telint), 25, 27,
37, 45–46
"Tempest," 185–86 n30
Silberman, Laurence, 157
Soviet Union. See U.S.S.R.
Surveillance, 19–20, 109–10, 210 n31
"brush pass," 19–20, 109
Foreign Intelligence Surveillance Act
(1978), 148
Freedom of Information Act, 210 n32
satellite, 28–29, 47–48, 206 n42

Technical intelligence collection (techint), 20–36, 107, 121, 165, 169,
   214 n19. *See also* Photographic/
   imagery intelligence; Signals intelligence
   compared to humint, 30–33
   and deception operations, 121, 178
   emission control (emcon), 121
   fiber-optic/laser-beam communications,
      32, 117
   satellite reconnaissance, 23–24, 28–29,
      118, 120–21, 124–25
   sensors, 28
   "signature," 33, 47–48
Terrorism, 5, 75, 89
Truman, Harry (S), 100, 164
Turner, Admiral Stansfield, 30–31, 60,
   90
Tzu, Sun, 159–60, 168–69

U-2 reconnaissance plane, 23–24, 92,
   166
United Kingdom, 8, 16, 107, 134. *See
   also* Cryptanalysis; Double-Cross
   System
   British Government Communications
      Headquarters (GCHQ), 107
   communications intelligence break-
      throughs, 25, 27, 40, 50
   and D-Day landings, 18, 59, 61, 114,
      119, 122–23, 127
   and development of infrared and radar,
      24
   Government Code and Cypher School,
      44
   MI5, 113
   MI6, 95, 123
   and not invented here syndrome, 66–
      67
   Special Operations Executive (SOE),
      123
   use of aerial photography, 21
United States
   Defense Intelligence Agency (DIA),
      54, 68, 191 n27
   Department of Defense (DoD), 101–2
   embassy in Moscow, 90, 183 n4
   intelligence community, 193 n43
   Iran-Contra affair, 93–94
   Secret Service, 155–56
   support for Nicaraguan resistance, 75,
      89

   use of double-agents against U.S.S.R.,
      111, 204 n25
U.S. Congress, 78
   Boland Amendments, 145
   House of Representatives Permanent
      Select Committee on Intelligence,
      135, 136, 141, 144–45
   Hughes-Ryan Amendment, 74, 93, 197
      n2, 200–1 n38
   "leaks," 146, 209 n21, 209 n23
   National Intelligence Reorganization
      and Reform Act (1978), 211 n39
   Senate Select Committee on Intelli-
      gence, 144, 181 n4, 194 n50
U.S. Department of State, 75, 85
   biographic materials published by, 13
   Black Chamber, 27, 41, 169, 186 n35,
      214–15 n25
   Bureau of Intelligence and Research
      (INR), 54, 68
U.S.S.R., 35, 56, 86. *See also* KGB;
   GRU
   in Afghanistan, 89, 91, 94
   agents of influence, types of, 80
   and "black" propaganda, 83–84
   disinformation, 81–82, 85
   embassy of, in Washington, D.C., 117
   glasnost, 31, 33, 53, 203 n9
   and "gray" propaganda, 84
   Khrushchev, Nikita, secret speech of,
      85, 93, 199 n22
   missiles in Cuba, 48, 191 n27, 191
      n28
   and use of front groups, 85

Vance, Cyrus, 60

Wilson, Woodrow, 40, 41, 144
World Peace Council, 76, 85
World War II. *See also* Cryptanalysis;
   Encryption; Germany; Japan; United
   Kingdom
   British cryptanalysis skills, 25, 43–45,
      114, 122
   Chicago Tribune article on Japanese
      codes, 42–43
   Double-Cross System, 18, 113–15,
      119, 120, 122–23, 127

Yardley, Herbert, 40

ABOUT THE AUTHOR

Abram N. Shulsky, senior fellow at the National Strategy Information Center (NSIC) in Washington, has served as the director of Strategic Arms Control Policy in the Pentagon and as minority director (Democratic) of the Senate Select Committee on Intelligence staff. He has been a consultant to the President's Foreign Intelligence Advisory Board and the acting representative of the Secretary of Defense at the U.S.-USSR Nuclear and Space Talks in Geneva. Dr. Shulsky is also the author of several articles on intelligence and related national security matters.